Eating Identities

Eating Identities

Reading Food in
Asian American
Literature

Wenying Xu

University of Hawai'i Press
Honolulu

13 12 11 10 09 08   6 5 4 3 2 1

Library of Congress Cataloging-in-Publication Data
Xu, Wenying.
Eating identities : reading food in Asian American literature / Wenying Xu.
    p. cm.
Includes bibliographical references and index.
ISBN 978-0-8248-3195-0 (pbk. : alk. paper)
    1. American literature—Asian American authors—History and criticism.
2. Gastronomy in literature.   3. Food habits in literature.   4. Dinners and
dining in literature.   5. Cookery in literature.   6. Asian Americans—Intellectual
life.   7. Asian Americans in literature.   8. Food habits—Social aspects.   I. Title.
    PS153.A84X8 2008
    810.9'3559—dc22

2007035581

Designed by Paul Herr
Printed by Versa Press, Inc.

To Henry and Alan,
who love my cooking

Contents

Acknowledgments

Many people have contributed to this book. If I had to name them all, the list would be embarrassingly long. My gratitude first goes to Florida Atlantic University for a research grant and two teaching release awards. Without this institutional support, I would not have finished this book. I thank my students in the graduate seminar Food and Identities in Asian American Literature (Fall 2004) for their enthusiastic exchange with me and their challenges that forced me to refine my arguments. Several friends have been instrumental to this project. Joanna Marshall read chapter 1 when it was a conference paper and offered insightful comments. Jane Caputi read chapter 2 twice and led me to connections I didn't imagine. Greg Richter copyedited my manuscript with a pair of unrelenting eyes. Carol Gould's conversations about fusion food informed my writing of the introduction.

Among friends a term has been circulating to identify people who love the activities of daily living; we call them "people of clay." It is these people of clay who have supported and legitimated my endeavor to convert my love for food into an academic project. They are Marina Banchetti, Clevis Headley, Tom Marshall, Mary Cameron, Mary and Chuck Niessen, Andy Furman, Bonnie TuSmith, and Jerry Bergevin. I want to thank the Department of English at Florida Atlantic University for travel funding and secretarial support. Colleagues from the Society for the Study of the Multiethnic Literature of the United States (MELUS) have been generous and constructive in responding to my papers on food and literature. These include Cheng Lok Chua, Fred Gardaphe, Mary Jo Bona, Irma Maini, Melinda de Jesus, Georgina Dodge, and Wenxin Li.

Masako Ikeda, editor at the University of Hawai'i Press, has been wonderful. I remain deeply indebted to her for her faith and support. Joanne Sandstrom, copy editor for the University of Hawai'i Press, did a remarkable job. Portions of chapters 1, 2, and 4 have appeared in *LIT, boundary 2,* and *Cultural Critique.* I thank the editors of these journals and their presses (Taylor and Francis, Duke University Press, and the University of Minnesota Press) for their permission to reprint these portions. To my family goes my final gratitude for their support, interest, and love.

Introduction

Allow me to begin with two stories.

During the Chinese Cultural Revolution (1966–1976), hunger dominated my life in Baoding, Hebei Province, China, as it did millions of others. Only a small elite had access to protein, and their currency was power. Unlike abject starvation, the hunger I experienced permitted fantasies, such as meats, sweets, and fancy pastries. My family often sat at the dinner table after a meal of corn bread and boiled cabbage to continue eating imaginary delicacies. We would share in great detail the most delicious dishes we had ever eaten—their rare ingredients, their elaborate cooking, their distinctive tastes, and their spectacular presentations. The hungrier we were, the more extravagant our descriptions. On one of these occasions, when I began talking about my favorite Southern dessert, *tang yuan*, my father told the following story: when the British went to China in the late 1600s, one of the things about China that puzzled the British was *tang yuan*. "They liked the sticky rice ball very much," he said. "It's chewy and creamy at the same time. A burst of rich, fragrant sweetness goes off in your mouth like a bomb. The British had never tasted anything like it. That's why it really bothered them that they couldn't figure out how the Chinese put the sweet filling inside seamless balls. They took a few samples of *tang yuan* to their lab and dissected them. What they found in the center was a dark mass. It didn't take them long to figure out that the dark substance consisted of brown sugar, lard, and sesame seeds. Since it congeals when cold and a mass is more difficult to insert into a ball than liquid, the Chinese must have melted the substance first. After repeated experiments, the English scientists finally came to the conclusion that the Chinese injected into sticky rice balls a sugar-lard-sesame seed syrup with a large hypodermic needle." My father laughed and slapped his thigh at this point. "Of course, they proudly sent their finding to Queen Victoria."

Now thinking back, I have no doubt that Father made up that story. But it is a story that dominated my childhood imagination about the West, about how curious, scientific-minded, and yet stupid the English were. Although I had never tasted English food, I already concluded that it must be artless, tasteless, and redolent of Lysol, even during those long years of hunger.

Story 2: In 1987 Den Fujita, McDonald's partner in Japan, made the following statement: "The reason Japanese people are so short and have yellow skin is because they have eaten nothing but fish and rice for 2,000 years. If we eat McDonald's hamburgers and potatoes for a thousand years, we will become taller, our skin will become white and our hair blond" (qtd. in Reiter 169).

Food and Identity

Both anecdotes illustrate the central argument of this book—that food operates as one of the key cultural signs that structure people's identities and their concepts of others. Although commonplace practices of everyday life, cooking and eating have far-reaching significance in our subject formation. The first anecdote reveals a Chinese sense of culinary superiority that sets the self over against the other. Given China's defeat in the Opium War (1839–1842) by the British and other European powers and the subsequent partial colonization of China, my father's tale can be interpreted as an act of revenge. The second shows the success of Western colonization of the minds and taste buds of the Japanese. There, culinary differences become the ground for racialization that brings about the denigration not only of one's own foodways but also of one's own blood as polluted by those foodways.

This book argues for and explicates the relationship between food and identities specifically in Asian American literature, which abounds with culinary fiction and poetry. By reading the writings of seven Asian American authors, I place in the spaces of food, cooking, hunger, consumption, appetite, orality, and the like a wide range of identity issues such as race/ethnicity, gender, class, diaspora, and sexuality. In doing so, I hope to contribute to and complicate the ongoing discussion of the relationships between food and subjectivity in food studies in general and in Asian American literary studies in particular. Only a few critics have studied the significance of food in Asian American literature, and thus far they have focused primarily on food and ethnicity and gender. In addition, my interpretations of these Asian American literary texts provide models for reading food and identities in other literary traditions.

Food, as the most significant medium of the traffic between the inside and outside of our bodies, organizes, signifies, and legitimates our sense of self in distinction from others who practice different foodways. In sociologist Claude Fischler's words, "Food not only nourishes but also signifies" (276). Cuisine, the process of transforming raw materials into safe, nourishing, and pleasing dishes, is central to our subjectivity, because this transformation operates in "the register of the imagination" more than of the material (Fischler

284). Every manipulation of the edible is a civilizing act that shows who we are, what values we uphold, how we interact with one another, and why we do food differently from others. Terry Eagleton sums up well the signifying properties of food: "If there is one sure thing about food, it is that it is never just food—it is endlessly interpretable—materialised emotion" ("Edible écriture" 204). And materialized emotions are vital to the health of a community. Benedict Anderson argues that human communities exist as imagined entities in which people "will never know most of their fellow-members, meet them, or even hear of them, yet in the minds of each lives the image of their communion" (6). He proposes the three things that structure identifications: the community's boundaries, sovereignty, and fraternity (7). It is unfortunate that Anderson fails to consider a community's cuisine as a daily and visceral experience through which people imagine themselves as belonging to a unified and homogenous community, be it a nation, village, ethnicity, class, or religion. Slavoj Žižek, in advocating philosophical attention to the nondiscursive forms of identification, writes,

> The element which holds together a given community cannot be reduced to the point of symbolic identification: the bond linking together its members always implies a shared relationship toward a Thing, toward Enjoyment incarnated. [...] If we are asked how we can recognize the presence of the Thing, the only consistent answer is that the Thing is present in that elusive entity called "our way of life." All we can do is enumerate disconnected fragments of the way our community organizes its feasts, its rituals of mating, its initiation ceremonies, in short, all the details by which is made visible the unique way a community organizes its enjoyment. (*Tarrying with the Negative* 201)

Without intending to do so, Žižek amends Anderson's lapse by underscoring the highly symbolic value of the material enjoyment of a community. Few people would dispute that, of all the forms of communal enjoyment, alimentary pleasure is the most frequent and visible one.

Sharing food plays a central role in the formation of social groupings. In many cultures eating alone is an uncomfortable if not a shameful act. Solitary eating is often associated with loneliness, unpopularity, social isolation, unhealthy lifestyle, or eating disorder. With humor Mary Lukanuski tells of her broaching this subject with friends, family, and colleagues: "The overwhelming response was one of embarrassment, as if we were discussing their masturbation rituals. And who wants to admit they're having it, food or sex, alone?" (115). We eat together, and sometimes cook together, to affirm our feelings of family, community, friendship, love, and comfort. As Lukanuski puts it, "In the sharing of food, the sense of community is continually defined and maintained" (113).

Each culture's foodways always already function in its system of representation as signs of sophistication or civilization over against others engaged in "crude and barbaric" food practices. In its variant ways of transferring Nature to Culture, therefore, cuisine inculcates eaters with a deep-seated (corporeal) sense of diversity and hierarchy within their social group and over against other groups. Lukanuski writes,

> How food is consumed is a powerful method of further defining a community.
> A group who follows proscriptions forbidding certain foods, and or
> combinations of foods, immediately separate themselves. A sense of order,
> place, and discipline is created: the tacit understanding, beside any divine
> command, is that without such regulations the community would fall victim
> to its individual appetites. Once members of the community were pursuing
> their own desires, the community would disintegrate. (113)

As much as cuisine induces an imaginary solidarity among members of a community, it stratifies us also in that our food practices and taste buds render us acquiescent to divisions along the lines of culture, region, race/ethnicity, religion, gender, age, class, and sexuality—a hegemony that is exercised via appetite and desire. This hegemony is probably more effectively inscribed in us than other ideological hegemonies. As we often express our intolerance of other cultures by our repugnance toward their food practices, so do we demonstrate our cosmopolitan and adventurous selves by trying and relishing exotic dishes. Eating is indeed inseparable from personhood.

The classic philosophy in the West, however, regards personhood as an autonomous and disembodied mind. Any philosophical attention to the embodied self is often deemed to be ordinary and banal. Such a split between body and mind, as Deane Curtin points out, "has tended to silence philosophical interest in food." Given the valorization of mind over body, "dualisms are not only dualisms of ontological kind, but also of value" (6). It is no surprise that many of those who grow and prepare food do not occupy the full status of personhood in the Western philosophical tradition, and these people are, more often than not, manual laborers, women, and people of color. To register food with ontological significance is not only to restore full personhood to those marginalized but also to politicize what has been perceived as common and banal. Deborah Lupton argues that cooking and eating "are the ways that we live in and through our bodies" (1). Who we think we are has everything to do with what and how we eat. The authors of *Food and Cultural Studies* treat food as an index to the British national identity. "The distancing of self from those others who eat curry or spaghetti specifically, or in general from consumers of 'foreign muck', has contributed significantly to the definition of Britishness" (Ashley et al. 83). During World War II, being American and being patriotic were also defined by eating habits. Donna Gabaccia writes about culinary nationalism in the chapter "Food Fights and American Value."

> To create a scientific, healthful, and national cuisine, domestic scientists
> proposed [...] programs of education for immigrants and minorities
> throughout the United States. [...] As late as 1940, the Home Economics
> Section of New York's Department of Welfare recommended that immigrants
> should eat the old colonial creoles: for breakfast, hominy grits with milk
> and sugar, bread with butter, and milk and coffee; for dinner, baked beans,
> coleslaw with carrots, bread with butter, and custard pudding with raisins;
> and for supper, cream of carrot soup with rice, cottage cheese and prune salad,
> bread with butter, and tea. (128, 129)

Homogenizing immigrants' and minorities' foodways was part and parcel of the project of assimilation.

In addition to nation building through culinary standardization, food and eating often serve as a set of gendering and gendered signs that circulates in everyday life. Not only are eating disorders most frequently associated with girls and women, but also certain foods are considered to be men's or women's. For instance, fish is considered a feminine food by the French working classes. Pierre Bourdieu writes, "Fish has to be eaten in a way which totally contradicts the masculine way of eating, that is, with restraint, in small mouthfuls, chewed gently, with the front of the mouth, on the tips of the teeth [...]. The whole masculine identity [...] is involved in these two ways of eating, nibbling and picking, as befits of a woman" (*Distinction* 190–191). Most of us are familiar with culinary myths that dictate our gendering activity. For instance, we regard sweet, pale, and delicate foods as feminine and most fit for women's constitution. Men, on the other hand, "are typically associated with red meat and large helpings of food" (Lupton 104). In the context of this country, femininity is often at the mercy of one's dietary habit, a point that Shirley Geok-lin Lim sums up well: "In the United States, eating and non-eating or starvation are often marked as gendered activities, bearing particular significance for women and deeply identified with images of female bodies valued as desirable or debased as contemptible and worthless" (304). A recent TV commercial for Hummers portrays a young male vegetarian who is embarrassed by the stares from other male shoppers checking out steaks, spareribs, and other red meats. In the second scene, the vegetarian man regains equilibrium by purchasing a Hummer.

More prominently than gendering, food stratifies in terms of classes and races/ethnicities. The diet of the poor living in the Appalachians differs greatly from that of the middle and upper classes of America both in kind and in quality, and the cuisine of Vietnamese Americans appears exotic if not alien to many white and black Americans. In differentiating foodways, we often believe that our food not only tastes better but is also more healthful and cleaner than others'. Our assessment of other food practices operates from *our* sense of order—edible versus inedible food, appropriate versus inappropriate place of cooking, clean versus dirty food, and so on. Our system of ordering culinary matters socializes our taste buds and metabolisms, which in turn stand in the front line of demarcating the border between them and us. Such demarcation is never simply a line drawn between good and bad cuisine or even clean and filthy food. It always informs the construction of a moral judgment of a particular social group. Those who eat "filthy" food are believed to indulge in filthy ways. An example is the nineteenth- and twentieth-century stereotype of the rat-eating Chinese men lying languidly in opium dens and engaged in turning innocent white girls into sex slaves.[1] Doris Witt, in *Black Hunger*, recalls a particular scene regarding chitterlings in Ralph Ellison's *Invisible Man* that is most suitable "for exploring the triangulated relationships among blackness, food, and filth prior to the valorization of soul food" (83). Ellison's narrator fantasizes about exposing Dr. Bledsoe as someone who aspires to assimilate into the white culture while secretly holding onto black habits. The narrator whips out "a foot or two of chitterlings, raw, uncleaned and dripping sticky circles on the floor" and shakes them in Bledsoe's face. He yells, "Bledsoe, you're a shameless chitterling eater! I accuse you of relishing hog bowels! Ha! And not only do you eat them, you sneak and eat them in *private* when you think you're unobserved!" (265). Witt insightfully interprets this scene as both racial and homosexual, fraught with ambivalent feelings of desire and repulsion.

Class and race/ethnicity are inextricably linked not only because of their significant intersections but also because of their frequent synonymy. The unforgettable and disturbing images of Katrina victims in New Orleans were predominantly of black Americans who were too poor to evacuate (because they did not own cars or did not have money for gas and motels). In *How Capitalism Underdeveloped Black America,* Manning Marable argues that the majority of black Americans have been subjected to economic and political exploitation.

> The most striking fact about American economic history and politics is the brutal and systemic underdevelopment of Black people. Afro-Americans have been on the other side of one of the most remarkable and rapid accumulations of capital seen anywhere in human history, existing as a necessary yet

circumscribed victim within the proverbial belly of the beast. The relationship is filled with paradoxes: each advance in white freedom was purchased by Black enslavement; white affluence coexists with Black poverty; white state and corporate power is the product in part of Black powerlessness; income mobility for the few is rooted in income stasis for the many. (1–2)

The great discrepancy Marable describes between the economic contribution and the economic earnings of African Americans has continually brought hunger, illiteracy, poor health, and powerlessness to the black community. After all, soul food—chitterlings, trotters, neck bones, pig's tails, and the like—is a cuisine born from poverty and necessity that transforms into nourishment parts of animals considered undesirable or filthy by the middle and upper classes.

Much as Marable argues about how capitalism impoverishes black Americans, Lisa Lowe, in *Immigrant Acts*, exposes the asymmetrical relationship between white America and Asian America in U.S. history. In centralizing the contradictions within capitalism and American democracy at the critical site of Asian immigration, she narrates how legal, economic, and social discriminations against Asian immigrants and Asian Americans have helped maximize economic profits for the dominant population of this country. "Capital in the 1880s utilized racialized divisions among laborers to maximize its profits; it needed the exclusion of further Chinese immigration to prevent a superabundance of cheap labor, and the disenfranchisement of the existing Chinese immigrant labor force, to prevent capital accumulation by these wage laborers" (13). It is generally agreed that an Asian American middle class did not begin to emerge until after the Immigration and Nationality Act of 1965 ended eighty-some years of Asian exclusion. Lowe places this shift of immigration policy within the demand for "economic internationalism to expand labor and capital, to secure raw materials and consumer markets, to locate areas in which to invest surplus capital, and to provide a safety valve for domestic tension" (15). Since 1965 most Asian immigrants have been low-wage workers or underpaid professionals, whose labor and skills are directly responsible for the growth of global capitalism, particularly of the dominance of the U.S. economy in the Pacific Rim. Accompanying the increasing professionalization of the Asian American population is "the increased proletarianization of Asian immigrant women's labor in the United States," a racialized, gendered, and exploited group used as "a 'flexible' work force in the restructuring of capitalism globally" (16). American media are mainly interested in economic success stories about Asian Americans and thus perpetuate the myth of the model minority. It rarely enters into the American consciousness that tens of thousands of Asian immigrants and Asian Americans continue eking out a living in ethnic ghettos with neither health care nor pension plans.

Food and Asian Americans

It is banal to claim that Asian Americans have a special relationship with food. Who doesn't? Every social group is bound by an interrelated system of food production, rituals, and ideology. Having said this, however, I must insist that food and eating occupy a significant place in the formation of Asian American subjectivity. First, the racialization of Asian Americans has been achieved prominently through the mainstream's representation and appropriation of Asian foodways. Second, in Asian American history, food and eating do not simply fulfill necessities; rather they serve as an index to a material history of survival, adaptation, ingenuity, and hybridization—a triumphant history of overcoming adversities.

"They eat rats." "They eat dogs and cats." "They eat monkey brains." "They eat snakes and grasshoppers." "They eat slugs." I could go on reiterating the many dietary accusations against Asians, for these sensational tidbits litter news reports, literature, scholarly studies, cartoons, TV shows, movies, and everyday conversations. Even though there is a certain degree of truth in some of these accusations, they are not made to simply offer facts about Asian foodways. Rather, these tales are told with the intention of defaming, of othering, and of abjecting Asians in America. American media's representation of Asian Americans is irrevocably associated with "the food of their ethnic ancestries," as Jennifer Ann Ho points out. "Indeed, it is fair to say that Asian Americans are almost invariably portrayed through foodways in television and film" (11). As recently as December 2005, such dietary othering was alive and well on television. In *Curb Your Enthusiasm,* episode number 49, Larry David's Korean American bookie is suspected of having stolen and killed Jeff's German shepherd, Oscar, for food. It also happens that this jolly, entrepreneurial Korean American man supplies flowers for a fancy wedding on the beach. Along with flowers he brings a meat dish, which the wedding guests find exceptionally delicious. When Larry (mis)informs the wedding crowd about the source of the meat, mass vomiting breaks out, everyone spitting, choking, and writhing on the beach. This episode's comicalness, though satirical of Larry's ignorance and misjudgment, depends upon racist stereotyping of Asian foodways.

When it's not representing Asian food as disgusting, mainstream culture exoticizes and romanticizes Asian food. The recent vogue of fusion cuisine creolizes the East with the West, offering foodies hip atmospheres and pretty, petite, and pricey entrees, such as fried calamari with creamy miso, pasta with curried vegetables, and green tea cake. In such fusion, the East and West often are not equal partners; European cuisines occupy a dominant position while Asian cuisines complement and embellish. Wolfgang Puck, the celebrated fusion chef who catered the 2006 Oscar party, has made a fortune in fusing Japanese, Chinese, Thai, Vietnamese, Korean, or Indian with European cuisines. Such appropriation of Asian foodways to satisfy culinary curiosities, the desire for thrills, and the drive for profit has earned it the name "cultural food colonialism," which Lisa Heldke aptly coins. Heldke points out that ethnic foods are "most frequently and most notably the foods of economically dominated or 'third world' cultures" (xv). The appropriation of Asian foods in fusion cuisine resembles the practices of "nineteenth- and early twentieth-century European painters, anthropologists, and explorers who set out in search of ever 'newer,' ever more 'remote' cultures that they could co-opt, borrow from freely and out of context, and use as the raw materials for their own efforts at creation and discovery" (xvi). But does this charge apply to Asian American fusion chefs such as Ming Tsai and Padma Lakshmi (who are the two best-known Asian American personalities on the Food Network)? Anita Mannur in her essay on fusion cuisine points out that both chefs appropriate more Asian cuisines than those in which they have life experiences or training.

> Tsai never explains how Indian or Vietnamese cuisine fits into his repertoire and yet he offers recipes for pho and lemon basmatic rice. Similarly, Padma Lakshmi never explains how recipes for "Oriental Shrimp Salad," "Thai Chicken Stew," or "Pan Asian Fried Rice" enter her repertoire. [...] They suggest that a knowledge of the range of Asian cuisines seeps through their pores merely by virtue of being Asian. ("Model Minority" 85)

While Tsai and Lakshmi resemble white chefs in appropriating and exoticizing Asian cuisines, they also invite an entirely different question, which Mannur phrases well: "How does the cooking style of each chef suggest that Asianness need not be understood as an unassimilable presence within the United States, but rather as something that can assimilate *quietly* and *subtly* into the U.S. culinary landscape?" (85, emphasis mine). The quiet and subtle food fusion of East with West serves as an emblem of U.S. multiculturalism, whose success chiefly rests upon the quiet and subtle coercion of multiethnic cultures into a highly commodified and self-exhibitionist performance. One good example in culinary multiculturalism is the (Japanese) TV show *The Iron Chef,* which entertains by performing exotic ethnicities in combat by knives and tongues. Furthermore, what disturbs many Asian Americans about the stereotype of the model minority is precisely the image of tolerance of racism and classism and compliance with mainstream norms, as though assimilability is contingent on how thoroughly ethnic minorities can dislearn the two quintessential codes of American democracy—discontent and dissent. Tsai, glorified as "the Asian American poster boy of cooking," is a model minority par excellence owing to the fact that he never talks about unpleasant racial encounters and moves smoothly in and out of the Eastern and Western worlds (Lan N. Nguyen 31).

In history the Asian American relationship with food had little to do with the thrill of creation and discovery or even profit (although creation and discovery did take place). It was survival and adaptation that governed the lives of generations of Asian immigrants and their descendants. Food production and service allowed the immigrants to gain a foothold in their adopted country. The Chinese went to San Francisco in the mid-1800s to participate in the gold rush, and facing the racist law that prohibited them from working new mines, many turned to farming, fishing, and cooking, among other things, for a livelihood. In the San Joaquin and Sacramento delta, Chinese immigrants turned marshes into lush, arable land by constructing a sophisticated system of drainage and channels. In 1870 only 18 percent of farmworkers in California were Chinese. By 1880 the Chinese made up 86 percent of the farming population in Sacramento County, 85 percent in Yuba County, and 67 percent in Solano County. Gabaccia writes, "In California, Chinese immigrants made up between half and three-quarters of the cultivators of specialized vegetable crops in the early 1880s. [...] In 1870 San Francisco had over a hundred Chinese truck gardeners; by 1880 Chinese truck gardeners were also prominent in Los Angeles and in the upper Sacramento Valley" (110–111). After the completion of the transcontinental railroad in 1869, the anti-Chinese sentiment in the West became so great that the state of California in 1878 held a constitutional convention to settle "the Chinese problem." The resulting constitution prohibited the Chinese from entering the state and empowered cities and counties to drive them out completely. Some Chinese fled from the West Coast to the South and made a living by growing and selling vegetables to "poor blacks and whites in rural towns in the 1870s" (Gabaccia 113).

The Chinese introduced several species of fruit to America, including the Bing cherry (bred by Ah Bing) and the frost-resistant oranges (bred by Me Gim Gong) that jump-started Florida's nascent citrus industry (Cao 22–23). Jack Chen is correct in claiming that "much of the development of the present multimillion-dollar fruit industry of California could not have been done without the Chinese farmers" (88). There were other Chinese who entered Californian history on the strength of their produce, such as Thomas Foon Chen, who was known as the "Asparagus King" of San Francisco, and Chin Lung, known as the "Chinese Potato King" in the Sacramento–San Joaquin delta (Chang 162). In 1850 a camp of Chinese fisherman was established at Rincon; in 1852 there were 25 boats bringing three thousand pounds of fresh fish to market every day (Jack Chen 57). The Chinese "introduced the use of funnel-shaped traps for shrimping and fishing" (Gabaccia 111). In 1888 Chinese labor in the salmon canneries of California and the Northwest coast made up 88 percent of the total work force (Jack Chen 83). In Hawai'i, "Chinese rice growers imported familiar fish varieties from Asia" (Gabaccia 66).

The Chinese were among the first to open eateries in San Francisco, despite the fact that cooking was mainly women's work in China. Chinese restaurants had been so popular that by 1920 they involved roughly a quarter of the Chinese population in America (Chang 163). Gabaccia remarks, "No enclave businessmen enjoyed greater success attracting culinary tourists in search of inexpensive exoticism than Chinese restaurants in the Chinatowns of New York and San Francisco" (102). Their signature entree in the late 1800s and early 1900s was chop suey, a dish invented by bachelors, who stir-fried a hodgepodge of vegetables, meats, seafood, and noodles. It instantly became a popular entree on the Chinese menu, so popular that some restaurants on the East Coast even offered chop suey sandwiches. The gold miner William Shaw in his memoir, *Golden Dreams and Waking Realities* (1851), wrote that "the best eating houses in San Francisco are those kept by Celestials and conducted Chinese fashion" and declared that they served not only the best but also the cheapest food in San Francisco (qtd. in Jack Chen 57). To Americans no Chinese meal is over until fortune cookies are served (they are unsettlingly absent to people visiting China), but few people know that fortune cookies were invented in America—by David Jung, who opened a noodle company in 1916, with the intention of turning San Francisco's Chinatown from a ghetto into a "quaint tourist attraction" (Chang 163).

The Japanese arrived in California roughly two decades after the Chinese. They first established the Wakamatsu Tea and Silk Colony north of San Francisco to grow tea and mulberry trees (whose leaves are food to silkworms). Large numbers of Japanese immigrants arrived in the 1890s in California, Washington, and Oregon to work in the salmon canneries and fishing fleets, and to grow vegetables. Gabaccia documents,

> In California, Japanese farmers introduced Napa cabbage and the radishes
> of their homeland. [...] By 1920 Japanese farmers raised 90 percent of
> snap beans; 50–90 percent of artichokes, canning beans, cauliflower, celery,
> cucumber, fall peas, spinach, and tomatoes; and 25–50 percent of asparagus,
> cabbage, cantaloupes, carrots, lettuce, onions, and watermelons. At that time
> they made up 3 percent of the farmers in California. (66, 119)

In Hawai'i large numbers of Japanese settled in the 1880s to work on sugar plantations that were begun by Chinese labor (Cao 84–92). In the early 1900s

Filipinos joined the Japanese in Hawai'i on these plantations. In California and Alaska, Filipinos worked on Japanese farms and in the salmon canneries (Cao 164–168).

Southeast Asians came to America after the end of the Vietnam War in the 1970s and brought new "exotic" cuisines with them. Vietnamese restaurants began to appear in cosmopolitan centers, many of them "pho restaurants," which serve as their signature entree rice noodles in beef broth heavily flavored with star anise. Thai cuisine has been a rage in America for over three decades. Its rich and fragrant curry-coconut dishes are popular among people of all ethnicities. In addition to traditional Southeast Asian cuisine, the hybrid cuisine of Asian and French cooking—one of the few happy consequences of French colonization of Indochina—was introduced and largely credited with the launching of the elite industry of fusion cuisine. Immigrants from Vietnam, Cambodia, and Laos have also been engaged in other food industries, such as shrimp and crab catching and processing. Mark Moberg and J. Stephen Thomas, writing in the late 1980s about Southeast Asian immigrant workers in the Gulf of Mexico seafood industry, remark,

> The Indochinese entry into the labor market has had a dramatic effect on the scale of local crab processing. Between 1979 and 1988 the number of crab shops operating in the area increased from thirteen to 23. Small processors that had once averaged 2,000 pounds of crab per day now processed 10,000 pounds. [...] By 1983 the character of the labor force in the crab processing industry had changed dramatically. [...] Nearly 70 per cent of the workers in the crab processing industry are now Asian. (50)

With the growing health consciousness and increasing demand for seafood by U.S. consumers, South Asian immigrants are playing a significant role in helping seafood industries keep up with the market demand.

My review of the Asian American history on food production presents a larger picture of Chinese Americans than of Japanese, Filipino, and Southeast Asian Americans because in U.S. history Chinese immigrants came in greater numbers, and they also have been in the country longer than most of the other Asian immigrant groups. Regardless of their numbers and lengths of history, Asian Americans have been invariably involved in food service and production. There is nothing natural or culturally predetermined about Asian Americans' vital relationship with food. Harsh circumstances made such work one of the few options available to them. To survive in this country and to be able to send money to loved ones left behind and barred from immigration, they did what others wouldn't, and did it with pride and dignity.

Food in Asian American Literature

Culinary and alimentary motifs and tropes abound in Asian American literature. On the one hand, this is in part due to the representational reinforcement of the association of Asian Americans with their food practices. To a certain extent, Asian cuisines serve as a medium for casual and safe exchanges between Asian Americans and white strangers. Many times when I have been introduced to white people, the icebreaker predictably is about Chinese food. For Asian American writers to succeed in attracting the interest of mainstream readers, they must scatter in their writings interesting if not exotic cultural details, among which food practices are most popular. Take for an example Jhumpa Lahiri's *The Namesake* (2003). The novel's hook comes in its two opening sentences: "On a sticky August evening two weeks before her due date, Ashima Ganguli stands in the kitchen of a Central Square apartment, combining Rice Krispies and Planters peanuts and chopped red onion in a bowl. She adds salt, lemon juice, thin slices of green chili pepper, wishing there were mustard oil to pour into the mix" (1). With this exotic food scene, Lahiri successfully pulls the reader into the story.[2] Let me offer another example. In *The Woman Warrior* (1975), Maxine Hong Kingston depicts the unforgettable scene of a monkey-brain feast told by her mother.

> "The eaters sit around a thick wood table with a hole in the middle. Boys bring in the monkey at the end of a pole. Its neck is in a collar at the end of the pole, and it is screaming. Its hands are tied behind it. They clamp the monkey into the table; the whole table fits like another collar around its neck. Using a surgeon's saw, the cooks cut a clean line in a circle at the top of its head. To loosen the bone, they tap with a tiny hammer and wedge here and there with a silver pick. Then an old woman reaches out her hand to the monkey's face and up to its scalp, where she tufts some hairs and lifts off the lid of the skull. The eaters spoon out the brain." (91–92)

When encountering this scene, almost everyone, including Chinese readers, inevitably experiences the mixture of shock, repulsion, and hilarity—a powerful emotional response almost all writers would die for.

On the other hand, the rich culinary materials in Asian American literature have also come about because Asian Americans have been racialized, gendered, and classed through their involvement with food by restrictive U.S. immigration laws, limited occupational options, and media representations. To portray the material existence of Asian Americans, food and eating become necessary not only for the sake of realism but also for their symbolism of the ontological conditions of the characters. For instance, in Gish Jen's *Typical American* (1991), eating fried chicken and operating Chicken Palace are symbolic of Ralph Chang's conceptualization and experience of the American Dream. As more and more cracks appear in the structure of Chicken Palace until it collapses, the American Dream sinks deeper and deeper into American reality.

In Asian American literary studies, several scholars recognize the relevance of food and eating to issues of race and ethnicity in Asian American literature. Sau-ling Cynthia Wong devotes one chapter of her 1993 book to the study of alimentary images in order to "explore issues of economic and cultural survival" of Asian Americans (12). Monica Chiu in *Filthy Fiction* spends one chapter discussing how the precarious divide between clean and filthy food structures ethnic and gender identification in Ruth L. Ozeki's novel *My Year of Meats*. Anita Mannur's work on food and Asian America has appeared in journals as well as in *Asian American Studies after Critical Mass* and *East Main Street: Asian American Popular Culture*, among others. She maintains that "consumption is a racializing process that warrants closer analysis" (*Asian American Studies* 57). Jeffrey Partridge, Eileen Chia-Ching Fung, Nicole Waller, and Wilfried Raussert have written journal articles on food in Asian American literature. The only book-length study on food and Asian American literature is by Jennifer Ann Ho; it focuses on the ambivalent relationship that young Asian American protagonists have with their ethnic foodways. All these scholars center their analyses mainly on the relationship between food and race/ethnicity.

Building upon their work, this book treats table narrative in Asian American literature as a dominant site of economic, cultural, and political struggle, not as a site to produce self-exoticism or food pornography. My contribution to this ongoing discussion lies in my broadening of the issue of food and identity to gender, class, diaspora, and sexuality. As none of these identities could be teased apart from others as a singular entity, I often work in the interstices between them. In chapter 1 I pair John Okada's *No-No Boy* (1957) and Joy Kogawa's *Obasan* (1982), with the former being the first American novel dealing with the subject of Japanese internment in the United States and the latter being a more recent portrayal of a similar experience in Canada. What fascinates me in this pairing is their very different approaches to the maternal, a psychosocial space in which food and rituals operate as an index to racial/ethnic consciousness. *No-No Boy*'s textual gesture directs the reader toward the rejection of the maternal and thus the erasure of food while *Obasan* enfolds the reader in the maternal manifested via food and rituals. I argue that the different treatments of the maternal in these two novels contribute to their protagonists' ethnic identification or disidentification. The characters' relationships with their ethnic forms of enjoyment demonstrate microcosmically their relationship with the dominant cultures in North America. By contextualizing both

Okada and Kogawa within their worlds, which hold different degrees of racism toward Japanese Americans and Japanese Canadians, this chapter traces the movement from self-loathing to self-affirmation through these two writers' delineations of their protagonists' relationships to food and rituals.

Chapter 2 centers on gendered consumption in selected works of Frank Chin. I choose to read Chin because he is the most vocal author in Asian American literature on the historical problem of Asian American emasculation. His novel *Donald Duk* (1991) and short story "The Eat and Run Midnight People" (1988) are saturated with references to the relationship between food and masculinity. Crucial to issues of Asian American masculinity is that of ethnicity, for both ethnicity and gender powerfully inform each other. I argue that it is through two sets of embedded discourses—cooking and violence, appetite and sexuality—that Chin produces the narrative energy to achieve his project of remasculinizing the Asian American male subject. By placing Chin's works within competing forms of masculinity and within the hetero-masculinist cultures of consuming the feminine in both East and West, this chapter demonstrates that Chin's construction of an Asian American manhood is not remote from the hegemonic white masculinity that he has fought against throughout his literary career.

Chapter 3 explores how culinary tropes underscore the intersection of race, class, and gender in David Wong Louie's *The Barbarians Are Coming* (2000), a rich novel that has received very little scholarly attention. I choose to focus this chapter on this single text in order to do justice to its sophistication in and abundance of culinary references. Placing the chosen vocation of French cuisine of protagonist Sterling Lung against his repugnance for his parents' Chinese foodways, I locate in alimentary matters the nexus of identity issues of class, ethnicity, and gender. Lung's class aspiration, inextricably associated with his gender and ethnic anxieties, is brought to light by his ambivalent relationships to both French and Chinese cuisines. By practicing a class critique that respects aesthetics, this chapter analyzes Lung's self-alienation as brought about by race, class, and gender ideologies manifested through and propagated by the cultural sign of food.

Li-Young Lee, a remarkable and prolific poet, resists his classification as an Asian American writer by appealing to the transcendental. Some other Asian American authors, such as Bharati Mukherjee,[3] find the ethnic label not only restricting but also ghettoizing. By identifying themselves as American writers, not just ethnic American writers, they demand integration into mainstream, if not canonical, literature. Lee, however, employs transcendentalism to subvert the practice of ethnic labeling. In chapter 4 I examine the ontological condition of Lee in several of his poems as diasporic and exilic and argue that his lyrical descriptions of Asian cuisines offer him a place from which to articulate the ethics and aesthetics of the exiled. I bring to the forefront the colonial history of the spice trade in relationship to Lee's central trope of "seeds" and the significance of orality in the Chinese culture to explore the dynamics between his transcendentalist polemics and his poetic reliance on ethnic signifiers such as Asian food and histories.

Food and sexuality, a highly symbolic domain of interchange, is the subject of chapter 5. Here, I focus on *The Book of Salt* (2003) by Monique Truong and *Eating Chinese Food Naked* (1998) by Mei Ng. Both novels, being wonderfully culinary, deal with the issue of sexuality—homosexuality and bisexuality. Truong juxtaposes two cases of diasporic gay existence in Paris in the 1930s, one of Gertrude Stein and Alice B. Toklas, and the other of Bình, their Vietnamese cook, both of which unfold chiefly via culinary tropes to reveal the truth that the ability to practice sexual transgression depends on one's race and class. It is also through alimentary imageries and tropes that Ng dramatizes the tensions between the ethnic, domestic space and the cosmopolitan space of streets—tensions that interlock motifs of food, ethnicity, and sexuality. I read *Eating Chinese Food Naked* against *The Book of Salt* so that the former, presenting a contemporary character whose sexuality evolves from hetero- to bisexuality, a fluid identity, invites me to critique the rigidity of hetero/homo bifurcation that is central to the latter.

These five chapters chiefly study Chinese, Japanese, and Vietnamese American authors. There is no representation of South Asian literature in this book, partly because I do not have an adequate knowledge of South Asian foodways and partly because I wish to yield space to Anita Mannur, who has written elegant essays on food and South Asian American literature and is currently completing a book on this very topic.

My last word here is in defense of literary reading or close reading, which is a significant methodology in this book. Many people from my generation (graduate schooling in the 1990s) and those coming after fear the label of close readers,[4] for it suggests not only discipleship with New Criticism that divorces literature from politics but also an inadequate grasp of theories, which is perceived as fatal for one's professional life as a scholar. As a result, we have witnessed a large quantity of contemporary scholarship that treats literary texts as testing grounds for theories and political positions. It is not that these approaches are intrinsically inappropriate for studying literature; the disciplinary demand for theoretical rigor, however, tends to produce literary criticism that imposes theory and politics upon literature, or colonizes literature, if I may, forcing it to speak words and yield meanings at the cost of its dismemberment. In the words of Lindsay Waters in his December 16, 2005, article in the *Chronicle Review,*

"This kind of literary criticism has nothing to do with aesthetic responses to art, only with conscious acts of will" (B7). He laments that "literary criticism no longer aims to appreciate aesthetics—to study how human beings respond to art" (B6). Surely, Waters does not mean to limit aesthetics to readerly or viewerly responses, for aesthetics invites not only the question "Do you get dizzy when you look at a Turner painting of a storm at sea?" (B6) but also the question "What did Turner do in the painting to make you dizzy?"

The latter question considers ideas and craft as well as emotions. Turner's subjects of shipwrecks, whaling, and slave ships, laden with his views on human conditions in the early and mid-1800s, considerably determined his choices of materials and techniques to evoke certain sensations in the viewer. Sense (meaning) and sensation, therefore, are necessary twins in aesthetic evaluation. One without the other reduces art and literature to ideology, for a purely emotional or experiential approach is suspiciously ideological as well. I want to advocate that a fair balance between theory and aesthetics can produce a happy union of sense and sensation, of writerly operation and readerly response, and I think that one of the significant ways to achieve this goal lies in the politically charged and theory-informed literary reading. Theory itself, being fragmented as Vincent Leitch points out, is a set of competing discourses that are "flexible, useful, and contingent devices" in a toolbox (123). Leitch's metaphor frees us from the demand for a singular and systematic narrative in our deployment of theory, such as being a Marxist, a feminist, or a postcolonialist, not being all three, in one essay or work. Coherence and homogeny in positioning often depend on a willful dismissal of contradictions between a text and a theory through which the text is processed. A sustained literary reading, not just that of a passage or two that perfectly suits one's theoretical position, wonderfully frustrates any attempt to keep one's theoretical position singular, because a responsible literary reading often leads a critic in various theoretical directions that sometimes converge or diverge on the terms the text dictates. In other words, to allow literary or aesthetic nuances to direct one's implementation of theoretical tools and modify one's argument promises rich and interesting discussions that respect both meaning and emotion. This is precisely what has happened in my reading of various Asian American texts, and the following chapters are an endeavor to bring theory and aesthetics into a politically charged conversation.

I

Enjoyment and Ethnic Identity
in *No-No Boy* and *Obasan*

She found enough barang to make up some noodles. Not all the
necessary things, but enough: dried mushrooms and prawns, fish sauce,
belacan—that beautifully fermented, fragrant shrimp paste that could
just as well have been labeled "Essence of Malaysia."
—Shymala B. Dason, "All the Necessary Things"

Food loathing is perhaps the most elementary and most archaic form of
abjection. [...] The abject confronts us [...] with our earliest attempts to
release the hold of maternal entity even before existing outside of her.
—Julia Kristeva, *Powers of Horror*

Most ethnic minorities in the United States desire to assert the constitutional
"we," a political identity that entitles them to rights and privileges granted to
all American citizens. This constitutional "we" has often competed with the
ethnic "we" in American history, with the former always wielding greater political and cultural power than the latter. The devastation to individuals caused
by such competition often finds expression in rudimentary matters like one's
preference for or loathing of the foods, rituals, and family relationships specific
to one's ethnic community. A healthy and secure community does not agonize
over its cuisine and rituals. On the contrary, by celebrating them a community
fortifies its unity and identification. In the context of the ethnic identity of
Greek Americans, Robert Georges comments that "in preparing and serving
[...] 'Greek' foods, my mother and other 'Greek' relatives display overtly their
sense of their 'ethnic identity,' or their pride in it, and symbolically reinforce
their 'bonding' with those present who share that heritage, while also distinguishing the 'ethnically bounded' from others present whose 'ethnic identification' has other national roots" (252). About the culinary habits of immigrant
communities in the United States, Donna Gabaccia writes that "immigrants
sought to maintain their familiar foodways because food initiated and main-

tained traditional relationships, expressed the extent of social distance between people, demonstrated status and prestige, rewarded and punished children's behavior, and treated illness" (51).

Food consolidates as well as demarcates eaters because what and how one eats engenders much of one's emotional tie to a group identity, be it a nation or an ethnicity. The famous twentieth-century Chinese poet and scholar Lin Yutang remarks, "Our love for fatherland is largely a matter of recollection of the keen sensual pleasure of our childhood. The loyalty to Uncle Sam is the loyalty to American doughnuts, and the loyalty to the *Vaterland* is the loyalty to *Pfannkuchen* and *Stollen*" (339). Such keen connection between food and national or ethnic identification clearly indicates the truth that cuisine and table narrative occupy a significant place in the training grounds of a community and its civilization, and thus, eating, cooking, and talking about one's cuisine are vital to a community's wholeness and continuation. In other words, the destiny of a community depends on how well it nourishes its members.

In this chapter I link the maternal with ethnic identity formation. Specifically, I look at the dynamics between enjoyment, the maternal, and ethnic identification as explored by John Okada and Joy Kogawa. I argue that enjoyment and the maternal occupy the same psychosocial space—the semiotic. To be more accurate, enjoyment is a manifestation of the maternal. A community whose fantasies (both linguistic and nonlinguistic expressions) about who they are suffer violation undergoes confusion, anguish, self-contempt, self-abjection, the loss of identification, and ultimately the devastation of the maternal. The community afflicted with such devastation faces cultural genocide and extinction. Both Japanese Americans and Japanese Canadians faced this crisis not only during their internment at the end of World War II but also decades afterward. My concern here is how Okada and Kogawa differ in their portrayals of the maternal and to what extent these portrayals of the maternal affect the ethnic identification of their protagonists.

Foodways and the Maternal

Food is one of the "keen sensual pleasures of our childhood" (Lin 339), and such pleasures register in "the semantic void," a term Žižek uses to describe a psychic space where lurks the (Lacanian) Real—enjoyment that is never exhaustively codified by language (*Tarrying* 202). In Julia Kristeva's theorization of the semiotic in *Powers of Horror*, the Real is tantamount to *jouissance*, which Žižek translates as "enjoyment" and which Kristeva associates with the maternal. The semiotic space that an infant experiences, without demarcations of inside and outside, self and other, is the space of enjoyment, the mother-child symbiosis where "the rhythms and sounds of their bodies fuse into one" (Oliver

34). At this stage antagonism and ambivalence, which dog us in life, are still kept at bay.

Many linguists interpret the symbolic order as whole and complete, paternal in its logocentricism. In becoming a subject, however, the child must break away from the maternal in order to enter the symbolic order of language, a difficult process that, Kristeva believes, requires the abjection of the semiotic and the maternal, for the semiotic fundamentally disrupts and frustrates the symbolic order. Kristeva explains, "It is thus not lack of cleanliness or health that causes abjection but what disturbs identity, system, order. What does not respect borders, positions, rules." "The abject confronts us [...] with our earliest attempt to release the hold of *maternal* entity even before existing outside of her, thanks to the autonomy of language" (*Powers* 4, 13). The specter of abjection hovers over and penetrates all efforts to produce unity and completeness solely at the symbolic level.

Kristeva calls our attention to the fact that the maternal and by extension the feminine[1] are frequently associated with food as well as filth. The association of food with the maternal, however, should not be taken as an essentialist link between women and food, because the maternal in Kristeva denotes the modality of the relationship between a caregiver and an infant regardless of the caregiver's gender. Kristeva's thesis that the abjection of the maternal and the feminine is often made on the basis of their association with food and filth finds a solid illustration in the study of soul food by Doris Witt, who interprets the gendered meanings surrounding soul food and social reactions to it. She argues that "the debate over soul food was constituted by, and in turn helped constitute, many of the contradictions inherent in postwar attempts to revalue or reconstruct black manhood, especially Black Power efforts to control, to contain, and [...] to 'abject' the often fungible category of the 'feminine'" ("Soul Food" 260–261). As she makes clear, the discourse of soul associates filth with femininity, particularly with lower-class black maternity. Witt further points out that the intraracial debate over soul food was volatile because of the underlying association of chitterlings with filth, with black femaleness, and with the fear of the "enslaved, enslaving black feminine within the self" (261). In linking black manhood's fear of soul food with its fear of the feminine in itself, Witt suggests that to jettison the feminine is to disavow the self and in consequence to sabotage not only oneself but also one's community.

Žižek, in his discussion of the ethnic conflicts in Eastern Europe, performs psychoanalysis of "the most elementary notions about national identification" (*Tarrying* 200). He argues that "the element which holds together a given community cannot be reduced to the point of symbolic identification"—the national flag, ideologies, the Lincoln Memorial or Tiananmen Square, national values, and citizenship. What also needs to be taken into account is "a shared relationship" among the members of a given community toward "Enjoyment incarnated" (201). It is the enjoyment manifested in the way a community cooks and eats, the way it organizes initiation ceremonies and rituals of mating, the way its women mother their children, and so on. Thus, Žižek critiques the deconstructionist tenet that everything, Nation in particular, has no biological or transhistorical essence but is only a contingent discursive construction, an overdetermined result of textual practices. Žižek contends that such deconstructionist "emphasis overlooks the remainder of some *real*, nondiscursive kernel of enjoyment which must be present for the Nation qua discursive entity effect to achieve its ontological consistency" (202), for a community's relationship toward "Enjoyment incarnated" is structured by means of fantasies. Though constructed out of social and cultural materials, fantasies are more than the symbolic, or are excesses of narratives.[2] By locating the implication of national identification in the nondiscursive or the semiotic, Žižek attributes issues of national or ethnic identity to the space of the maternal or the semiotic.

Operations of the Maternal

Readers of *No-No Boy* (1957) generally experience feelings of urgency and frantic depression. The sentences move at such a tempo that one's heartbeat quickens as though catching the end of a sentence were paramount to the successful rescue of the suffering protagonist, Ichiro Yamada. John Okada's breathless narration in Ichiro's voice may make one wonder: Why is there such a race? From what is the text (Okada?) running away? The first American novel to treat the subject of the Japanese American internment, *No-No Boy* was born out of rage, fear, ambivalence, and revulsion—powerful emotions that persist at the tenuous border between order and chaos, reason and unreason, or in psychoanalytical language, between the symbolic and the semiotic. It seems that running away from chaos/unreason and into the shelter of order/reason is a fundamental impulse of Okada's novel, with these two binaries at his time being the familial (mother's) demand for loyalty to Japan oppositional to the social and cultural (American) demand for assimilation. Although Okada is ahead of his time in his unflinching description of the devastation inflicted by the internment experience on his community, he is nevertheless held hostage by the ideology of assimilation that inculcates a myth about the racial and cultural inferiority of U.S. ethnic minorities. This state of being a hostage is shown in his traumatic and painful portrayal of the mother figure, Mrs. Yamada, and in his impulse to reject and degrade the maternal, whose manifestations include food practices and rituals. In so doing Okada unwittingly rejects a vital component in his ethnic identity and heritage—enjoyment specific to the Japanese American community.

At the opening of the novel, Ichiro returns to Seattle after serving two years in a federal prison for answering negatively to both of the loyalty questions put to all men of Japanese descent.[3] He returns to a home that is both broken and divided, with his mother clinging to the belief that Japan was victorious in the war, his father dominated by his wife painfully and bitterly keeping her belief intact, and his brother Taro dropping out of high school and joining the army to spite his parents. Part of Ichiro's confusion and pain, conveniently, finds an easy outlet in his agonizing hatred of his mother. "Ma is the rock," he cries,

> that's always hammering, pounding, pounding, pounding her unobtrusive, determined, fanatical way until there's nothing left to call one's self. She's cursed me with her meanness and the hatred that you cannot see but which is always hating. It was she who opened my mouth and made my lips move to sound the words which got me two years in prison and an emptiness that is more empty and frightening than the caverns of hell. She's killed me with her meanness and hatred and I hope she's happy because I'll never know the meaning of it again. (12)

Ichiro is aware of, but incapable of confronting, the role that the U.S. government has played in his suffering. His rage at the government is displaced not only by his hatred of his mother but also by self-blame. In the first half of the book, he is locked in the ideology of personal culpability in one's misery— "You're crazy. I'm crazy. All right, so we made a mistake. Let's admit it" (14). Madness is apparently the only thing he can blame, which is not exactly a logical explanation for the kind of "mistake" he has made. His impoverished language of self-indictment speaks volumes about his willful deflection of the real cause of his punishment and misery.

It is only after meeting Kenji, a wounded veteran who serves as a voice of reason in the novel, that Ichiro begins to complicate his hatred for his mother.

> Right or wrong, she [...] had tried harder than most mothers to be a good mother to him. Did it matter so much that events had ruined the plans which she cherished and turned the once very possible dreams into a madness which was madness only in view of the changed status of the Japanese in America? Was it she who was wrong and crazy not to have found in herself the capacity to accept a country which repeatedly refused to accept her or her sons unquestioningly [...]? (104)

Okada's portrayal of the mother-son relationship points to the psychological violence committed by the ideology of assimilation and legalized racism. Ichiro's tormented relationship with his mother offers a complication of Kristeva's and Žižek's interpretations of the mirror stage at which a child begins to develop its subjectivity. For Kristeva, this happens when a child identifies with the father and the symbolic order, and abjects the mother and the semiotic. For Žižek, in the mirror phase the child begins to see itself and the symbolic world as unified wholes, something neither one ever is. Although Ichiro enters the novel at age twenty-five, one can argue that he is very much like a child seeking selfhood. After two years in the camp and another two in a federal prison, he has experienced the destruction of his personhood. Now returning home from the prison, he is thrust into a world that makes little sense and in which he is nobody. A constant victim of verbal and physical violence, Ichiro feels powerless and naked in the face of abjection. In the opening of the book, he is spat on by his childhood friend Eto, who swears, "Rotten bastard. Shit on you, [...] I'll piss on you next time" (4). As his mother asks him questions, she uses "the tone of an adult asking a child" (13).

Ichiro cannot form his identity by looking at himself from the place of his mother because she is shattered like a mirror by her madness, her love having been turned into an irrational pride over her and her son's loyalty to Japan. Okada impresses upon the reader that Ichiro's mother's fervent allegiance to the old country splits her American-born son into halves. Ichiro cries, "I don't understand you who were the half of me that is no more and because I don't understand what it was about that half that made me destroy the half of me which was American" (16). His rejection of his mother, however, doesn't engender an identification with his father, for his father "was neither husband nor father nor Japanese nor American but a diluted mixture of all" (116). In other words, the Japanese father, emasculated and decultured by U.S. racism, is no longer in Ichiro's mind the unquestioned lawgiver, the unified symbolic order. In Žižek's terms, Ichiro's effort is doomed to fail because it depends on the false assumption that there could be a rational symbolic order, a unified self. Given that presumption, woman has to become that order's irrational other, even as woman is the traumatic, irremovable kernel that makes impossible any manly master signifier. Thus, Ichiro's mother, Mrs. Yamada, is given many symptoms of a madwoman.

Without the usual mechanism for seeking a working identity, Ichiro is doomed by a perpetual identity crisis. This explains why Okada is unable to give his protagonist a resolution. The best he can offer Ichiro Yamada is a "faint and elusive insinuation of promise" for a community (251). Okada's novel suggests that when the maternal sphere of a given community becomes embittered and violated, there is little hope for the community as a whole. The mother figure in No-No Boy is described as a "rock," one who blocks her son's path to selfhood and wholeness—"the woman who was only a rock of hate and fanatic stubbornness and was, therefore, neither woman nor mother" (21). Okada's unwitting degradation of the maternal robs the mother figure not only of femininity but also of motherhood, dehumanizing her into a cold, hard, and hateful vessel of fanatic nationalism. She is now empty of love and nourishment. Bryn Gribben identifies Mrs. Yamada's insufficiency in the cans of evaporated milk that she repeatedly lines up and knocks down (Okada 139): "The metaphor of the evaporated milk works to indicate how the mother is constructed as a lack even if she has something to provide. [...] She can provide, but what she can provide has been deemed 'lack,' an evaporation of nourishment" (Gribben 39). Such characterization of Mrs. Yamada dictates that her creator kill the mother character in order for the son to grow and become a man. "You're dead," Ichiro speaks to the body of his mother, "and I feel a little peace" (Okada 187). Mrs. Yamada's suicide serves as the peak of the rising action, and only from that point on does Ichiro begin his process of healing. The evening of his mother's funeral, Ichiro and Emi go dancing in a bar, an occasion described by Jinqi Ling as "a symbolic celebration of life after Ma's suicide" ("Race, Power, and Cultural Politics" 371). It is at the bar on the dance floor that Ichiro's path toward (ir)resolution begins with such reflections as "I've got to love the world the way I used to. I've got to love it and the people so I'll feel good, and feeling good will make life worthwhile. There's no point in crying about what's done" (Okada 209). The injunction to feel good and to love the world remains hollow as Ichiro is unable, even at the end, to love himself; such love of self would become possible only if he embraced his heritage and its unique forms of enjoyment.

The disturbing portrayal of the mother and the use of her death as an instrument for character development suggest the author's own bitter ambivalence toward his ethnic community, an internalization of racism most Japanese Americans failed to escape between the 1940s and 1960s. That the mother figure is devoid of tenderness and love and that the father is soft and weak disrupts a most important stability in Japanese culture. What denigrates the maternal in Okada's novel lies in the unwitting but unrelenting presentation of Mrs. Yamada as an unapologetic social man, a woman who has become an incarnation of a patriarchal ideology, a guardian of Father's law, which in this case is fanatic nationalism. Thus, she is "neither woman nor mother," but a "dried and toughened" embodiment of antagonism (10). Such denigration of the maternal denies its properties of sexuality, tenderness, intimacy, nourishment, and music, all that which Kristeva names the "semiotic chora,"[4] all of which are vital for a community's growth.

Okada's inability to resolve Ichiro's identity crisis also lies in the absence in the 1950s of an alternative discourse to American assimilation or Japanese nationalism. Ichiro's entrapment in the dark schism between these two discourses "keeps his own voice contradictory and problematic" (Ling, "Race, Power" 375). The same thing can be said about the author and many people of his community as well. According to Žižek, "The [shared] nondiscursive kernel of enjoyment" (*Tarrying* 202), which is central to the cohesion of a given community, is the psychosocial space that gets structured by means of fantasies, uncircumscribed by language. This "nondiscursive kernel of enjoyment" is the space of the semiotic, of the maternal. The "bad" mother occupying the central place in *No-No Boy* signifies an ethnic community going awry, a community at the brink of destruction. With the denigrating portrayal of the mother figure, the novel offers its reader a glimpse of the trauma that its author has undoubtedly attempted to suppress. Ichiro's hatred of his mother and loathing of things Japanese allegorize Japanese Americans' profoundly painful ambivalence toward their ethnicity and the impossibility of coming to terms with their rejection by America, the country of birth for many of them.

Okada's powerful picture of the effect of racism, centering on the mother-son relationship, therefore, is also ironically complicit with the very object of his critique. At the level of discursive consciousness, Okada is remarkably successful in challenging racial myths in his characterization of Ichiro and Kenji and in critiquing the discourses of fanatic nationalism (embodied by Mrs. Yamada) and American assimilation at all costs (represented by Bull and Taro). At the nondiscursive level, however, or within "the semantic void," Okada, in his unease with Japanese forms of enjoyment, proves vulnerable to the racism that reduces the Japanese Americans to the abject Other. Along with the rejection of the mother figure comes the rejection of the eating habits particular to her culture. Hence comes the denial of the enjoyment vital to the survival of the Japanese American community under siege.

In *No-No Boy*, the moments of enjoyment, with their therapeutic power for Okada and his protagonist, are distinctively non-Japanese. The only significant picture in this novel of wholeness and harmony in a Japanese American family, curiously motherless, is Kenji's last supper with his family before he leaves to die in the veterans' hospital in Portland, Oregon. Kenji's father, walking home from the market, feels glad that he has bought "such a fine roasting chicken" from the market and thinks, "There was nothing as satisfying as sitting at a well-laden table with one's family whether the occasion was a holiday or a birthday or a home-coming of some member or [...] even if it meant someone was going away" (126). The entire family feasts on the roasted chicken, the American salad that Kenji's sister Hanako has made, and for dessert the lemon meringue pie that his brother Tom has purchased from a bakery, and the utensils they use are forks, not chopsticks (128). After dinner they sit in the living room and watch a baseball game on television, and the snacks are "coffee and milk and pop and cookies and ice cream" (130). Despite the fact that Kenji and his siblings are no less troubled about their ethnic identity than Ichiro, this dinner scene nevertheless presents a fine picture of successful assimilation by the "patriotic" Japanese Americans. Given this prominent culinary scene, no reader of *No-No Boy* can miss Okada's point that Kenji's home life is the healthiest one in the entire novel.

In contrast, Okada gives Ichiro a Japanese home life, where foodways are strictly ethnic with chopsticks and "eggs, fried with soy sauce [...] boiled cabbage, and tea and rice" (12). His home is one where his mother waits for the ship from Japan to take them home, where letters from the old country are read aloud, and where Japanese competes with English, as "his parents [...] spoke virtually no English" (7). Okada fills this very Japanese home with destructive conflicts, intensifying self-loathing as well as ethnic pride. In opposition to his parents' food preferences, Ichiro associates with home "the life giving fragrance of bacon and eggs sizzling in a pan" (39). Their different culinary desires bespeak a somatic manifestation of difference between the first generation and the second generation. Such conflict of desires seems to be widespread, for "the young Japanese [...] thirst for cokes and beer and pinball machines or fast cars and deluxe hamburgers and cards and dice and trim legs" (34–35). Anita Mannur remarks succinctly, "Food was a visible way to mark ethnicity and difference" ("Food Matters" 210). To dedifferentiate oneself in the eyes of the mainstream culture, one is compelled to disavow one's ethnic foodways, and such disavowal exacts a very high emotional price. In discussing the relationship between emotions and eating habits, Gabaccia remarks, "Psychologists tell us that food and language are the cultural traits humans learn first, and the ones that they change with greatest reluctance. Humans cannot easily lose their accents when they learn new languages after the age of about twelve; similarly, the food they ate as children forever defines familiarity and comfort" (6). The change of taste in these Japanese American characters, particularly during the years of "enclave eating," is an unquestionable consequence of social and cultural coercion.[5]

Okada's choice of the menu for Kenji's family versus that for Ichiro's is significant. In *No-No Boy*, the juxtaposition of the relative harmony present at the dinner table of Kenji's home to the alienating and alienated lunch at Ichiro's home serves to demonstrate the symptom of the most detrimental form of racism—self-loathing. This ugly feeling is evident in the narrator's gaze at Chinatown as Ichiro and Kenji enter it—"the *ugly* street with the *ugly* buildings among the *ugly* people which was a part of America and, at the same time, would never be wholly America" (71, emphasis mine). Self-loathing in this case expresses itself not only in one's hatred of one's own being but also in one's revulsion of the significant markers of one's ethnic community. The consequent self-sabotage resulting from such hatred and revulsion manifests itself fully in the drive for assimilation at the cost of self-erasure, particularly unrelenting in the cases of Freddie and Bull. Freddie, another "no-no boy," seeks self-destruction to vent his hatred for being a "Jap." Ichiro sees in Freddie the potential damage he is capable of against himself—Freddie "who, in his hatred of the complex jungle of unreasoning that had twisted a life-giving yes into an empty no, blindly sought relief in total, hateful rejection of self and family and society" (241–242). Bull, a Japanese American himself, displays his hatred of "Japs" by humiliating his fellow men and flaunting his red-haired girl in front of the Japanese American young men in Club Oriental. Near the end of the novel, Freddie picks a fight with Bull in the bar. In his frantic getaway, Freddie drives his car into a wall and kills himself.

This tragic event around the Club Oriental in Chinatown is placed side by side with a high moment occurring in a bar away from the ethnic ghetto. On the dance floor he thinks, "There's a place for me and Emi and Freddie here on the dance floor and out there in the hustle of things if we'll let it be that way. I've been fighting it and hating it and letting my bitterness against myself and Ma and Pa and even Taro throw the whole universe out of perspective. I want only to go on living and be happy. I've only to let myself do so" (209). Stan Yogi points out, "The dance floor becomes a metaphor for America, and dancing becomes a metaphor for the constant cooperation and respect necessary to maintain a truly pluralistic nation" (242). As Okada designs this moment to be the most critical one where a space opens up for reconciliation, he introduces another scene of healing. A Caucasian man, "slightly drunk," approaches Ichiro and Emi. Contrary to Ichiro's anxious anticipation of insult, the man says, "I saw you and want to buy you both a drink" (210). After offering different interpretations of the man's motive, Ichiro and Emi happily settle on the universalist closure that "he saw a young couple and liked their looks and felt he wanted to buy them a drink and did" (211). These moments of enjoyment possess the power of healing precisely because they are divorced from these characters' ethnic background and because they reiterate universalist values that are part and parcel of the ideology of assimilation.

On the one hand, Okada's presentation of Japanese enjoyment as either absent or detrimental to identity formation in the United States truthfully pictures the atrocious impact that institutional racism had on Japanese Americans in the 1940s and 1950s. On the other hand, his presentation also reveals the extent to which he and his people have internalized the repugnance toward forms of enjoyment specific to their ethnicity. However, these forms of enjoyment are the very expressions of the maternal, and it is the maternal that has the power to sustain a community at a time of deep trouble and to nurture it back to health. Joy Kogawa's *Obasan*, dealing with the same topic and era, reveals exactly this truth. Her unapologetic presentation of Japanese enjoyment, such as food and the ritual of communal bathing, resists the abjection of people of Japanese descent in North America. The deeply feminine and maternal sensibility, projected via poetic language and dream motif, present in Kogawa's narrative is anchored in the embracing of enjoyment, of the maternal. Unlike *No-No Boy*, which must kill the mother so that the son can begin to resolve his identity conflict, *Obasan* charts the journey of its protagonist, Naomi Nakane, from repression to knowledge that is aided by the maternal, and her completion is signaled by her return to the maternal.

Obasan, centering on the mass relocation of West Coast Japanese Canadians during World War II, begins with Naomi Nakane's visit to Obasan (Aunt) upon receiving the news of Uncle's death. Raised by Aunt and Uncle since the relocation, Naomi is haunted by questions regarding her parents' disappearance, particularly that of her mother, who had gone back to Japan before the relocation and has never been heard from again. Uncle's death, bringing back the rest of the family—Aunt Emily and brother Stephen—becomes the occasion for memory, revelation, and truth, much of which Naomi is reluctant to face. The rest of the novel is narrated mainly from Naomi the child's point of view.

The most prominent alimentary trope in this novel is "stone bread," a black loaf made by Uncle, which Naomi finds on Obasan's kitchen counter. This food item interestingly reverberates back to the recurrent description of Mrs. Yamada as a "rock" in *No-No Boy* that signifies the death of the maternal sphere when it ceases to nurture. The rock figuring for Mrs. Yamada becomes stone bread in *Obasan* figuring for Uncle. Both rock and stone bread are products of persecution, poverty, and powerlessness, as Uncle makes stone bread out of leftovers, such as oatmeal and barley, carrots and potatoes, after the family is relocated/displaced to Alberta, a dust-stormy beet country (13). Stone bread and the hardened Mrs. Yamada, however, differ in signification: she is completely devoid of the maternal quality while the stone bread maintains that quality by being both stone and bread, for Uncle's existential modality is largely maternal in his gentleness, kindness, patience, silence, and quiet suffering. He is stone because he is stoic; he is bread because he is nurturing and loving.

Sau-ling Wong's reading of the stone bread constructs a multifaceted interpretation ranging from the personal to the religious. What is relevant to the thesis of this chapter is stone bread's metaphorical and metonymical relationship to Aunt Emily's package of relocation documents and family correspondence, which can reveal the truth that Naomi wants but is unable to stomach (*Reading Asian American Literature* 20–21). Handing Naomi the package, Aunt Emily says, "Read this, Nomi [...] Give you something to chew on" as she is "eating a slice of Uncle's stone bread with a slab of raw onion" (43). Unlike Aunt Emily who has a "tough digestion" (43), Naomi fears the truth about Mother's disappearance and silence (for reasons I explore later); rejecting the stone bread as food is figuratively a rejection of knowledge: "If you can't even break it, it's not bread," Naomi says (16). One may argue that knowledge and truth seem to belong to the symbolic order, but the kind of knowledge *Obasan* offers is so tragic and overwhelming that it borders upon unreason made unspeakable and unbearable by repression and death. Uncle's death, however, shocks Naomi into action. As she reluctantly opens up and reads Aunt Emily's package, the stone bread becomes transformed into wafers symbolizing the inner change in Naomi. "In Aunt Emily's package, the papers are piled as neatly as the thin white wafers in Sensei's silver box—symbols of communion, the materials of communication, white paper bread for the mind's meal" (217). Wong remarks, "The thick, hard stone bread, having broken down into paper-thin wafers, is ready to be absorbed. The mystery that propels *Obasan's* plot is finally solved when the letters disclosing the mother's fate are read to the now middle-aged children" (*Reading Asian American Literature* 21). The trope of stone bread is instrumental to Naomi's rebirth from her long years of emotional paralysis.

In *Obasan* expressions of resistance to racism and its internalization center on enjoyment or pleasures specific to Japanese culture. At the time of relocation, Stephen, Naomi's older brother, is old enough to feel the shame of being Japanese, of being regarded as the enemy of the country of his birth. The feeling of shame is intensified by a Somerville game, The Yellow Peril, a Christmas gift to Stephen. It is a game about war: "Over the map of Japan are the words: 'The game that shows how a few brave defenders can withstand a very great number of enemies'" (181). The game pits fifty small yellow pawns against three big blue checker kings: "To be yellow in the Yellow Peril game is to be weak and small. Yellow is to be chicken" (181). Stephen's powerlessness and shame over the fact that the Japanese Canadians have suddenly become enemies of the state and are shipped in cattle cars to forlorn places finds concrete expression in his rejection of Japanese food. When offered a rice ball by Obasan, Stephen scowls, "Not that kind of food" (136). After that, Obasan learns to pack two kinds of lunch—one for Naomi of "two sticky rice balls with a salty red plum in the center of each, a boiled egg to the side with a tight square of lightly boiled greens," the other for Stephen of "peanut-butter sandwiches, an apple, and a thermos of soup" (182). In time Stephen rejects nearly everything Japanese. The child Naomi sees in Stephen "Humpty Dumpty—cracked and surly and unable to move" (136). She seems to understand that it would take an enormous effort to make Stephen whole again: "If I could take all the rice pots in the world, dump them into a heap, and tromp all the bits to glue with my feet, there would be enough to stick anything, even Humpty Dumpty, together again" (137). Naomi instinctively knows that Stephen's healing will require all the power of alimentary comfort that their community can offer. But unfortunately, Stephen no longer eats rice.

In contrast to the repugnance toward Japanese forms of enjoyment in *No-No Boy*, Kogawa presents several Japanese Canadian characters in *Obasan* as clinging to their ethnicity even at the most difficult time by continuing their food and ritual practices. Naomi remembers the warm dinner being prepared as snow falls outside the two-room hut at the Slocan: "The miso shiru, smelling of brine and the sea, is on the stove [...]. [...] The dried fiddleheads with their slightly tough asparagus texture have been soaked and are cooking in a soy sauce base with thin slivers of meat and mushroom. Salty, half-dried cucumber and crisp yellow radish pickles are in a glass dish" (157). This Japanese dinner prepared by Obasan welcomes Uncle home from an internment camp, restores family, and regenerates kinship. Such an enjoyment is unmistakably linked with the maternal that possesses the power to heal, to give and defend life, and to restore sensuality.

One of the Japanese enjoyments vital to the sense and sensuality of ethnic community is the ritual of communal bathing. Robin Potter is insightful in seeing the manifestation of the maternal in such a ritual. He writes, "That bathing is a time of utmost bliss for Naomi reveals a close identity with the Mother and with the semiotic. When the language of F/father has interceded in usual communication, these scenes serve to unite the daughter to the pleasures of the (infant) body, to regenerative processes, to the real and primal M/mothers" (130). That nudity is accepted as natural in the bathing ritual, untouched by the Judeo-Christian language of sin and impurity, reminds us indeed of Kristeva's mother-child symbiosis before the separation from and abjection of Mother by the demand of the symbolic.

> The bath is a place of deep bone warmth and rest. It is always filled with a
> slow steamy chatter from women and girls and babies. It smells of wet cloth
> and wet wood and wet skin. We are one flesh, one family, washing each other
> or submerged in the hot water, half awake, half asleep. The bath times are like
> a hazy happy dream. (*Obasan* 191)

Kogawa's language of the senses strongly evokes the primordial, preverbal world where bodily pleasures dominate an infant's consciousness, where Self is indistinguishable from the Other—"one flesh, one family." Žižek insists that our suppressed memory of the Real or *jouissance* lurks in the unconscious: "it is precisely and only in dreams that we encounter the real of our desire" (*Looking Awry* 17). The bath times compared to "a hazy happy dream" recall the fetal sleep of the child in the mother's womb.

Unlike *No-No Boy*, which is peopled mainly by men, *Obasan* presents the world of women. For Naomi there are three mother figures: the mother who is missing; Grandmother Kato, who delivers the "freeing word" in her letters from Japan; and Obasan, the surrogate mother who raises Naomi and Stephen. As Potter observes, Grandma Kato's language is that of "the body, of murmurs, gaps, and bliss; of survival, not of power structures" (129). The same can be said of Obasan. These three women constitute the sphere of the maternal in which Naomi is both frustrated and comforted by silence but, more important, sustained by intimacy, nourishment, tenderness, and love. Another bath scene of Naomi and Grandmother Kato serves "to salvage the remnants of a time during which neither the mother nor the child have experienced separation and abjection" (Potter 131).

> She urges me down deeper into the liquid furnace and I go into the midst of the flames, obedient as Abednego, for lo, Grandma is an angel of the lord and stands before me in the midst of the fire and has no hurt, neither is a hair of her body singed nor has the smell of fire passed her. She is sitting directly beside the gushing boiling hot-water tap and the steaming froth plunges around her bony buttocks. [...] I will suffer endless indignities of the flesh for the pleasure of my grandmother's pleasure. [...] My body is extended beside hers and she makes waves to cover my shoulders. Once the body is fully immersed, there is a torpid peace. We lie in this state forever. (58)

The hot bath, elevated with an allusion to the persecution and divine intervention in the biblical history of the Jews, merges the bodily and the spiritual, the semiotic and the symbolic, the East and West, allowing the Real (pleasures) to bubble up to frustrate the codified world, the world of rules, order, and asymmetrical binaries. Its power to cleanse, to heal, and to commune is vital to the preservation of the identity, dignity, and hope of the Japanese Canadians. Kogawa seems to offer us a lesson that the best defense for an ethnic community against gross injustice and denigration lies in the embracing of its enjoyment, for an ethnic community, as Žižek proposes, "*exists* only as long as its specific enjoyment continues to be materialized in a set of social practices" (*Tarrying* 202).

In discussing the amniotic deep in *Obasan*, Christina Tourino points out that this maternal site of reproduction is the highly contested one between "ethnic family" and the Canadian government (134). She argues that "abortion of that reproduction is the novel's central metaphor" (134), as evident in the crisis of regeneration among the female characters (two stillbirths for Obasan and the childlessness and celibacy of both Naomi and Emily). The amniotic space "as alternatively nurturing and destructive" pictures the barely living state of the Japanese Canadian community during and after the internment, of which Naomi's suspended state serves as an apt metonymy (137). Despite the fact she has been surrounded by the forces of Mother, not only in the maternal space constituted by the women in her family but also in the poetic language and dream motif that Kogawa lavishes upon this character, she remains traumatized and repressed until the end of the novel, when she is returned to the maternal. The sources of her trauma and repression are what she considers abandonment by her mother and the memory of sexual molestation by Old Man Gower. When she recalls Gower's repeated molestation and a similar encounter later with a boy named Percy in Slocan, Naomi faces her ambivalence—"I am filled with a strange terror and exhilaration"—with a painful question: "When does this begin—this fascination and danger that rockets through my body?" (73). Here in a dream Naomi links her sexual trauma with the plight of the three mother figures. In this dream, three Asian women lie naked in the muddy road guarded by rifle-bearing soldiers. When one of them touches her hair, she wiggles her body "seductively"; she is "trying to use the only weapon she had—her desirability" (73). Naomi reflects, "This is what a punished dog feels—this abject longing, wretchedness, fear, and utter helplessness. She lay on the edge of nausea, stretched between hatred and lust" (73–74). That the desperate, abject seduction doesn't save the women from mutilation and death is traumatic to Naomi, for she has rationalized her "cooperation" with Old Man Gower by thinking that "the only way to be saved from harm was to become seductive" (73). Kogawa travels deep into the wounded psyche of Naomi by picturing similar scenes where the victim is, wittingly or unwittingly, complicit with the perpetrator, such as the chicks approaching the hen that pecks them to death, highly symbolic of the Japanese Canadians' trust of and persecution by the Canadian government (70). Naomi can't separate her sexual molestation from her mother's "abandonment." Both experiences fold in the double image: her mother's leg she clings to is "a flesh shaft that grows from the ground," echoing the sexual foliage in Gower's garden where hornlike fiddleheads grow (77). The image further complicates Naomi's reasoning of Mother's disappearance: "The shaft of her leg is the shaft of my body [...]. But here in Mr. Gower's hands I become other—a parasite on her body [...]. My arms are vines that strangle the limb to which I cling [...]. I am a growth that attaches and digs a furrow under [...] her skin" (77). In Naomi's subconscious, it is her secrets with Mr. Gower that have injured Mother and caused her to disappear. "The secret is this: I go to seek Old Man Gower in his Hideaway. I clamber unbidden onto his lap. His hands are frightening and pleasurable. In the center of my body is a rift" (77). In her childhood dreams, Naomi sees the "rift" yawning apart like a chasm between two mountains, forever separating her from her mother, and separating her from her own motherhood. Tourino is right in her interpretation that "Kogawa connects Naomi's abuse by Gower to the abuse of the Japanese Canadians by white Canada in that both interrupt Japanese Canadian procreation" (146).

The traumatic separation from Mother, facilitated by Gower, initiates Naomi into the symbolic, an order whose maxim is reason. In her waking life, Naomi has questioned repeatedly why Mother has left her and Stephen and why Mother never writes. In questioning Mother, she has accused Mother of abandonment. In demanding an answer, she has judged Mother. After Naomi learns the truth of Mother's departure, of her disfiguration during the bombing of Nagasaki, of her injunction not to tell for the sake of the children, and of her silent, lonely death, Kogawa evokes the metaphor of the Grand Inquisitor to free Naomi from the entrapment of the symbolic that demands answers and explanations for what cannot be rationalized.

> The Grand Inquisitor was carnivorous and full of murder. His demand to
> know was both a judgment and a refusal to hear. The more he questioned her,
> the more he was her accuser and murderer. The more he killed her, the deeper
> her silence became. What the Grand Inquisitor has never learned is that the
> avenues of speech are the avenues of silence. To hear my mother, to attend her
> speech, to attend the sound of stone, he must first become silent. Only when
> he enters her abandonment will he be released from his own. [...] At the age
> of questioning my mother disappeared. Why, I have asked ever since, did
> she not write? Why, I ask now, must I know? Did I doubt her love? Am I her
> accuser? (273–274).

In structuring the plot of *Obasan*, Kogawa makes a liberal deployment of the maternal, and the semiotic operates fruitfully in the novel. This is evident not only in Kogawa's poetic and sensory language but also in the major motifs of dream and intuition and their significant role in the novel's resolution. Even before Naomi is finally allowed to learn about her mother's tragedy through Grandma Kato's letters, she is visited by a dream that prepares her for the final knowledge. In her dream,

> the maggots are crawling in [a kitten's] eyes and mouth. Its fur is covered in
> slimy feces. Chickens with their heads half off flap and swing upside down in
> midair. The baby in the dream has fried-egg eyes and his excrement is soft and
> yellow as corn mush. His head is covered with an oatmeal scab, under which
> his scalp is a wet wound. (188)

One may wonder why Kogawa evokes food metaphors to paint such a horrific scene. I think that the juxtaposition of filth and decay to food is highly symbolic of the maternal that disobeys the divide between the pure and impure, for mother's milk and blood both nourish and disgust. This socially constructed and reinforced divide between food and filth characterizes the ambivalent relationship of the symbolic with the maternal in that the symbolic order both comes from and retains the maternal. As the symbolic can hardly keep at bay the threat of contamination by the maternal despite its insistence on order and law, so is food highly unstable, continually threatening to become dirt. "Delicious food is only hours or days away from rotting matter [...]. As a result, disgust is never far from the pleasures of food and eating" (Lupton 3). Kogawa's commingling of food and filth metaphors presents an apocalyptic vision in which the symbolic has collapsed into the maternal, which orchestrates the primal scenes of birth and death. Kogawa's apocalyptic scene folds nearly perfectly into the picture of nuclear devastation that Grandma Kato paints in one of her letters.

> Beneath some wreckage, she saw first the broken arm, then the writhing body of her niece, her head bent back, her hair singed, both her eyes sockets blown out. [...] Grandma Kato touched her niece's leg and the skin peeled off and stuck to the palm of her hand. [...] Men, women, and in many cases indistinguishable by sex, hairless, half clothed, hobbled past. Skin hung from their bodies like tattered rags. One man held his bowels in with the stump of one hand. [...] one evening [...] she sat down beside a naked woman she'd seen earlier who was aimlessly chipping wood to make a pyre on which to cremate a dead baby. The woman was utterly disfigured. Her nose and one cheek were almost gone. Great wounds and pustules covered her entire face and body. She was completely bald. She sat in a cloud of flies, and maggots wriggled among her wounds. (284–286)

And this woman turns out to be Naomi's mother. Naomi's dream serves as a premonition that imparts knowledge in a way that is often deemed by the symbolic order as irrational or superstitious. In *Obasan* there are abundant moments of dreams and intuitions whose images echo those appearing at the climax, where the protagonist gains the full knowledge of her mother's suffering and death. Instead of being shocked into psychosis, Naomi, having been prepared by earlier visions, moves beyond shock and begins the process of healing soon after: "I am back with Uncle again, listening and listening to the silent earth and the silent sky as I have done all my life. I close my eyes. Mother, I am listening. Assist me to hear you" (288).

The semiotic or the Real is a domain in which unreason, like the undergrowth of a forest, dominates its space. What is considered dreamy, illogical, absurd, filthy, or ungrounded often governs or creates tension in our waking, rational life, and this is precisely Lacan's anti-Cartesian thesis: "I think where I am not, therefore I am where I do not think" (166). Kogawa uses the power of unreason without hesitation in the portrayal of the maternal forces (Japanese food, communal bathing, dreams, and intuitions) that assist the protagonist in her journey into "the underground stream"—the unconscious, the suppressed—to eventually emerge in the "brooding light" (295).

Naomi's journey from repression to understanding is thus made possible by the maternal and urged on by the power of the word embodied in Aunt Emily. Naomi's deliverance from repression comes at the end, when she willingly embraces the maternal. Naomi puts on Aunt Emily's coat, "warmer than [her] jacket," and visits the coulee Uncle used to take her to every year on the anniversary of the bombing of Nagasaki (296). Unlike before when she has preferred to stay on the top of the slope, listening to the sound of "muddy river sludge along its crooked bed," Naomi this time wades through the coulee grass: "I inch my way down the steep path that skirts the wild rose bushes, down slipping along the wet grass where the underground stream seeps through the earth" (296). She lets the river wet her pajamas and coat and the mud clog her shoes, fully submerged in the deeply buried knowledge of Mother's departure, love, silence, and death. In such a symbolic action, Naomi submits herself to the semiotic, the maternal where sounds, sensations, smells rule: "The perfume in the air is sweet and faint. If I hold my head a certain way, I can smell them from where I am" (296).

In comparison, the maternal operates quite differently in No-No Boy. There the maternal forces are either controlled (such as the choices of food) or rejected (the traumatic portrayal of Mrs. Yamada and her suicide). In addition, Okada's language and plot remain heavily rational throughout, with their emphasis on the conflict centering on whether Ichiro is American or Japanese and on the distinction between sanity and insanity. The reins Okada wields over the power of the maternal, as I've pointed out earlier, are symptomatic of ethnic insecurity caused by racism and its internalization. His unease with his ethnicity, vividly portrayed in Ichiro, Kenji, Freddie, Bull, and others is a powerful criticism of U.S. culture.

In critiquing No-No Boy for its vulnerability to racism at a deep level—the Japanese forms of enjoyment and the mother figure made abject by racism—I am not denying the fact that Okada has, to a large measure, broken free from the hold of the racist ideology. He brilliantly shows the dark abyss between two equally devastating models—that of Freddie's self-contempt and self-destruction and that of Kenji, who has served in the U.S. Army but whose war wound robs him of his manhood inch by inch (symbolized by the amputation of his leg) until it kills him. Ironically, Kenji, the "sane" voice and the war hero in the novel, speaks his last words fraught with self-loathing: "I got to thinking that the Japs were wising up, that they had learned that living in big bunches and talking Jap and feeling Jap and doing Jap was just inviting trouble" (163). His final advice to Ichiro is, "Go someplace where there isn't another Jap within a thousand miles. Marry a white girl or a Negro or an Italian or even a Chinese.

Anything but a Japanese. After a few generations of that, you've got the thing beat" (164). In presenting both Freddie (a no-no boy) and Kenji (a yes-yes hero) as irreparably maimed by the experience of internment, Okada effectively pictures the inhumanity of racism and the great challenge in constructing positive ethnic identification at his time.

As I am arguing that the denigration of the maternal and the unease with Japanese forms of enjoyment in No-No Boy reveal Okada's own ambivalence toward his ethnicity, I must also point out that Okada has done a superb job in portraying the Buddhist funeral for Mrs. Yamada as an occasion when a non-mainstream ritual is practiced with the effect of forging the community. When the community comes together to mark the passing of one of its members, with the burning of incense, the banging of "an urn-like gong," and the holy chanting, a transformation takes place in Mr. Yamada (191). Ichiro, uneasy with the too ethnic funeral, becomes aware of the change in his father, feeling "the presence of his father beside him like a towering mass of granite" (193), an image in sharp contrast to the frightened, feeble man, whom Ichiro also describes as "a goddamned, fat, grinning, spineless nobody" (12).

With Obasan coming twenty-four years after No-No Boy, Kogawa has the advantage of having witnessed movements against racism and toward ethnic recognition, particularly "the redress movement" of Japanese Americans. Kogawa's security in Buddhism and Japanese forms of enjoyment reflects the general ethos of a budding multiculturalism in North America. To acknowledge the relatively friendly cultural milieu does not diminish Kogawa's amazing accomplishment in Obasan. Making a comparative study of both No-No Boy and Obasan addressing their different approaches to the maternal and ethnic enjoyment and using the strength of psychoanalytical theories expounded by Kristeva and Žižek can shed light upon issues of ethnic identification that provide a powerful critique of interpretations where the symbolic or the superstructure rules.

Food and rituals, as manifestations of the maternal, are unmistakably gendered feminine in this discussion. Ethnic identification, viewed from the perspective of the maternal, is understood not as an individual's will to identity but as a communal endeavor to secure its members' comfort and pride in belonging. Food and cooking rituals, however, can also be masculine and masculinizing. Ethnic identification and masculinity, fraught with tension in Asian American culture and literary tradition, are the subjects of the next chapter, in which I explore how an ethnic masculinity becomes constructed in selected works of Frank Chin via food, cooking, and eating. If this chapter has misled the reader to assume the essentialist connection between women and food/cooking (which I have tried to avoid), chapter 2 challenges that assumption by introducing a male chef.

2

Masculinity, Food, and Appetite in Frank Chin's *Donald Duk* and "The Eat and Run Midnight People"

[T]*he male body is understood as powerful, big and strong, "with enormous, imperative, brutal needs" which are asserted when eating.*
—Deborah Lupton, *Food, the Body, and the Self*

[T]*he stereotype of male eating habits originated in the bush, and included a lack of table manners for the expression of a rude, hearty appetite, simply cooked meat, damper baked in the ashes of camp fires and meat pies and tomato sauce.*
—Michael Symons, *One Continuous Picnic*

The name Frank Chin provokes controversy among Asian American readers and scholars, but almost all agree that masculinity has preoccupied his entire literary and critical career. Almost all his writings aim at dismantling the U.S. hegemonic, emasculating representations of Asian American males, even when this agenda must sometimes be carried out at the expense of Asian American women and gay men. Recognizing his homophobic and macho tendencies, I nevertheless value Chin's literary attempts to assail the prevailing stereotype of Asian American male sexuality. His is not only an important but also a necessary project in the evolution of Asian American aesthetics. Moving away from the black masculine model (such as in *The Chickencoop Chinaman*), Chin in his imagination of a proud Chinese American manhood turns to Asian and Asian American cultures in his 1991 novel, *Donald Duk*. While *Donald Duk* is no exception in its goal, it is a departure from the angry tone that dominates his earlier works, such as "Racist Love" (1972), "The Chickencoop Chinaman" (1981), and "Come All Ye Asian American Writers of the Real and the Fake!" (1991). In *Donald Duk* Chin is more humorous than angry, more tolerant than accusatory. Unlike his earlier works, whose angry tone, directed at the mainstream culture, only painfully reveals Chin's unwitting obsession with the "white gaze,"[1] *Donald Duk* offers a witty and confident portrayal of several Chinese American men whose gender formation is largely anchored in pan-Asian cultures—Chinese literature, Chinese cuisine, and Hong Kong kung fu movies. Yet Chin's new construction of Chinese American manhood is, unfortunately, not very remote from the hegemonic white masculinity that he has fought against throughout his literary career.

Food is a crucial signifier in this novel's gender imaginary.[2] Eileen Fung's essay on this novel, an inspiration for this chapter, argues convincingly that "food becomes a discourse of a masculine culture which reinscribes male aggression and domination" (259). In *Donald Duk* the kitchen becomes a site for the assertion of masculinity, with the language of cooking repeatedly evoking images of martial arts and war. Chin's short story "The Eat and Run Midnight People" (1988) also employs tropes of food and appetite in capturing the voice of a hypermasculine narrator. There Chin portrays a Chinese culture whose prowess resides in its gastronomic promiscuity and a Chinese American man whose sex act travels between the signifiers of food and trains. Alimentary references in both works help pave the most conventional path to the construction of masculinity—the path of violence. With *Donald Duk* and "Eat and Run" juxtaposed, we will see that Chin the writer, produced by as well as productive of transcultural and competing forms of masculinity, cannot help but rely heavily on the masculine pleasures of consumption, sex, and violence in his effort to remasculinize the Asian American male subject.

Chin's effort to rescue Asian American manhood, as King-Kok Cheung points out, is based upon a hegemonic conception of masculinity that is largely white, heterosexual, and propertied.[3] Although there are critics favorably disposed to Chin's evocation of the Chinese male heroic tradition, such as Jinqi Ling, who advocates "a more nuanced and less reductive" reading of Chin, their appreciation of Chin's struggle does not compromise their disapproval of his masculinist agenda (*Narrating Nationalisms* 83). Robert Connell attributes hegemonic masculinity to "the cultural dynamic by which a group claims and sustains a leading position in social life," one that is maintained by "the dominant position of men and the subordination of women" (77). In exploring the complexity of minority masculinities, Jachinson Chan remarks,

> Men of color, who are excluded from the hegemonic model of masculinity, may unwittingly buy into this notion of [masculinity]. In spite of exclusions based on race, men of color can still benefit from patriarchal dividends and they may demonstrate a longing for inclusion to a hegemonic masculine identity. The seduction of a hegemonic masculinity can be a powerful force that lures men of color from a place of complicity to an aggressive pursuit of being a part of an elite group. (10)

Hegemonic masculinity is by no means a secure and stable identity.[4] Michael Kimmel in his study of American masculinity demonstrates that the story of "manhood as a relentless test [...] has been and continues to be a dominant one in American life" (ix). Furthermore, "It is a story of a chronically anxious, temperamentally restless manhood—a manhood that carries with it the constant burdens of proof" (x). Gender anxiety manifested through this "relentless test" takes an even heavier toll on men of color.

In much of his earlier works, as Daniel Kim outlines, Chin offers "a literary self-portrait of an Asian American masculinity in ruins, of men who seem only to hate themselves for their inability to be men" (296). Chin's anger and longing seem to be interwoven in a painfully ambivalent relationship to the normative model of masculinity. His knowledge that it is through the desexualization of Asian American men that white American patriarchy forges itself cannot free him from the desire to identify with this very model. In *Donald Duk*, however, he seems to be less preoccupied with the model of white patriarchy and more engaged in constructing an Asian American manhood that relies on Chinese icons of masculinity, such as Kwan Kung and Lee Kuey. Different from his earlier works dominated by themes of insurmountable alienation and nonidentity, *Donald Duk* is driven by a homing plot that, in Goldstein-Shirley's words, "transcends the traditional bildungsroman, offering a protagonist whose coming-of-age represents a counter-hegemonic gesture" (1). Chin's counterhegemonic gesture, however, gains only a small measure of success inasmuch as the "new" model of masculinity turns out to resemble, more than differ from, what he sets out to subvert. By pointing this out, I am not so much chastising Chin for his failed effort as underscoring the seductive power of hegemonic masculinity and its demand that one must prove oneself to be a man. Neither am I suggesting that it is impossible to construct a Chinese American masculinity that is not an ethnicized version of the hegemonic model.[5]

From Sissy to Man

The tale of *Donald Duk* takes place before the Chinese New Year, a major threshold in its protagonist's life as the title character is about to become twelve, completing his first zodiac cycle to signify his transition from boyhood to manhood. The novel's central conflict is Donald's self-loathing instilled by the orientalist education he receives in a private school—"a place where the Chinese are comfortable hating Chinese" (2). The education he receives is a process of what Frantz Fanon calls "cultural estrangement." Fanon writes in *The Wretched of the Earth*,

> Colonialism is not satisfied merely with holding a people in its grip and emptying the native's brain of all form and content. By a kind of perverted

logic, it turns to the past of the oppressed people, and distorts, disfigures, and destroys it. [...] [In] the efforts made to carry out the cultural estrangement [...] nothing has been left to chance. (210)

In Donald's case his private education schools his shift of social norms and cultural allegiance in its effort to erase ethnic identification in favor of assimilation, and this process of cultural estrangement has rendered the ethnic practices ridiculous and shameful.

Much like Stephen's in *Obasan*, Donald's repudiation of his ethnicity also occurs in his relationship to food. In desiring and consuming what he thinks of as "pure American food. Steaks. Chops" (8), as though ingesting American food would turn him white inside out, Donald practices what Camille Cauti calls "culinary passing" (10). Such passing offers an anxious identity because it requires the passer to revile his or her own kind, and in Donald's life, it is the Chinese cuisine that he must spurn. At the New Year Eve's lunch, for example, he denigrates the king clam dish as looking "like the sole of my Reeboks sliced real real thin" (46). "By comparing a rubber sneaker to an authentic Chinese dish, Donald demonstrates his sense that Chinese American food and culture is [...] literally inedible" (Ho 31). Furthermore, Donald regards everything Chinese as "funny": "the *funny* things Chinese believe in. The *funny* things Chinese do. The *funny* things Chinese eat" (3, emphasis mine). In this ambivalent, slippery word "funny," Donald exhibits what Fanon coins as "the colonized personality" (*Wretched* 250).[6]

In speaking of the affects of the culturally estranged, Fanon remarks that "the emotional sensitivity of the native is kept on the surface of his skin like an open sore which flinches from the caustic agent; and the psyche shrinks back, obliterates itself and finds outlet in muscular demonstrations" (*Wretched* 56). Donald's debilitating embarrassment with his ancestral culture and his ethnicity, symptomatic in the word "funny," displays an open sore that inflicts emotional and physical discomfort. "[W]hen Mr. Meanwright talks about Chinatown, Donald Duk's muscles all tighten up, and he wants Mr. Meanwright to shut up" (34). What becomes apparent in Chin's portrayal of Donald is that the boy's ideological indoctrination has given him a heightened emotional sensitivity toward and repugnance for his home culture—the culture in Chinatown. However, his repeated usage of "funny," or his lack of concrete descriptions, also reveals that the process of cultural estrangement remains fortunately incomplete, which is evident in his incompetent ventriloquy of the colonial/Orientalist discourse. Significantly, this leaves the possibility of the character's development and initiation into a proud Asian American manhood.

Donald's self-loathing is often expressed in the enmeshed lexicon of race and gender. He tends to believe that being Chinese is no different from being sissy and ridiculous. To him "Chinese are artsy, cutesy and chickendick," a language that has proved durable in American culture and an image fraught with the culturally enforced inferiority of Asian American men (3). In this adolescent character, Chin creates an allegory of the open sore that inflicts many Asian American men in the sense that Donald's self-loathing recapitulates the Asian American male subjectivity as masochistic in the face of "the predicament of being yellow and male, of being formed as masculine subjects, in a culture in which most of the dominant images of manhood are white" (Kim 293). Donald's obsessive yet frustrated identification with whiteness purports a self-splitting that David Eng names "a melancholic form of racialized subjectivity" (72).

The white iconic figure that preoccupies Donald's consciousness is Fred Astaire, with whom he carries on imaginary conversations. "I'm like you. We speak the same language. We talk the same lingo. We dig the same jive" (93). His idolization of the Hollywood star is resonant with Daniel Kim's observation of Frank Chin that "many of his [...] literary endeavors betray his own intense and loving obsession with an array of iconic American images of white manhood" (270). One might view in Donald's characterization Chin's own obsessive relationship with the icons in American popular culture. Donald's identificatory complex with Astaire turns on a degrading differentiation from the alienness and awkwardness of the Chinese. In his imaginary conversation, he tells his idol that the Chinese in Chinatown are not "American! Like you and me. The kind of people who make American history. The kind of people actors play in American movies" (91). Having been trained to speak from the regime of American history, Donald cannot but represent Chinese Americans as nonactional and thus unworthy of heroic portrayals. In this demarcation between "us" and "them," Donald participates in the hegemonic process of "othering" that produces a schizophrenic self—a self torn between body (yellow and foreign) and mind (white and American).

To loosen the assimilationist hold on Donald's consciousness, Chin employs the narrative strategy of dream scenarios that thrust the boy repeatedly into the male world of the transcontinental railroad construction. Interestingly, Chinese food punctuates each of Donald's dream sequences, in which he becomes an eating and laboring member of the Chinese community, remaking Asian American history. Ho succinctly points out, "To consume Chinese food is to consume Chinese history" (38). Donald's preference for American food and rejection of Chinese dishes are an overt expression of his subscription to white culture and his belief that only white people are men enough to make history. When shopping with his father for the New Year's banquet, the most important and elaborate meal of the year, he asks for "a filet mignon wrapped in bacon" (39). But in his dreams he feels at home among the Chinese and relishes their cuisine. In the morning before work, he follows the crowd to "the *deem sum* people's camp."

"The *juk* is made, hot and fresh. For a penny he gets a steaming bowl of fresh white *juk* and a dish of three steamed pastries stuffed with fish and chicken" (72). Nourished by dim sum, Donald enters the heroic, historical event of the record-breaking track-laying contest between the Chinese and Irish workers.

Donald's dream world is populated not only with familiar people from San Francisco's Chinatown but also with mythical characters from the Chinese classics. Through these dreams that spill from time to time into his waking consciousness, Donald comes to understand and value Chinese American prowess, and eventually comes to embrace his ethnicity. Donald's dreams constitute the heroic history of the Chinese contribution to the building of the United States—the return of the repressed that renders real the officially erased history, which, via the oral lore, has become the Chinese American collective memory. In his dreams Donald lives this history, visceral in its triumph and disappointment, its toil and dignity, its violence and pride.

The construction of the transnational railroad, therefore, becomes a privileged site for the attempt to constitute a new Asian American male subjectivity. This new subjectivity, however, challenges as well as colludes with the dominant culture. As Viet Thah Nguyen notes, "Donald embarks on his masculine young adulthood through a journey from the Chinese ghetto to the frontier West, a space of violent character formation [...] fundamental to the American imagination" (135). Powerfully shaped by Hollywood representations of the West and cowboys, Chin locates the primary site of Donald's character formation in the body politic. Ironically, this bodily based subject making has always already been inscribed in the practices of domination "because the history of American legislation concerning Asian immigration has been explicitly a biopolitics of bodily regulation, shaping the Asian American community through acts targeting gender, sexuality, race, and class" (V. T. Nguyen 133). What Nguyen refers to are the numerous laws that prohibited the entrance of Chinese women (the Page Law of 1875 and the resulting formation of the bachelor societies), Chinese laborers (the 1882 Chinese Exclusion Law and its ensuing revisions), and a variety of city ordinances of San Francisco that targeted the Asian body as the object of discipline and punishment (regulations on living space, the cutting of the queue as a penalty, etc.).

The masculine presence in Donald's dreams is no longer the white iconic figures Chin has evoked elsewhere—John Wayne, Gary Cooper, and the Lone Ranger. Instead, it comes from Chinese literary tradition. Kwan Kung—a legendary figure in the Chinese classic *The Three Kingdoms*—leads the Chinese railroad workers. In a significant scene, Kwan seizes Crocker's "sixgun in his hand" and leaps onto Crocker's white horse, "splashing mud all over Crocker" (78). Single-handedly, Kwan secures the first victory for his followers. "Kwan lifts Donald Duk into the saddle behind him and rides off to the Chinamen's camp. Crocker chases after on foot, a white suit in a crowd of black" (78). Sitting high and proud on Crocker's horse, Kwan boldly declares to his followers, "They say it is impossible to lay ten miles of track in one day. We begin work at dawn. By sunset we will look back on more than ten miles of track. Do that and Crocker's horse here is ours to eat" (78). Here Kwan's offering of the enemy's horse for a celebratory feast constitutes a hypermasculine act. To eat the white horse, to assimilate the power of one's enemy by eating him or his horse, is metonymic of the neutralization of white men's power and of the feminization of the dandy owner of the Central Pacific Railroad dressed all in white. (In both the East and West, a man's relationship to food and appetite gauges his virility, a connection I explore in the next two sections.)

Under Kwan's tutelage, Donald shifts his identification away from Fred Astaire. Kwan places on him the demand of loyalty and revenge—loyalty to Chinamen and revenge for the injustice against them. Donald performs his vengeance through reconstructing the obliterated history of the Chinese railroad workers. It is through his vengeance that Donald unlearns his identification with whiteness. Three-fourths of the way into the novel, Donald, for the first time, is able to turn the tables on Fred Astaire with a poignant question, a question with a tone of vengeance: "I have always dreamed of being Fred Astaire. Did you ever dream of being like me?" (124). Astaire replies, "Oh, no. I have always dreamed of being Fred Astaire" (124). To both Donald and the reader, Astaire's answer illuminates the asymmetrical nature of the minority's identification with white icons and thus the coercive power exerted at the site of subject interpellation by the hegemonic culture, particularly by the ideology of assimilation. Anne Anlin Cheng writes,

> Racialization in America may be said to operate through the institutional
> process of producing a dominant, standard, white national ideal, which is
> sustained by the exclusion-yet-retention of racialized others. The national
> topography of centrality and marginality legitimizes itself by retroactively
> positing the racial other as *always Other* and lost to the heart of the nation.
> (10, emphasis mine)

Astaire's answer to Donald's question denies the possibility of a two-way traffic of looks between the white national Self and the racialized Other—the possibility for Donald to see Astaire looking at himself through Donald's eyes. Both lost in and angered by the chasm that Astaire's answer has opened up, Donald falls back on a cliché, but one with some edge: "All that matters to you is you are what you always dreamed you'd be" (125). The palpable melancholia in Donald's remark seems to initiate an effort to break free from his obsessive identification with the white icon. This small vengeance constitutes the first act of what Anne Anlin Cheng calls "the conversion of the disenfranchised person from being subjected to grief to being a subject speaking grievance" (7).

In becoming a subject speaking of grievance, Donald avenges the wrongs done to the Chinese railroad workers by first researching the history of the transcontinental railroad construction in Chinatown's library and then, when finding nothing about the Chinese in that particular history, by articulating the injustice of the historical elision. "Report[ing] a crime," as defined by Maxine Hong Kingston, "is vengeance" (53). In Donald's character development, his realization of the historical erasure of Chinese labor becomes a defining moment. He says to his father, "I dreamed *we* set a world's record [...]. I dreamed *we* laid the last crosstie, and it's true. [...] *We* made history. Twelve hundred Chinese. And they don't even put the name of *our* foreman in the books about the railroad" (137, 122, emphases mine). Donald's claim to the collective marks the beginning of the novel's resolution.

Before his journey concludes, Donald confronts the hegemonic culture epitomized by Mr. Meanwright and thus proves to be a man. In the classroom when the teacher begins to lecture on the Chinese, Donald feels for the first time "flashing hot blood and angry [...] at what he hears all the time" (149). He raises his hands and says,

> "Excuse me, Mr. Meanwright. You are incorrect, sir." [...]
> "Mr. Meanwright, what you just said about the Chinese is not true." [...]
> "Yessir, I am offended." [...]
> "You are...sir, Mr. Meanwright, not correct about us being passive, noncompetitive. We did the blasting through Summit Tunnel. We worked through two hard winters in the high Sierra. We went on strike for back pay and Chinese foremen for Chinese gangs, and won. We set the world's record for miles of track laid in one day. We set our last crosstie at Promontory. And it is badly informed people like you who keep us out of that picture there."
> (150)

In this public fashion, Donald finally faces and triumphs over his worst fear: being identified and identifying himself as a Chinese. Chin ends this chapter with Donald wishing Mr. Meanwright a Happy New Year in Cantonese—"*Goong hay fot choy*"—a language he has disowned until now (152).

Cooking as Martial Art

Donald Duk's plot, centering on the rite of passage of a Chinese American adolescent, in the form of instituting his ethnic as well as gendered identity, hinges chiefly on four father figures, two real and two mythical—his father King Duk,

Uncle Donald Duk, Kwan Kung, and Lee Kuey. The real men incarnate the mythical men by playing them in a Cantonese opera. In the portrayal of the father character, the owner and chef of a thriving Chinese restaurant in San Francisco's Chinatown, Chin's strategy is to embed the discourse of masculinity in that of food. One of the recurring scenes is King's kitchen, where Donald and his white friend Arnold often observe and sample Dad's cooking. It is a kitchen in which the "steam and smoke bloom and mushroom-cloud about Donald Duk's father as he tosses piles of raw shrimp paste and bowls of cold sliced fish and fruit, and waves his tools into and out of the roiling atmospheres" (63). Larry Louise, the Chinese Fred Astaire, appropriately describes this scene as "Godzilla versus the nuclear missiles" (64).

Alluding to the original Japanese "Gojira," a cautionary tale against nuclear escalation, this image invokes a samurai-informed masculinity rising up to avenge its annihilation by America's wanton power and technology. Even though in *Godzilla* the giant lizard is created by French nuclear testing, it is Manhattan, the birthplace of the atomic bomb, not Paris, that is trashed. With this allusion, Chin transforms the kitchen into a symbolic site of violence and destruction. In this kitchen the wok becomes "the hot steel," the spatula the sword, and the chef a "swordsman" (64, 65). The military ambience surrounding this chef is further enhanced by the history of his training, for King has learned to cook "in the kitchens of the most powerful men in the world" and often tells "the story of how he passed the war in the kitchens of presidents, prime ministers, premiers, lords and generalissimos" (9). Painstakingly, Chin eradicates all feminine vestiges from King's kitchen not only with analogies of war and martial arts but also by making his cooking performative.[7] Like a martial artist, King takes on challenges. Donald and Arnold often sit in the kitchen and "challenge the extent of Dad's knowledge of food and cooking. Whatever the boys read about and ask for, Dad cooks without a book. Whatever it is, he cooks it" (9).

Others often address King Duk as *sifu,* which means simultaneously a master chef and a kung fu master. The interchangeability between these two identities becomes apparent in the scene of ancestral worship, a ritual always performed via food and drink. The family shrine is set up on the altar table in the dining room. In front of it "stands an incense burner with smoldering sticks of incense punk. A steamed chicken on a platter and three little rice bowls filled with perfect mounds of rice [...]. There is a bottle of Johnny Walker Red [...]. The red envelopes of *lay see* are the donations of the immediate family to immediate family causes [...], the war chest" (65). Family and friends take turns paying respect to the ancestors' shrine. Their stylized manner is unmistakably associated with martial arts. "He lights a stick of incense and holds it in his right hand and covers his right hand with his left, like a swordsman in a kung fu movie meeting a swordsman on the road of life" (65). With one sweep of the pen, Chin transforms what has been demeaned as a demonstration of Chinese heathenness and passivity into a masculine scene of militancy.

Metaphors of war and martial arts thus sustain the descriptions of this kitchen and its owner—a semiotic site where the enjoyment of masculine assertion colludes with that of cooking and eating. Chin's predilection for food is gleefully indulged in this novel, as it is set significantly around the Chinese New Year, a time of cooking and feasting and performing rituals. This is also a time when King must incarnate his mythical model, Kwan Kung, "the god of fighters, blighters and writers," by playing, or more accurately by becoming, him in the Cantonese opera (67). King fits this role not simply because he is a good actor but because he embodies the god's virtues—fierceness, loyalty, and self-discipline. It is significant that Chin makes Kwan Kung (or Guan Yu), the most worthy warrior in *The Three Kingdoms*,[8] the god of both literature and war, who thus embodies the *wen-wu* dyad that has been central to the historical construction of Chinese masculinities. *Wen* means "cultural attainment," and *wu*, "martial valor."[9] While these two qualities have been given different weight at different moments in Chinese history, their balance has never ceased to be the ideal. As Kam Louie explicates, "Ideal masculinity can be either *wen* or *wu* but is at its height when both are present to a high degree" (16).

Chin's transformation of the god of war into the god of literature and war serves to idealize King as a cosmopolitan model of the balanced *wen-wu*, with his American birth, martial arts training in Hong Kong, military service in the U.S. Army, opera performance, and culinary arts. All of these contribute to King's Asian-American-ness as the new model of Chinatown masculinity "to replace," as Ho points out, "Hop Sing of *Bonanza*" (24). In *The Three Kingdoms*, however, Kwan Kung is not known for cultural attainment; his reputation as the best warrior rests on courage, loyalty, and discipline when it comes to women. He regards desiring and desirable women as obstacles to true brotherhood; he "would rather decapitate a beautiful woman than be tempted by her" (K. Louie 46).[10] Therefore, for King to take the Kwan Kung role, he must exercise the ultimate self-control. He explains to Donald,

> Nobody wants to play Kwan Kung. Too risky. What if they accidentally forget and eat a hotdog? Or one bite of a *cha siu bow* goes down their throat before they remember? Kwan Kung does not accept the mess up of responsibility allowed by Western psychology. Real men, real actors, real soldiers of the art don't lose control. Just like Doong the Tattooed Wrestler in *The Water Margin*, when the most beautiful woman in the empire [...] coos and croons all her seductive know-how on Doong, he never gives in and never forgets his mission. Never. (68)

Here Chin's distinction between real and fake men pivots on a man's relationship to appetite, both sexual and alimentary. The punishment for undisciplined appetite, curiously, falls on women. "There are stories about the actor who played Kwan Kung recently and did not take the part seriously, and maybe slept with his girlfriend that night before [...] and when he takes the stage his girlfriend's hair turns white and she has a miscarriage" (67). Misogyny is an indisputable component in this model of contained masculinity.

Ironically, the mainstream culture's distinction between "real" and "fake" men is precisely what has incited rage in Chin, but only because the mainstream's distinction has been made along racial lines. He writes in *The Big Aiiieeeee!*

> It is an article of white liberal American faith today that Chinese men, at
> their best, are effeminate closet queens like Charlie Chan and, at their worst,
> are homosexual menaces like Fu Manchu. No wonder David Henry Hwang's
> derivative *M. Butterfly* won the Tony for the best new play of 1988. The good
> Chinese man, at his best, is the fulfillment of white male homosexual fantasy,
> literally kissing white ass. (xiii)

Fraught with homophobia, Chin's rage doesn't simply derive from the white man's stereotype of Asian American manhood but also from Asian American men's own subscription to it. It would become particularly maddening to Chin if he had any inkling, however slight, of the near totalizing extent of this stereotype, so much so that he himself has operated within its matrix as well, and that is exactly what Daniel Kim charges. In reading Chin's "Riding the Rails with Chickencoop Slim," Kim argues persuasively that Chin has put "his own libidinal investment in white men and the manhood they embody"; "his fervent loathing for Fu [Manchu] also expresses a kind of homophobic self-loathing: what he sees and hates in Fu—an eroticized desire for the white man—is something he sees and hates in himself" (286). Though a victim of this mainstream distinction between "real" and "sissy" men, Chin nevertheless reevokes the same divide in *Donald Duk* in his attempt to remasculinize its Chinese American male characters.

Buttressing Chin's delineation of "real" Chinese manhood in *Donald Duk* is the intertextuality of another Chinese classic, *The Water Margin*. This warrior tale, which portrays 108 exiled and self-exiled renegades, whose code of ethics is nothing but fraternal loyalty, is essential for advancing *Donald Duk*'s narrative and for achieving its final resolution. This classic is also the source of the third father figure for Donald, Lee Kuey, representing another competing form of masculinity, the singularly *wu* model. At the onset of the novel is the description of the 108 balsa-wood model planes that King's family is making. Each of them is painted with the face of and named after one of the 108 warriors. King plans to fly these airplanes off Angel Island on the night of the fifteenth day, a day customarily called the Little New Year, and watch them burst into flames over the Pacific Ocean. Chin's choice of Angel Island is patently significant as it is the most historical and thus most recognizable site where America has exercised its emasculating power over Chinese immigrants by confining, interrogating, traumatizing, and sometimes deporting them. What could be a better symbol of revenge than launching the 108 renegades, firing and afire, into the sky off Angel Island? Donald doesn't understand yet the symbolic value of his father's plan and steals one of the planes on New Year's Eve for an early taste of the thrill. He sets it flying and in flame over the rooftops of San Francisco's Chinatown. This stolen and consummated plane, bearing the nickname the Black Tornado, happens to be Lee Kuey's, thus establishing Lee's relationship with Donald early on in the narrative. Deserving the nickname, Lee Kuey is a killing machine and a dark and fearless devotee of the outlaw brotherhood in the marshes. Chin's description of this mythical character runs amok. "All the Black Tornado's muscles balloon and pull at their roots pounding rage. It's the battle-axe freak who likes to run naked into one end of a battle and come out the other covered in layers of drying blood, with a bloody axe in each hand" (159). In this presentation of a warrior is an extravagant masculinity that Chin glorifies and covets. In a ventriloquist moment, Chin becomes Lee Kuey by having King declare publicly, "I wish Pearl Buck was alive and walk into my restaurant so I can cut out her heart and liver" (135).

Lee Kuey becomes the means of Donald's final identification with the Chinese heroic *wu* tradition and thus instrumental to the young protagonist's completion of the rite of passage. Like Kwan Kung, Lee appears in Donald's dreams, demands Donald's attention, and imparts lessons of pride and valor in his own right. "'You better remember me!' Lee Kuey talks in a voice of crunching gravel, 'Cuz I am out to get ya! I have the blood of punks like you drying into scabs all over my body!'" (114). Although Lee, invariably appearing in disarrayed, bloodied clothes with one axe over his shoulder and another in the other hand, is not exactly a model of manly responsibility, as Kwan is, he nevertheless exemplifies characteristics that are bedrocks of masculinity in both the East and the West, qualities such as valor, loyalty, and a big appetite.

Chin revises the classical character of Lee Kuey to enhance masculinity with the other extreme: undisciplined appetite. Lee boasts to Donald, "I am the only one to eat the flesh of his dead mother, because I was hungry and knew she loved me"—an episode Chin has invented despite the original character's reputation as a filial son (159). The plot that Chin suppresses goes like this. One day Lee carries his mother over a mountain, and when his mother becomes thirsty, he leaves her sitting on a big rock while going off to find water. When he returns, his mother is gone. Upon a closer look, he finds blood and shreds of clothing scattered in the rock's vicinity. Following the blood trail, he comes to the opening of a cave where two tiger cubs are eating a human leg. He kills the cubs and their parents.[11] On the surface, Chin's deliberate reworking of this classical character serves to incarnate the male catechism: a man must do what he must do. In other words, a real man cannot be bothered by female scruples. But more disturbing is its deep, subliminal root in patriarchal religions that supplanted original matriarchal religions by killing and devouring the Mother Goddess (who bore variant names such as Isis, Demeter, Gaia, Shakti, Dakinis, Astarte, Ishtar, Nu Wa, Rhea, Nerthus, Brigid, and Danu).[12] For instance, Zeus swallowed Metis, Goddess of Wisdom, when she was pregnant with Athena.[13] Abundant in Greek mythology, Judeo-Christianity, Islam, Hinduism, and many other religions are tales of slaying dragons and demonizing serpents. Prehistoric dragons and snakes, known as the energy source of life—"of healing and oracular power, fertility and maternal blessing" (Sjöö and Mor 251)—are often associated with female deities such as the Amazonian Medusa, the Chinese Nu Wa, and the Hebrew Lilith.[14]

In light of these motifs of mother killing and devouring in the cultural landscape in which and against which Chin operates as a writer, his offering of a mother eater as a father figure cannot be read simply as an expression of male bravado. Male cannibalism, commencing with Zeus' swallowing of the pregnant Metis and striking again recently in Thomas Harris' character Hannibal Lecter, has been repeatedly reenacted in literary and cultural productions, including Chin's own (such as "Eat and Run," which I discuss in the next section). Carol Adams defamiliarizes us with the daily representations that collapse sexuality and consumption by unveiling the linguistic, imagistic, symbolic, and literal relationship of animal slaughter and meat consumption with violence against women. "Images of butchering suffuse patriarchal culture. A steakhouse in New Jersey was called 'Adam's Rib.' [...] *The Hustler,* prior to its incarnation as a pornographic magazine, was a Cleveland restaurant whose menu presented a woman's buttocks on the cover and proclaimed, 'We serve the best meat in town!'" (60). Although in Chin, Lee Kuey's cannibalistic appropriation of his dead mother is empty of the connotation of sexual violence, the archetypal impulse to strangle and usurp the feminine power of creation is implicit. To devour Mother is to denounce one's connection with the feminine and to usurp the maternal power in the attempt to give birth to oneself. (Zeus, after swallowing pregnant Metis, birthed from his head Athena, who became his mouthpiece. After killing Semele, the mother of his son Dionysus, Zeus sewed the fetus in his thigh for it to reach full term.) Chin furnishes Donald with four father figures that embody competing and yet overlapping masculinities. Their task is delivering him from his eroded and threatened psyche and giving birth to a confident and proud Chinese American man. These father figures find no rivalry in the mother Daisy Duk, who effaces herself quite jocularly. Daisy, after all, is not meant to be a mother. With its unisexual origin in Walt Disney, the Disney Duck family knows no mother figure.

The father figure of Lee Kuey is indisputable, given claims to both Donald's ancestral history and biology. Chin insists that Lee Kuey remains a hero in Chinese history despite his senseless killing of the innocent and has him proclaim, "I am the only one to murder a little boy and still be counted a hero. Because I did it out of stupid loyalty [...], everything sort of worked out" (159–160). As it is, Chin also makes Lee Kuey Donald's ancestor, for Uncle Donald Duk tells the child, "[Y]our Chinese name is not Duk, but Lee, Lee, just like Lee Kuey" (160). This blood connection entitles Lee to his claim to Donald's education and well-being. Thus, he commands, "Don't back away from me, boy. I thought you and me were alike, kid. Anger! Hate! I thrive on it" (160). Then "he pulls a red envelope out of his bag. '*Goong hay fot choy!*'" wishing Donald Happy New Year like a regular uncle (160).

The novel's first resolution takes place at this moment, having established the kinship between our young protagonist and Lee Kuey, having succeeded in schooling Donald in the proper behavior and attitude that comport to masculine conduct, and having forged an ethnic identity secured in the Chinese heroic tradition. Hence, near the end of the novel, Chin revisits the scene of male competition (Donald's encounter with the Chinatown "gang kids") that initially demonstrates Donald's "sissy" self (5). Donald watches a "tall thin Chinatown kid in a camouflage field jacket, military web belt with an army plastic canteen [...], plastic helmet-liner and steel helmet [...], blue jeans bloused into the top of highly polished black jump boots laced with white parachute cord [...]." As this kid approaches, "Donald says, 'Don't mess with me,' with his shoulders, his chest, his neck, his face, his eyes, and walks on. No one messes with him" (134).

Both Donald's masculinization and ethnicization are partially made possible through an embedded discourse of food/appetite and masculinity, and this discourse becomes actualized in part by ridiculing women as well as by excluding their participation in food production and ethnic existential choices. In other words, the portrayal of women as culturally impoverished consumers is one of the necessary conditions for Chin's restoration of Chinese American male dignity. His language describing the food practices in King's kitchen evokes cooking's affinity to martial arts and war. This affinity further disassociates the two kinds of cooking—restaurant and home cooking. The traditional divide between these two modes of the same activity solidifies the system of value in gendered labor. While restaurant cooking has been regarded as male and professional, categorized as production and generating exchange value, cooking at home has been seen as female and domestic, thus belonging to the categories of reproduction and use value.[15] Cooking at home as nonremunerative work does not even enter into the orthodox Marxist analysis of labor and capital. Chin's masculinization of King's kitchen not only relies on the gendered divide between professional and domestic cooking but also attempts to banish the association of cooking with women by excluding Donald's mother and twin sisters from productive labor. Rather, they are but passive consumers.

As representatives of passive consumers, these women necessarily lack individuality. All three female members of the Duk family are given identical character traits, so identical that it is hard to tell them apart; they are cheerful, uncomplicated, theatrical, cartoon funny, callow, and whitewashed. Eileen Fung points out that Daisy Duk's "subjectivity—if there is any sense of that at all—stems from her theatrical impersonations of performers in American cinema (i.e. Greta Garbo, Katherine Hepburn), which further reinforces her distance from Chinese traditions and cultures" (262). With the erasure of her ethnicity, Daisy Duk must relinquish her parental responsibility toward her son and must leave his ethnicization to her very ethnic husband, to Kwan Kung, to Uncle Donald, and to the mother eater Lee Kuey.

Indeed, none of the women agonize over their ethnic or cultural identity as their men do. Their primary presence in the novel comes through their naïve bantering with each other and cute interjections into men's conversation. Chin describes, "The twins often talk as if everything they hear everybody say and see everybody do is dialog in a memoir they're writing or action in a play they're directing.[16] This makes Mom feel like she's on stage and drives Donald Duk crazy."

"Is that Chinese psychology, dear?" Daisy Duk asks.
"Daisy Duk inquires," says Penelope Duk.
"And Little Donnie Duk says, *Oh, Mom!* and sighs."
"I do not!" Donald Duk yelps at the twins.
"Well, then, say it," Penelope Duk says. "It's a good line [...]."
[...]
"I thought it was narrative," Venus says.
"Listen up to some Chinese psychology, girls and boys," Daisy Duk says.
"No, that's not psychology, that's Bugs Bunny," Dad says.
"You don't mean Bugs Bunny, dear. You always make that mistake."
"Br'er Rabbit!" Dad says. (5–6)

Although this dialogue also presents King in a somewhat cartoonish manner, his characterization gets plenty of time and space to develop into a unique individual. Yet the Duk women remain flat and stunted throughout the novel. Fung correctly charges that Chin denies these women "any sense of human authenticity" (263).

As their characterization precludes much possibility of agency, these women serve to set off the men as agents, producers, and providers. King's kitchen regularly feeds crowds of diners, and when it is closed for the New Year holiday it offers free dinner to more than "150" relatives and friends at one time (31). Such a highly productive site banishes the association of cooking with domesticity. In creating such a situation, Chin places women outside the kitchen and assigns them the position of passive consumers. Except for one occasion in which Daisy is found "shelling shrimp, busting crab, blanching chickens for Dad to finish and sauce in the woks," all the women in the novel are denied participation in the now masculine economy of cooking and feeding (69). King as the primary producer/provider not only cooks for armies of people but also offers free food to the community. The Frog Twin sisters "wait outside Dad's restaurant when the garbage is put out. Now and then, when Dad knows they are out in the alley, he gives them a fresh catfish to take home" (10). On New Year's Day, King drops fifty-pound sacks of rice at his neighbors' doorsteps. As Chin bestows the glory of generosity on King, he assigns the disgrace of being charity cases to women. Fung writes of *Donald Duk*,

> Here, the ethnic men are both laborers and consumers, displacing the ethnic women from both public and domestic work as well as denying them their consumption. As the men construct a kind of social reality based on the context of market economy and nationalist discourse, the women, like food, embody exchange and fetishistic values. In other words, the process of producing and consuming food constructs complex power dynamics based on gender and class differences that ultimately lead to a language of legitimacy and exclusion: namely, deciding who gets to obtain, cook, and/or eat food signals an economy of power, exchange, and desire. (256)

Chin's presentation of cooking as masculine/productive labor in this novel engenders a class divide and thus an economy of asymmetrical power relationships between men and women, between the working and the nonworking, between producers and consumers, and between consumers and charity cases. One may argue that the masculinization of cooking succeeds in breaking down the binary between the public and the private in blurring the distinction between home and restaurant. It is precisely through this breakdown, however, that Chin exiles the Duk women from their traditionally gendered space without offering them an alternative location for meaningful labor and subject formation.

Appetite, Trains, and Masculinity

The demonstration of masculinity via disciplined appetite as exercised by King during his preparation to impersonate the god of war and literature disturbingly accompanies another masculinity of undisciplined appetite, embodied by Lee Kuey, who brags about his cannibalization of his dead mother. Both models register masculine prowess in Chin's gender imaginary. A flippant, undisciplined, and corporeal masculinity finds its playground in Chin's short story "Eat and Run," in which indiscriminate appetite gauges the virility of a culture. Chin's narrator defines "Chinaman" this way:

> We were the badasses of China, the barbarians far away from the high culture of the North [...] sending our fingers underground grubbing after eats. We were the dregs, the bandits, the killers, the get out of town eat and run folks, hungry all the time, eating after looking for food. Murderers and sailors. Rebel yellers and hardcore cooks. Our culture is our cuisine. There are no cats in Chinatown. [...] We eat toejam, bugs, leaves, seeds, birds, bird nests, treebarks, trunks, fungus, rot, roots, and smut and are always on the move, fingering the ground, on the forage, embalming food in leaves and seeds, on the way, for the part of the trip when all we'll have to eat on the way will be mummies, and all the time eating anything that can be torn apart and put in the mouth, looking for new food to make up enough to eat. [...] I'm proud to say my ancestors did not invent gunpowder but stole it. If they had invented gunpowder, they would have eaten it up sure, and never borne this hungry son of a Chinaman to run. (11)

This equation of an exotic (peasant) cuisine with Chinatown culture has its class orientation, differentiating "the barbarians" from "the high culture" of Confucianism, whose ideal, couched in the *wen*-over-*wu* (culture-over-valor) paradigm, is often represented in the West as soft masculinity. *The Analects* states, "The master said of the *shao* [music] that it was perfectly beautiful and perfectly good but of the *wu* that it was perfectly beautiful but not perfectly good" (Lau III.25.71). In the Confucian classic *Spring and Autumn Annals*, it is said, "The virtues of *wen* are superior, the greatness of *wu* is lower, and this has always and will always be the case" (qtd. in K. Louie 18). Chin's description of tough Chinamen as bandits and murderers contemptuous of the elite Confucian culture resonates with his essay "Come All Ye Asian American Writers of the Real and the Fake," in which he chooses to militarize Confucianism, insisting that Asian children grow up with "the Confucian ethic of private revenge" (*The Big Aiiieeeee!* 34). This revision energizes Chin's mantras: "Life is war. Every human is born a soldier." "All art is martial art. Writing is fighting" (xv, 35). Interestingly,

Chin unifies the *wen-wu* dyad in this moment by equating the scholar with the soldier, rather than balancing the two, in order to make Confucian masculinity resemble the Western normative masculinity, rendering brain equivalent to brawn.[17] Chin's unification of the *wen-wu* dyad also directly subverts the Chinese literary tradition of scholar-and-beauty romance in which a pale-faced scholar falls in love with a beautiful girl. In this tradition, masculinity and sexual attraction reside in the scholar's intellectual ability or artistic creativity rather than in his physical strength, wealth, or political power.[18] To assert a masculine dignity that is acceptable in the West, Chin must turn the scholar into a soldier.

Chin's maneuver invites further meditation on food. If our cuisine is our culture and our culture is Confucian, then his logic follows that the way we eat is inseparable from the ethic of revenge and war. This masculinized complex of gender, food, and culture finds its precursor in Chin's play, *The Chickencoop Chinaman,* in which the emasculation of the Chinese male is allegorized by the reference to the protagonist Tam as a dish. Via an alimentary metaphor, Tam remarks on the futility of racial mimicry. "My whiteness runneth over and blackness...but people still send me back to the kitchen" (63)—a dish being sent back to the kitchen for being underdone (too white) or overdone (too black). Chin's play concludes with Tam entering the kitchen, where he recalls the Iron Moonhunter; thus he is connected with the heroic in his Chinese American forefathers, a forefather figure that he had been seeking erroneously through the black boxer and Charley Popcorn. It is in the kitchen, too, that Tam appears to realize an identity for himself as a food provider (hence a father figure). This conclusion anticipates the appearance of a new Chinese American chef figure, King Duk, who is a father, a warrior, and an actor as well.

In contrast to King, the narrator of "Eat and Run" enacts a diasporic breed of masculinity that can trace its sources to both East and West through the signifiers of appetite and trains. Both versions are heteromasculine in surfeit, defined by unappeasable hunger, as though masculinity is consolidated only through the consumption of a female body. The story begins with the hyperbolic trope of food and appetite that not only casts the Chinese subject as male but also attributes to it a hypermasculine quality—aggressive potency. Chin's alimentary figuring of the Asian American male subject can be interpreted as an act of transcoding, which Stuart Hall defines as "taking an existing meaning and re-appropriating it for new meanings" ("The Spectacle of the 'Other'" 270). Inescapably operating from the maxim of white masculinity ("T.V. movies were in my blood" ["Eat and Run" 10]), Chin transcodes the cowboy ethos of guns, horses, and solitude to bizarre food matters, bottomless stomachs, and indiscriminate appetite, and he encodes this new Asian American masculinity with a mighty power residing within the physiology of its male body rather than in weaponry. Although not a radical departure from the cowboy cliché, which also aggrandizes the male body's power and stamina, Chin's transcoding of masculine prowess via food and appetite nevertheless subverts the white masculinity in its self-deprecating and ironic tones: "I'm proud to say my ancestors did not invent gunpowder but stole it. If they had invented gunpowder, they would have eaten it up sure" (11).

Such transcoding, however, goes only so far in challenging the hegemonic codes of masculinity. More than having a subversive value, Chin's endeavor unwittingly collaborates with the very discourse he intends to combat in that the relationship between appetite and sexuality is a stable fixture in Western culture. Carol Counihan, in her study of European women's fasting, points out the long-standing association of sexuality with the appetite for food and the limited space in which women were permitted to exercise agency in dominating their bodies through controlling their appetite (105–106). Similarly, Victorian culture also regarded appetite as a barometer of sexuality (109). Chin's picture of a culture and its people who frantically convert nature into nourishment that enables them to "run in your mother country like a virus staying a step ahead of a cure" invites this very association; eating and running and eating around the clock are unmistakable acts of masculine aggression as well as transgression that are appropriate for "bandits," "killers," and "[m]urderers" ("Eat and Run" 11). In this context, the concept of "[f]ood pornography" seems apt in describing the sexualized relationship between the eaters and their food ("Railroad Standard Time" 3).

In this story the Chinese gustatory prowess and gastronomic indiscrimination symbolize the virility and sexual appetite essential in Occidental masculinity. Knowingly or unknowingly, Chin also falls back into the masculinist discourse of ancient Chinese *ars erotica,* which teaches men how to bring women to orgasm without themselves emitting semen, thereby converting female fluids into nourishment. Van Gulik explains a standing belief in Chinese sexology that "during the sexual union the man's vital force is *fed* and strengthened by that of the woman, supposed to reside in her vaginal secretions" (17, emphasis mine). Judith Farquhar correctly points out that in this belief "nurture life" (*yang sheng*), not pleasure, is its primary concern (although in practice pleasure is essential to the production of the vital force, *jing*), and it is the health of the males that is the gravitating center in this sexual/medical discourse.[19] The mutual production of *jing* in coitus benefits men only when ejaculation is interrupted, with *jing* being "a fundamental substance that constitutes and maintains the living body" (Farquhar 265).[20] All benefits (men gain) in this practice are strictly dependent on a man's abstinence, a virtue Chin celebrates in his characterization of both King and Kwan Kung.

Contextualized in this Chinese tradition, Chin's masculinization of Asian American males via food and appetite can be interpreted to hinge on the conversion of the feminine into nourishment. What becomes compelling in the juxtaposition of *Donald Duk* to "Eat and Run" is the apparent intertextuality between Lee Kuey's cannibalistic appropriation of his dead mother and Chin's analogy of the Chinaman to a virus parasitic on the "mother country." Implicit in the gendering and sexualizing of food and appetite is a not-all-metaphorical subthesis that the masculine consumes the feminine (nature and women). Here, masculinity takes on the forms of an unappeasable hunger that devours whatever lies in its way and of a tough digestive system that metabolizes all that it encounters.

"Eat and Run," after its presentation of a spectacle of Chinese gastronomic excesses, enters into the narrative of a literal sexual metabolism enacted by the male narrator upon a former Catholic nun named Lily.[21] The language describing the sexual act is couched in that of food and appetite. "I rolled over onto her sandy breasts, her sandy belly, her sandy thighs, and stuck it in. [...] my grumbling snarling stomach wringing itself out after food. [...] All around sizzling meat. [...] going and going with my thing [...] pointing it into the sound of a stove cooking up a feast" (13–15). With this imbricated language of sex and food, Chin participates in the patriarchal traditions (of both the East and West) in which the female body assumes food metaphors to be sampled and devoured by men. Not only is Lily's body narrated as "sizzling meat" and "a stove cooking up a feast," but she is made an active and willing participant in her own consumption. Lily initiates the sexual act by moving "her hand back and forth, flat, round and round my breast, sanding off a nipple. She breathed in my ear, put her tongue inside, dribbled beer off her kiss" (10). Symbolic of her bodily fluids (*jing*) that are famed for their nourishing properties, she "poured Primo beer down her belly to wash my prick off on the outstroke" (13–14).

The male narrator, fully conscious of the allegory of sex for consumption, momentarily confuses the consumer with the consumed—"Her twat was feeding on me" (23)—but soon the confused state mutates back to the paradigm of the male consuming the female through a reevocation of the initial spectacle of exotic food that defines a masculine Chinese culture. "It [her twat] gnawed on me with fat lips, bone gums, bombardments of marshmallows, rosy slugs, swelling dough" (23). Chin's linguistic contortion disguises this inequitable sexual relation between the consumer and the consumed by a brief illusion of circularity: he consumes her and she feeds on him. Yet the unmistakable conversion of her body to "bone gums," "marshmallows," "rosy slugs," and "swelling dough" directs the image of consumption to his eating of her. Consequently, Lily's body-turning-into-food-matter empowers male virility and inflames Chin's language to such an uncontrollable extent as to become an unabashed, hilarious male fantasy. "The beer down my spine killed everything of me but my prick. The prick that grew bigger than New York and nudged the moon in outer space was loose" (23).

Food, sex, and male virility in both *Donald Duk* and "Eat and Run" are major motifs that enact the masculine discourse of violence, whether contained or unleashed. Its enactment happens through an association, both metaphorical and literal, of food, cooking, and eating with what Viet Thah Nguyen describes as "the performance of violence by the male body" (134). In the previous section, I have demonstrated how Chin transforms the kitchen into a masculine space underscored by the references to war and martial arts. Similar strategies are employed in "Eat and Run," and the male narrator in this story performs his masculinity by evoking the signifier of trains as male violence and virility. "Eat and Run" makes a collage of food, sex, and trains that attests to the sexual aggression of the narrator. Soon into the story he declares, "I am the Iron Moonhunter mounted in the cab, rigged for silent running" (8). Chin's Iron Moonhunter, a significant symbol for Asian American manhood, appears first in *The Chickencoop Chinaman*. Tam tells the story in act 2:

> "[G]randmaw heard thunder in the Sierra [...] and listened for the Chinaman-
> known Iron Moonhunter, that train built by Chinamans who knew they'd
> never be given passes to ride the rails they laid. So of all American railroaders,
> only they sung no songs, told no jokes, drank no toasts to the ol' iron horse,
> but stole themselves some iron on the way, slowly stole up a pile of steel [...]
> builded themselves a wild engine to take them home." (31)

At the end, afflicted with both racial and gender anxiety, Tam reaches a resolution by marrying the kitchen to this uniquely Chinese American train story. While he "works out with the cleaver on green onions," he declares, "a Chinaman borne, high stepping Iron Moonhunter, lifting eagles with its breath! [...] Listen, children, I gotta go. Ride Buck Buck Bagaw with me... Listen in the kitchen for the Chickencoop Chinaman slowin on home" (63, 65, 66). The Iron Moonhunter returns to "Eat and Run" as "the vengeance train" and brings home both the narrator and Grandfather (16). "Ride with me, Grandfather. Going home, Grandfather, highballing the gate down straight rail to Oakland" (8). By summoning the narrator's grandfather to take a ride with him, Chin assigns the narrator the task of assuming the collective body of "Chinamen." The narrator's sexual encounter with Lily, therefore, becomes a collective act, if not of all Chinese American men, at least of him and Grandfather. The fantastic language, in which sex, food, and trains cut and spill into each other, pictures the male body as a potent machine, an engine unstoppable in its racing and "digging" (13).

Inside her twat was like I was mixing concrete. It was wet cement and sand
inside there. I moved back and then I moved in, in cold blood, in and out,
fascinated with the motion, pistoning grit, digging an escape tunnel out of
camp, banging down the right of way, going home, Grandfather. This is my
ancient ship. The Iron Moonhunter is out of the devil's roundhouse, called out
to roll a Chinaman Special down the mainline home, out of the mountains of
night. (13)

Even Lily's body takes on a machine-like quality—"her oily aluminum skin,"
"[h]er cunt clutches me like a baseball bat"—to serve as the instrument of
masculine assertion (9, 14). Lost in his train fantasy of power and velocity, the
narrator "grunted while [...] fucked. Fucked and grunted, beating up a railroad song to make sense of this Hawaii" (13).

Engaged in sex, the narrator rides and becomes the Iron Moonhunter all
at once. In a seamless manner, his narration races from sex to trains and back
to sex again. "I ran it in a long time, panting behind my dong, exploring the
terrible length of her cavernous sigh with it, pushing toward the source of her
heat. [...] Highballing deep into the night [...]. Making the stillness whistle off
the shells of my ears with my speed" (15). After this, the narrative flashes back
to a literal train ride. Like the author, the narrator is "[t]he first Chinaman to
brake on the Southern Pacific line" (15). A long reverie cuts into the scene of
sex: the narrator "was off the train" and walks through the "railyards," burst-
ing with pride (16). When the narrative returns to the present, the narrator has
morphed into a train himself. "My blood has turned into thin gas" (17). When
Lily speaks and interrupts his fantasy, he screams, "Shuddup! [...] Don't talk
to me" (17). Within this brief moment of narrative rupture from the railroad
memory, the narrator is transformed into a bandit and Lily into a hostage. The
scene of sex takes a step closer to real violence. Just as if the interruption didn't
occur, his reverie returns to the railroad without a gap. The language of trains
now, however, reverberates with sexual innuendo.

> The loudness of our four locomotives [...] increased [...] the rising pitch
> of vibrations and concussive thunders that reached right through the flesh
> and clutched the heart and deeper into the valves of the heart, the lips of the
> valves. [...] The racket of the engines had settled into my flesh, my muscle, all
> of me and become the sounds of me alive. (17)

Appropriate to the coupling of trains and sex, the narrative goes on to
describe a scene of violence in sexually charged language. Shannon, the narrator's co-worker, in the process of "coupling" two cars, becomes "coupled up"
himself and dies a violent death (18). Chin's diction blatantly associates male

sexuality with trains and sex with violence. As if the language of coupling were inadequate for this association, the narrator moves on to tell us of his drunken self who couples with Shannon's widow. "[T]hat night! That night! I learned once and for all that I am rotten to the core, and she was too. Well, after we proved that, to get the smell [...] to [...] come clean, we went swimming bareass naked" (19). With all of the imaginative leaps between times, trains and sex, the female body and nature, Lily's "twat" and food, violence and virility, the narrative predictably gravitates toward one maxim—the aggrandizement of masculine aggression.

Just as the sign of trains travels between male sexuality and violence, so does the sign of the female body vacillate between nourishment and danger, between food and eater. Lily's body becomes equated to nature that feeds and comforts as well as threatens to harm the narrator. "Her body, the moon, the beach, breath, splash, sea heaving, through the sand, her body all one, grinding in my euphoric hunger pangs" (14). The ambiguity of Lily's body as a sign serves both to propel the surreal morphing of Chin's imageries and to denote the danger of female power. The transcultural misogynistic discourse warning men of the threat of women is rich in references to food and consumption. The danger of the feminine materializes either through the incorporation of inedible or tabooed food into the male body or through the consumption of male virility by women. In the West, other than the biblical story of the Fall in which a fruit becomes the incriminating evidence against Eve, it is the lore of witches and witchcraft that best demonstrates this discourse.[22] After all, the witch is a cook who stews natural ingredients into potions that heal, transform, or kill when necessary. According to Neumann, the witch's three-legged cauldron has been a symbol of female transforming power; "the magical caldron or pot is always in the hand of the female mana figure, the priestess, or, later, the witch" (288).[23] The witch threatens the patriarchal power so much that she is called "an anti-cook" (Fischler 284). Only in a culture in which female transforming power is feared is there a frenzy to identify and eliminate witches. Their shamanic practices have presented such peril to the male institutions of medicine and cuisine that witches are perceived as a diabolic antithesis to health and epicurism. Although an admirable scholar, Fischler collaborates with this patriarchal interpretation. He notes that "cookery [...] serves to tame the wild, threatening forces that inhabit nature and the universe, the same ones that the witch's anti-cookery is able to unleash" (285). In this contrast between cookery and anticookery, cuisine takes on a masculine identity ("to tame the wild") in distinction from the female form—the witch's malicious mimicry of cookery.

The fear of female power in classical Chinese culture finds expressions in the figure of a glutinous female ghost or fox spirit who preys on pale-looking and romantic male scholars. In the famed Qin collection of ghost tales, *Liao zhai zhi yi*, female ghosts in the form of beautiful maidens seduce sedentary young men, ironically the future of the Chinese patriarchy, who have been slaving over the four great books in order to score well in the civil service exam and therefore to obtain official positions. Once they succeed, and they always do, these beautiful maidens take on vampiric qualities and consume their victims. Through sexual intercourse, they extract male virility to nourish and empower themselves, a fact frighteningly antithetical to traditional Chinese *ars erotica* that values the very opposite.

Straddling both Eastern and Western cultures and their mythical and literary traditions, Chin projects his misogynous fear in infusing the description of sex with motifs of ghosts and vampires. "We were corpses skull to skull, full of worms, adjoining buildings in an earthquake. Bats in the upper hollows. Wrestlers grunted and smacked the floor with their bodies. Footsteps click out of the dark of a long corridor" (14). Chin's ambivalence toward the female body, both an object to be acted upon to demonstrate heteromasculine prowess and an agent that presents peril to the male body, results in a dizzying narrative. "Exploding war all around. [...] I heard the rumble before maniacal laughter. [...] Something coming, I heard, too late to get out of the way" (14). Chin's narrative breathlessly enacts the most staple motifs in the lore of witches and vampires, with "worms," "bats," "corpses," "skull," and "maniacal laughter" driving the narrator's sexual act violently frantic. Out of this symbolic war between the two characters, the narrator or (shall we say?) Chin emerges triumphant, replete with all the masculine glory deemed necessary in his gender imaginary. "I'd been Shanghaied by my monster dong that was rocketing me away with one long hysterical streamline sensation toward parts unknown. I was the great rider, Jonah in the whale, a load of shot in my dad's primed hardon pumping grease out of Ma's little cunt that night in a backyard chicken-coop, in Chinatown, Oakland, California" (23). The collective act of masculine assertion is therefore accomplished in this completion of a circle beginning with Grandpa and ending with the conception of the narrator himself. One cannot help detecting, however, an undertone of caution in Chin's last image of the narrator being "Shanghaied" by his "monster dong." Too much corporeality can result in deviancy and loss of control, thus not being a "real" man. Set alongside the martial arts ideal of self-discipline, we may interpret the East as the repository of "real" men exemplified by King and his mythical counterpart, Kwan Kung.

Chin seems to be traversing in a contradictory field of competing masculinities in the hope of finding or negotiating an alternative model that restores masculine dignity to the Asian American man while still affirming his "yellow pride" (Ho 29). As admirable and necessary as this project is, it is, however, sadly trapped in a diasporic cross fire of masculinities, without one that is sensitive to women and nature. Concretized by food references, this project becomes unfortunately pinioned to many conventional traits of patriarchy and machismo. In "Eat and Run," he offers the narrator's sexual encounter as a voyeur's feast. Yet it is a feast prepared by men to benefit men as it glorifies the submission and the objectification of women and as it proves the power of masculinity via aggressive and indiscriminate appetite, velocity, and violence. Although Chin's beefing up of culinary arts in *Donald Duk* promises a departure from U.S. hegemonic patriarchy, which has emasculated Asian American men precisely through their association with food service, his narrative remains irresistibly drawn to existing discourses of masculinity. Cuisine and appetite in Chin solidify rather than dismantle a transcultural paradigm of patriarchy by equating cooking with martial arts, by relegating women to the positions of consumers and charity cases, and by converting the feminine into food matter that fuels the masculine subject formation of Asian American males.

It becomes apparent that the intersection between ethnicity and masculinity is a site of conflicts and contradictions. To further complicate their relationship, I next introduce the issue of class, because race/ethnicity often determines class position and in turn class and race/ethnicity often affect gender formation. These three are generally inseparable in the study of ethnic literature. In the next chapter I juxtapose these three forces in the lives of the male characters in David Wong Louie's culinary novel *The Barbarians Are Coming*.

3

 Class and Cuisine in
David Wong Louie's
The Barbarians Are Coming

_____

Pigeons. Only recently did I learn that the name for them was squab.
[...] A good meal at forty cents a bird. [...] Mah said they were special,
a nutritious treat. She filled our bowls high with little pigeon parts. [...]
But Mah always sat alone in the kitchen sucking out the sweetness of the
lesser parts: the neck, the back, and the head.
—Fae Myenne Ng, *Bone*

David Wong Louie's novel *The Barbarians Are Coming* (2000) is a culinary event, but one that totters agonizingly between hunger and feast. It is a hunger that no feast can satisfy, and a feast that only accentuates the pangs of hunger. This novel is remarkable in troping food to dramatize the interlocking tensions among race, gender, and class in the psychic development of its protagonist, Sterling Lung. By centering on Sterling's relationship with food in the harrowing formation of his subjectivity, Louie argues that food practices organize individuals' identities and that one's discomfort with home cooking is engendered by ideological demands. Via food tropes Louie constructs a layered narrative moving from melancholia to rage and from rage to recognition, encompassing some of the perennial themes of Asian American literature, including racial emasculation, class identity inseparable from race/ethnicity, and the model-minority complex. Sterling's self-alienating subjectivity is articulated through his class inferiority, which is laced with ethnic and gender insecurity, and Louie's literary, culinary tour de force helps articulate the truth that the social etiology behind Chinese American men's (Genius' and Sterling's) feelings of powerlessness and inchoate anger lies in the nexus of their race, gender, and class oppression.

Although we are currently witnessing an academic revival of class analysis,[1] the field of Asian American studies continues to be preoccupied by issues of race and gender, an Asian American discourse that Jinqi Ling calls "the reigning racial and gender ideology" (*Narrating Nationalisms* 14).[2] Back in 1995

Peter Kwong already cautioned us, "While few works in Asian American literature focus primarily on class, class formation within the Asian American community is very much a reality," and yet "Asian American studies rarely engages it as an issue" (77, 79). This field's concentration on race and gender traps itself in a limited concern from which a critical vantage point is maintained often by silencing the question of class. In blocking out class, it fails to engage in a discussion of the systemic structure of domination in which all forms of oppression network en masse.

In *The Political Unconscious*, Fredric Jameson advocates a literary analysis that reveals "cultural artifacts as socially symbolic acts," acts that allegorize class conflicts in characters and their transpersonal realities (20). Class analysis is significant because the language of class is one of the few public discourses (together with those of race, gender, and sexuality) that openly acknowledge the existence of social conflicts. In this chapter I show how class analysis can yield politically engaged readings of literature without sacrificing literariness. Among the myriad contemporary interpretative apparatuses, few would reject the position that a text's aesthetic exercise and organization are deeply political, but not many give class the central role Jameson does. À la George Lukács, Jameson writes, "[T]he cultural text is [...] an essentially allegorical model of society as a whole, its tokens and elements, such as the literary 'character,' being read as 'typifications' of elements on other levels, and in particular as figures for the various social classes and class fractions" (33). In the context of *Barbarians*, the lives of Genius and Sterling not only serve as allegories of class conflicts but also of race and gender struggles, for Louie's novel exemplifies remarkably well the crosscurrents among class, gender, and ethnicity that saturate the characterizations of its major figures and propel its plot. My main focus is on how Louie employs culinary tropes to articulate these crosscurrents. Because of the organizational difficulty of running all three tracks simultaneously, I center the first section on class and ethnicity and the second on class and gender.[3]

"The best were Swanson TV dinners"

Barbarians begins with two key words—"Feast or Famine"—throwing into question its protagonist's status as an upward-moving minority, or in other words a model minority (3). Twenty-six years of age, Sterling Lung, a graduate of the CIA—the Culinary Institute of America—is a French cuisine chef. With his skill capital funded by a large loan,[4] he obtains his first position as "the new resident chef at the Richfield Ladies Club" (3). This position in the [r]ich [f]ield appears at first to be the realization of the American Dream. His exuberance is palpable at the first sight of the club.

When I drove up for my job interview and first laid eyes on the big white house, with its dark green shutters, vast lawn, ancient oaks and elms, bounded by imposing stone and wrought-iron fences, I felt I had arrived. After spending the majority of my years growing up in the back of a Chinese laundry, I was on the verge of ascending to a new station in life, home in this stately patrician edifice, planting my feet firmly in the American bedrock. (27–28)

To live inside such a mansion, he believes, is his arrival at the promise of America—the promise of full citizenship and economic success. Soon, however, he realizes that his true station is no better than his parents'. The feast of the Richfield makes cruelly apparent his famine. He is "devastated by the news my residence would be the carriage house apartment. [...] I saw things for what they were. I occupied the servant's quarter. And I was undeniably the servant" (29). His education, his apprenticeship in haute cuisine, and his hard work fail to change the fact that he, like all working-class people, lives a life of hunger in the face of the feast he has prepared for others.

The fact that Sterling moves out of his parents' laundry into the suburbs to serve the white and wealthy doesn't move him out of his parents' class position. To mainstream Americans, Asians are a model minority, a reputation historically produced partially by and productive of social obedience. According to *U.S. News and World Report*,[5] Chinese Americans have "become a model of self-respect and achievement," and they "are getting ahead on their own with no help from anyone else" (Wu 158). Against the backdrop of the civil rights movement, this report uses Chinese Americans' frugality and tenacity to denigrate other disenfranchised racial minorities, particularly African Americans. What the report refers to as "achievement" and "success" are no more than racialized occupations such as hand laundry and restaurants, which pose little economic threat to white America.[6] In addition, the Chinese Americans were engaged in a subsistence economy without any government assistance and without instigating social unrest. It is precisely because of the rarity of organized class struggle in Chinese American history that the report names the Chinese Americans a model minority.

Mike Savage points out, "Class identification is usually ambivalent, defensive, and hesitant" (36). Sterling's class consciousness initially exhibits all these qualities. He is ashamed of his background, quietly bitter in the face of injustice, and desires power and dignity via the socioeconomic ladder. As in most immigrants' class identification, Sterling's is inextricably intertwined with his discomfort in his ethnicity. Louie shows this complex of class and ethnicity through Sterling's ambivalent relationship with his parents and their foodways. What used to be "a childhood favorite of" his (104) he reviles now as "barefoot food, eat-with-stick food" (75). He opens his parents' refrigerator to expose mockingly "greens, and roots: bundles of medicinal herbs, twigs, bark, berries, and what look like worms bound with pink cellophane ribbon [...]. Under harvest moons, rinse off the maggots, slice, and steam. It is squatting-in-still-water food. Pole-across-your-shoulders, hooves-in-the-house food" (75–76).

In appealing to our sense of pure/impure, inside/outside, and filthy/clean, Sterling's description renders his parents' foodways almost unfit for humans. Monica Chiu comments, "Food's status as either disgusting or delectable has always pivoted in the space of the slash (/), based on human classification by one (dominant) subset of people for their own finicky and fluctuating tastes in a manner that shapes its meanings for other groups of people" (138). Sterling's white, middle-class preference structures his tastes and sensibilities to such an extent that the slash (/) between delectable and disgusting food also cuts across white America and Asian America, elevating European (read "civilized") cuisines over against Chinese food, seen as barbaric and degenerate.

The further othering within the Other becomes a necessary condition for the assimilated self to organize and maintain its tenuous borders. Sterling's self-appointed affinity with white and middle-class Americans not only deems Asian American foodways filthy but also deems its people outside the borders of the national imaginary. In desiring the "real food," "[w]hat real people ate," he demonstrates the operation of the ideology of assimilation that equates "real" people with white middle-class Americans and Asian Americans with poor foreigners (76). Anne Anlin Cheng remarks, "Racialization in America may be said to operate through the institutional process of producing a dominant, standard, white national ideal, which is sustained by the exclusion-yet-retention of racialized others" (10). To white America, Sterling is unquestionably among those to be simultaneously excluded and retained so that American nationality can continue defining its ideal over and against the racial Other. His identificatory complex with American nationality thus feeds upon the very ideal that castigates him. To identify with the national ideal the racialized Other must desire its own denigration. Or as Cheng puts it, "[T]he education of racism is an education of desire" (19). From a young age, Sterling feels compelled to imitate how "real" people eat, "[w]ith forks and knives, your own plate, your own portions, no more dipping into the communal soup bowl. Food from boxes and cans" (76). In demarcating the civilized (read "white") table service and manner from the ethnic (read "barbaric") communal dipping, Sterling meets the objectives of the racist, binary pedagogy that introduces political domination into the seemingly apolitical sphere of personal experience.

The distinction between civilized and barbaric food practices elucidates how the national ideal inscribes not only racial/ethnic but also class differentiations. Class ideology has always been a significant component in American nationalism, which projects its ideal through media images that are predominantly white, heterosexual, middle class, able-bodied, educated, and professional. In Sterling's life such ideological and imagistic coercion manifests itself in his relationship with food. To him Chinese cuisine with everything mixed together symbolizes the way his family lives, while American food shows "[h]ow real people live" (76). He recalls his childhood impression: "The best were Swanson TV dinners. Meatloaf, Salisbury steak. I was convinced Salisbury steak was served in the White House every night. Meat in one compartment, vegetable medley in another, apple crisp next door. What a concept! Everything had its own house or its own room" (76). The young Sterling's comical association of Swanson TV dinners with the first family links food practices with a classed national identification in which everyone has his own house or his own room. In this picture real Americans do not live in a cramped space as the Lungs do.

Capital demands that space be organized hierarchically, with classes ordered in their appropriate places both to minimize social and class conflicts and to maximize productivity. Lisa Lowe, writing about Fae Myenne Ng's *Bone*, defines Chinatown as a heterotopia, a term that Michel Foucault uses to describe "[a site] of crisis and deviation" in a system of hierarchically organized social space (122). In its condensed space where no easy demarcation can be made between private and public, leisure and work, legitimate and illegitimate, and commercial and residential, Chinatown frustrates capitalist rationality for spatial organization. The Lungs' laundry is such a space, with business conducted in the front of the house and family life lived in the back and basement. Such a spatial arrangement is a residue from a pre- or infant capitalist era and resists advanced capitalism's disciplinary ordering of space and, as Lowe puts it, "marks the disunity and discontinuity of the racialized urban space with the national space. It's a space not spoken by or in the language of the nation" (122). Pockets of resistance such as Chinatowns and the Lungs' laundry challenge the rigidity of national borders. As we sometimes hear from tourists, Chinatown feels like a foreign country. This explains why Sterling regards his parents' laundry as un-American and their class difference from others as a race matter. "Oh, the privilege of being an American," Sterling ponders, "cars and quick escapes! Until I was fourteen or fifteen my family never owned a car. That fact was consistent with the profile of Chineseness that was forming in my young brain: We don't own cars, we don't live in houses, we don't eat anything but rice. Each one a racial trait" (45). Louie remembers that he himself, having internalized the othering of Asian Americans, saw his family "as somehow abnormal" (Hirose 199).

The ideology of assimilation is instrumental to capitalism in demarcating civilization and barbarism along the lines of class and race/ethnicity based on consumption patterns. Bourdieu argues that "art and cultural consumption are predisposed [...] to fulfill a social function of legitimating social differences" (*Distinction* 7). Such ideological demarcation produces in the people of color and the poor a self-alienating subjectivity that is manifested through self-faulting, self-loathing, and self-abjection. Part of the self-alienation one experiences is due to the ideological demand that one renounce one's relationship to one's heritage, which may very well be a precapitalist mode of existence such as self-sufficiency. Louie uses references to food consumption to portray Sterling and his mother, Zsa Zsa, as embodying two very different systems of value, and thus their contrasting perspectives on what is considered civilized eating. For example, Zsa Zsa never wastes time and money on serving dishes, but serves "English muffins" in the pan in which they are cooked. "Why do more work than necessary; isn't there enough to do already? Who cares how food is served, just as long as there is food to serve?" (367). Sterling, however, begins to question this home practice after he visits his classmates, for he is "shamed and mesmerized by their table manners, by their glasses for cold drinks, cups and saucers for hot, dishes of different sizes for different purposes, the dizzying array of utensils, big and small, the beautiful gilt-edged platters on which food was served" (367). Conspicuous consumption and trivially specialized commodities preoccupy people's notions of self-worth and belonging. Those who are not bothered by how the Joneses live are often perceived as poor, dumb, and crude. In copying the table manners of his classmates, Sterling feels self-conscious and unnatural, "like dogs trained to walk on their hind legs." But to assimilate, to appear American, Sterling must mimic; "even coarse mimicry [...] was belonging" (367).

> On another occasion, Sterling takes his mother Zsa Zsa for a ride through
> the narrow, maple-lined streets of split-level houses, fresh paint, and two-
> car garages where many of my schoolmates and her customers lived. In
> front of one house she had me stop, and she exited the car and inspected
> the shiny-leafed bushes and shrubs, clipped at crisp right angles, stately as
> the Parthenon. [...] "Why plant so many plants you can't eat?" she said in
> Chinese. "These people are stupid." [...] "If it were left up to you," I said [...]
> "those nice garages would be stables, the lawns vegetable gardens." How stupid
> she was, ignorant of the look of success, of civilization at its height. (37)

Fundamentally frustrating to capitalist rationality, Zsa Zsa's peasant mentality disregards the look of success and evaluates things for their use value alone. What does not contribute to survival is wasteful, and looks mean little in her value system. Sterling on the other hand marvels, "What a luxury unused land is" (37). He fantasizes about his ownership of a place projecting the look of success. Sometimes when he cooks in the club, he looks out its kitchen window at the Puerto Rican gardener with his son working in the grounds. "From *my* position inside the house, I feel as if he were *my* gardener, working under *my* orders, keeping each of *my* blades of grass trimmed to the same height" (37, emphasis mine). Instead of viewing the gardener as a fellow worker, another exploited ethnic minority member who serves the rich white ladies, Sterling separates himself, cooking *inside* the kitchen of the mansion, from the gardener, working *outside* in the sun. The repeated usage of the possessive pronoun underscores his imaginary power derived from imaginary ownership of property.

It is not surprising that a collective class consciousness is foreign to Sterling, for class in America is a taboo subject. Perrucci and Wyson attribute this fact to "the national reluctance to examine how the class system of the United States operates on a day-to-day basis" (4). For this class system to work, they point out, "the majority of disadvantaged Americans must be persuaded to believe that the way things work out for people is fair. This is done by distracting attention from class inequality and focusing the national spotlight on conflict between Blacks and Whites, women and men, gays and straight, prochoice and antiabortion partisans" (4–5). As a result, class has been forced underground and remains deeply "embedded in the recesses of our cultural and political unconscious" (Aronowitz 30). The class unconscious manifests itself via Sterling's class aspirations. The fact that he aligns himself with the Richfield ladies, whose social station he aspires to achieve through his skill capital, over against the Puerto Rican gardener demonstrates that class hierarchy remains a dominant feature in the United States. Despite the sustaining myth that all Americans are middle class and, therefore, America a classless society, millions of Americans like Sterling continue to experience class anxieties in their daily lives.

Sterling's marriage to Bliss Sass is highly motivated by his class ambition. His half-hearted relationship with her, resulting in pregnancy, begins the novel as its major conflict. While he tries to persuade her to have an abortion, he becomes attracted to Yuk, a Hong Kong girl his parents intend for him to marry. When he agrees to visit Bliss at Thanksgiving, he has no intention of marrying her (134). Things change, however, when he lays his eyes on the Sass estate in New Canaan. Driving up the private road, he experiences a mixture of voyeuristic pleasure, envy, and inchoate anger.

> I finally find the Sass property, [...] and immediately my eyes are filled with
> the bright whiteness of the vast groves of birches on both sides of the asphalt
> drive. The trees are so densely packed in the endless acreage that the moment
> is dazzling: it's like *tearing* through clouds at thirty thousand feet. All I see are

the tall, papery-barked trees and the long black drive that *cuts* through them to *oblivion*. I blink, inhale deeply, *set and reset my jaws:* I'm adjusting my body to the new light, air, and sounds.

The road narrows and winds, five-mile-an-hour curves as tight as *fish hooks*, to the right, to the left, *tortuously* luring me in. [...] At last, I see the house plainly—a giant tease, like *gold littered on American streets*, set among somber centuries-old trees, the ultramodern glass-and-steel jewel Bliss calls home. I am in love! (137, emphasis mine)

Symbolic of the Gold Mountain, a fantasy that lured tens of thousands of Chinese to America, the Sass estate is "gold littered on American streets." With the metaphors of "tearing," "cut," "fish hooks," and "tortuously," Louie suggests the danger of this lure. Preconsciously, Sterling understands the peril that the bait of the Sass property presents: once caught he will become their fodder. His white preference and class aspiration, however, propel him forward regardless of his fear. He is described as "set[ing] and reset[ing]" his "jaws" as though anger prepares him for the hook to take him to "the new light, air, and sounds," a new environment that is fatal to him. Louie's language depicting Sterling's state of mind at this moment powerfully evokes contrary emotions with "oblivion" paired up with "new light" and "cut" with "love." In discussing Toni Morrison's *The Bluest Eye,* Anne Anlin Cheng writes about such paradoxes: "White preference is not a phenomenon that simply gets handed down from society to black women and then to black girls; instead it travels a tortuous, melancholic path of alienation, resistance, aggression, and then, finally the domestication of that aggression as love" (17–18). This insight illuminates the painful operation of class envy, class anger, ethnic inferiority, and rage in the psyche of Sterling, who at the end converts aggression to love and personal displeasure to social pleasure. The lack of institutional space for class discourse effectively sends class anger and grief into hiding.

Social pleasure at such personal costs leads to a symbolic death for Sterling, which commences as soon as he enters the Sasses' house. By now not only does he no longer resist Bliss' proposal of marriage but also considers giving up his name for hers.

A switching of names is, in a certain light, like the trading of fathers. Trading hers for mine, Sass for Lung. Anyone can see what a swindle that is. I would gladly accept such a one-for-one swap. And why not? Look at this land, this house, those fine automobiles! He makes tons of money without having to press a single shirt, without having to kiss a single customer's starch-or-no-starch ass. What's so bad about that? Change my name, slip free of the old yoke, refathered, reborn, Sterling Sass? Absolutely. (141)

Sterling Lung must die in order for Sterling Sass to be "refathered, reborn," and mesmerized by the wealth around him, he chooses suicide. In the logic of money and power, such trade of a poor, colored father for a rich, white one can only be considered a "swindle." Taking in the wealth of the Sass property, Sterling measures it with what he understands and appreciates—the riches in the kitchen:

> The bulging bowls of fruit, Golden Delicious, Red Delicious, Granny Smith, Pippin, Empire, Jonathan, McIntosh, Cortland apples: Bartlett, Bosc, Anjou, Comice pears; expensive out-of-season peaches, cherries, plums, and nectarines; crystal dishes brimming with walnuts, pecans, almonds, hazelnuts, brazil nuts, chestnuts; pumpkin, spaghetti, hubbard, acorn, turban squash for show; loaves of white, rye, challah, and pumpernickel [...]; twenty pounds of turkey, and the best ingredients money can buy for sides, blue point oysters, Iowa pork sausage, Idaho russets, Carolina yams, Long Island corn, Cape Cod cranberries, Florida oranges. (147)

Rather than sensuality and splendor, the quantity and variety of foods inspire awe and repulsion. The Sasses' kitchen, more like an upscale supermarket than a home kitchen, presents a cornucopia of the best in the world that money can buy—a truly decadent scene of promiscuity and wastefulness. No wonder "an emergent madness surfaces on my [Sterling's] face, lost as I am in such a magnificent jungle of goodness" (147). Louie's craft in language vividly portrays Sterling's class anxiety and ambivalence. As a French chef in the midst of such a "jungle of goodness," he is both overwhelmed by the joy of recognition of good living and the fright of senseless consumerism that is a jungle with no outlets. And in this "magnificent jungle of goodness," nonexistence awaits.[7]

Louie's choice of Thanksgiving for this occasion requires some meditation. Thanksgiving, one of the two major American holidays underscoring the national imaginary, perpetuates the myth of racial harmony and promotes ideological amnesia of genocide and colonization. It conjures up the rosy picture of the first meal shared by the exiled and their hosts. Through gustatory assimilation, Thanksgiving presents the bounty of this land and the goodwill of its first people. Sterling's entrance into the Sass family on this holiday stages a parody of Thanksgiving, in which he arrives as an outsider at the bountiful estate of the Sasses, who posture as native American, opening their door and offering their hospitality to the exiled (in two senses: the prevailing perception of Asian Americans as perpetual foreigners and Sterling's self-exile from his ancestral culture). The American deed of goodwill by sharing Thanksgiving dinner with foreigners often exacts religious and cultural conversion. In

Sterling's case, the staged racial and class harmony leads him onto the path of further self-alienation.

In the face of the Sasses' wealth, Sterling is filled with gratitude and self-contempt. He is grateful that the Sasses are civil to him in spite of Bliss' pregnancy, now that he fully realizes the severity of the matter—that Bliss is the precious daughter of rich and powerful people and that they could make his life miserable if they wished. Selma Sass' first question to him is caustic and insulting: "Is it true that your parents work in a laundry?" Sterling's immediate answer attempts to narrow their apparent class distance: "They own the business." Selma's response shows a touch of ironic condescension: "That must make it nicer for them" (143). Sterling quickly changes "the subject, nothing gained stumbling along that path. It's guilt by association" (144). His self-contempt illustrates that the ideology of the American Dream conditions one's sense of self-worth, for it enjoins self-blame for failing to succeed in the land of promise. Consequently, he feels undeserving of his new fortune.

> I know then, in my most honest heart, that I don't belong here, absorbing
> their heat, eating their food, getting high on their good fortune. New Canaan
> is mine because of their charity. Bliss is my pipeline to this bounty, and I don't
> even love her. [...] Isn't this love I feel? I find it in a crease inside me like a
> utility bill I've lost, sandwiched between other papers, and neglected to pay.
> My unworthiness of this bounty explains my vague love. What in my history
> allows for such presumption? It's my back-of-the-laundry soul clanging inside
> her beautiful house; it's my bigoted immigrant parents who'll remain, until
> their deathdays, bottom-feeders, washing and ironing for others. (154)

The analogy of his finding a vague love for Bliss to his discovering a utility bill he has neglected to pay sets in motion Sterling's inner turmoil in the language of class. An unpaid utility bill entails powerlessness, starvation, or both, and yet to pay this bill requires him to marry a woman he doesn't love. Ultimately, the payment for class promotion is further self-alienation. The evocation of his parents' class position in this context reveals his inarticulate anger and bitterness, for deep down he knows that it is not his parents' laziness or stupidity that render them "bottom feeders," as the discourse of the American Dream would like him to rehash. Yet such knowledge without a collective class consciousness and its desire to engage in class struggle simply produces melancholia and masochism.

Louie shows the psychological drama centering on class inferiority in Sterling via the objective correlative of a deer battling the expensive electric fences Morton Sass has erected. It is here that his masochism neutralizes his otherwise explosive rage. When Sterling is first introduced to the fences, he reaches out to test the wires' tension. Sass doesn't stop him, knowing fully well the voltage of the fences. "I'm jolted back by a sharp electrical charge that brings tears to my eyes. [...] I shout, shaking, then inspecting, my fried hand. Morton Sass laughs. In a dark corner of my mind I register the moment as a milestone in our brand-new relationship: I have made Morton Sass laugh" (140). Sass' pleasure at Sterling's expense is weirdly perceived as a reward in a "dark corner" of his mind, and this dark corner of repression converts his rage into love. To let his rage out of hiding would jeopardize the social pleasure he is seeking. As they walk to the house Sterling spots a deer. Sass cusses, picks up a stick, and throws it at the deer. "Here, eat this!" Sass shouts. "Get off my property" (141). Sterling's identification with the deer comes effortlessly. "His voice thumps off my heart and echoes in my chest, as if the anger were really meant for me. When the deer bounds away, part of me runs with him" (142). Sterling subconsciously recognizes himself in the deer that intrudes onto the Sass property to feed on a few leaves of lettuce in the garden. During the Thanksgiving feast, which Sterling has helped cook, the deer returns, this time coming threateningly close to the window of the dining room.

> Framed in the sheet of glass is the same magnificent deer, its antlers
> spanning the window. He stands inches from the pane, his ears cocked
> and wary, eyes bright, tender, gleaming like oil in a cast-iron pan. [...] We
> recognize we are in the presence of a force we are not going to understand.
> As he absorbs our abrasive stares he stares back at us: his dark eternal gaze,
> bulging with longing, eats right through me, and I feel undressed, dissected,
> unsexed. (154)

Sterling's identification with the deer tightens here via the mirror image: "the reflection of my face is superimposed on the deer's body," as though it were himself outside the window looking in (154). It is ironic that the electric fences Sass has erected around his property to prevent the trespassing of humans and animals keep out neither Sterling nor the deer. The deer's magnificence, audacity, and defiance, which Sterling clearly admires, drive fear into the hearts of these rich people. Its dramatic arrival at the Thanksgiving feast represents the return of the repressed in Sterling—the outrage over blatant social inequality and the longing for the same affluence and comfort. Confronting the deer's courage and maleness, Sterling feels helpless, impotent, and ashamed. When the deer bounds off, he feels as though it had carried "my heart away like a tick," another metaphor of his symbolic death (155).

Sterling's class aspiration calls for the disavowal of his ethnicity because in his mind being Chinese is tantamount to being poor. While his parents pin their hope of class mobility on his becoming a medical doctor, he chooses to pursue a career as a French chef, for in the hierarchy of culinary art, French cuisine occupies an elite position. In his own words, French cuisine is "aristocratic" and Chinese "the plebeian fare" (210). Bourdieu employs "habitus" to describe a socially and historically acquired disposition that is both classified and classifying (*The Logic of Practice* 54). Because of its consistency through regularities and repetitions, habitus acquires the status of necessity and naturalness. Habitus thus is an existential condition of which one is often unconscious—a state of ease in a social locale. One can say that Sterling has been brought to consciousness of his habitus by his heightened sense of racial and class differences manifested in matters of taste, and his spoiled habitus results in his hopeless class aspirations and painful alienation from his kind. With his vocational choice, he believes he has managed to distance himself from his ethnic origin, has gone mainstream or even highbrow in his taste and sensibility. He finds comfort in the apolitical rhetoric of desire and passion: "My purest desires are in the kitchen: for the exact flavor, the clearest consommé, the perfect meringue, precise paysanne-cut potatoes [...]. My great desire, the one that inspires the others, is to please my diners, that they love my food and love to take me into their bodies, into their hearts" (88–89). It is cooking and serving French food that allows him to conjure the illusion that the rich white ladies at the club accept him as one of them and that he assimilates by being assimilated into their bodies.

His notion of purest desires existing in the kitchen serves as his opium to put to rest any inkling that his activities in the kitchen are far from being innocent and apolitical. To accentuate this point, Louie places Sterling in his mother's kitchen where his "purest desires" vanish; instead he feels disdain mixed with awe. It occurs to him "that, improbable as it may seem, I'm watching Zsa Zsa perform the meal's *mise en place*. To think such similarities exist between her casual, capricious, undisciplined style of cooking and what I learned at a cost of thousands of dollars in student loans" (102–103). Zsa Zsa looks at French food with equal disdain. "That *lo-fahn* [foreign] food you cook," she says, "don't tell me that's what you eat too! I worry for you" (103). To her Americans are "more concerned with how the food looks than how it tastes" (105). In a moment of exasperation, Sterling grabs at the rice pot Zsa Zsa is carrying and "accidentally hook[s] her arm, and the rice spills out, each grain crashing on the linoleum, crackling like static" (103). Louie sets this scene to be highly symbolic of Sterling's rejection of his rice-dominated culture. The hyperbolic sound effects—"crashing" and "crackling" of each grain—loud with Louie's disapproval of his protagonist, underscore Sterling's own inkling of guilt, vividly conveying the agony he suffers in his self-alienating effort to assimilate into the mainstream by rejecting his parents.

The central allegory that organizes this novel's plot is the abduction of Baby Sterling by Lucy, the white woman with whom Sterling's father Genius has had a brief affair (284–285). Sterling's brief abduction symbolizes his loss to his parents and his ethnic origin. "Days after the incident his [Genius'] wife insisted the baby was not the same baby that had been stolen from her. In the short time they were apart something had happened, though she was unable to pinpoint a single characteristic that was different. She just knew" (286). With this allegory, Louie impresses upon his reader that Sterling's alienation from his parents, his ethnicity, and ultimately himself is an outcome of ideological abduction. In other words, he has been orphaned by the ideology of assimilation. His acquiescence to the socioeconomic demand that "real" Americans be white and middle class is symptomatic of a U.S. cultural hegemony that promises racial minorities economic rewards for self-abnegation. Speaking in Genius' voice addressed to Sterling, Louie condemns this ideological coercion with a parable.

> You grow up with wolves, you are theirs your whole life. You howl like them, rip the meat like them. They raise you from infancy, and then the day comes when you wake in dew-wet grass, your feet aching from a hard night's hunt, and you realize you're not a wolf after all. The wolves, of course, know this all along. [...] You are confused; you think you had unlearned your wolf days, but the wild's furry edges still must show. As you shake your head, vehemently denying you ever ran with wolves, your lips involuntarily peel back, baring your teeth, and you snarl and growl. (347–348)[8]

Genius' parable powerfully indicts capitalism for having turned human beings into predators. Implicating the ideology of assimilation, this tale also reveals the painful truth that the racial Other remains Other to the national Self even as the former believes otherwise.

Despite his disavowals of ethnic identification, Sterling can never live outside his skin color and physiognomy. Lisa Marie Cacho in her review of *Barbarians* says it well: "Completely invested in and taking all the right steps to American assimilation [...], Sterling still finds his socioeconomic success dependent upon his compliance with being marked and marketed as foreign" (380). He is force-fed with racial stereotypes when he is constantly asked to cook Chinese and to sound comically "Chinese" on a cooking show. Libby Drake, the president of the Richfield Ladies' Club, doesn't understand why Sterling cannot and will not cook Chinese, because in her mind his ethnicity naturally guarantees authentic Chinese cooking regardless of his training, as though the knowledge and art of Chinese cuisine were in his DNA. Sterling's response, however, is "I'm a chef, one who specializes in continental not communist cuisine" (146). While divorcing culinary art from the notion of ethnic authenticity, he appeals to another U.S. ideological fixture—that communism is evil—to legitimate his choice of vocation and to certify his American-ness. Subscribing to the discourse of assimilation, he believes that America is a culture where a man reinvents himself and where his arbitrary racial makeup matters less than his conscious choice of self. "[W]hat I am is a chef," Sterling thinks. "Damn it, Morton Sass should know better than label me Chinese. This is America" (148). When Libby Drake finally realizes that Sterling will never cook Chinese for the ladies, she hires a Chinese cook, whom she introduces as an "authentic" Chinese, implying that Sterling is not (198).

The other face of ethnic authenticity is exoticism, and in the global capitalist circulation of commodities, ethnic exoticism generates profit and degrades the ethnic laborer. Sass orchestrates a TV cooking show that stars Sterling; its name, *Enter the Dragon French Kitchen,* plays on his last name, Lung (dragon), and its ethnic ambiguity (Bliss Frenchifies it as "Lunge."). Sterling proposes to blend "the aristocratic cuisine in which I was schooled with sprinklings of the plebeian fare [Chinese cuisine] that the masses apparently want" (210). But Sass, a shrewd businessman, insists, "Why do you want to compete with that crowd already cooking normal food?" (210). By labeling French food as "normal," Sass exoticizes Chinese cuisine. "That Chinese guy is where you go if you want to egg foo yung," he tells Sterling (211). In other words, normal people cook and eat normal food, and the Chinese, exotic food. Bell Hooks points out, "The commodification of Otherness has been so successful because it is offered as a new delight, more intense, more satisfying than normal ways of doing and feeling. Within commodity culture, ethnicity becomes spice, seasoning that can liven up the dull dish that is mainstream white culture" (21). Understanding the increasing desire to eat the Other, Sass invests in televising ethnic cuisine for one purpose only—profit. With Bliss' mediation, Sass finally concedes that Sterling will cook Chinese every fourth Sunday and the rest of the month, French. A significant characteristic of being the exploited class is one's inability to define the product of one's labor or to determine its market value.

Alienated labor produces alienated selfhood. By shifting points of view, the author further reveals the extent to which such self-alienation afflicts the protagonist. Through Genius' eyes, the reader sees how Sterling prostitutes himself on TV.

The shiny cleaver chases the knuckles along the stalk of cabbage, a blur of a blade that slams hard against the cutting board, just shy of his hand. Where did this technique come from? All for show. Americans eat this crap up. And what are they really after? They want to see him slip, see the chink lop off a digit. If he had any real balls, he'd drop his trousers, hoist his dickie bird onto the chopping block and give them a real thrill, something to remember. [...] Shameless. Making a fool of himself. Like his dick's already been cut off.

His son finishes the last stalk of cabbage with an emphatic *whomp* of the cleaver. "Wow!" he says, smiling into the camera, eyes as big as Ping-Pong balls. "Velly, velly fast!" (228)

Genius feels deeply pained by his son's TV persona, "his flesh and blood on display like a rare zoo creature for everyone to gawk at" (229). Through his performance of the racial stereotype of a Chinese chef, eager to please and unabashed with foreign accents, Sterling commodifies himself in a market that craves the exotic and the comical in the name of multiculturalism. In Sterling's own words, "I act like an ass on TV because I don't know how else to act. How am I supposed to be Chinese? By being myself? I'm not the kind of Chinese that viewers want to see [...]. So I try to give the people what they want: a goofy bucktoothed immigrant bastard who is humbled and grateful he's been let into their homes" (348). He is so successful in denigrating himself and his people that he begins to accrue value as a commodity, which Sass sells to San Francisco public TV. "Congratulations," he tells Sterling, "you finally turned a profit" (295–296). With this business transaction, Sterling's self-alienation deepens. His complete loss of autonomy is powerfully evoked in his conversation with the butcher, Fuchs. "So now I'm a piece of meat," Sterling says despondently. "You're being *sold* like a piece of meat," Fuchs replies (296). Sterling's early illusion that in the kitchen he is a man has become shattered, and instead he himself becomes feminized—an object, a piece of meat, to be bought and sold, to be manipulated, cooked, and consumed. In San Francisco his show is given another name, "*The Peeking Duck* ('evvy week I peek into your life!'—another voice I borrowed from another TV Chinese chef, Hop Sing, the houseboy on *Bonanza*)" (296). The obscenity of the show's name renders no agency, for a TV chef is the object of gaze, not at all in a position to peek into anyone else's life. The intertextuality with *Bonanza* solidifies Sterling's lack of agency, with the TV character portrayed as a powerless, asexual, grinning, and bowing houseboy.

The ultimate self-loathing in Sterling is allegorized in his ambivalent relationship with his sons. At the birth of Moses, his older son, Sterling feels relieved that the baby "at least in his first hours of life, has chosen to resemble Morton Sass, and not Genius or some mutty blend of the two" (182). Sadly, it is the baby's white looks that form a bond with Sterling. "He is my child, precisely because he is loaded with Sass genetic material" (182). After a few days, however, he is dismayed that Moses has lost the Sass look. "It doesn't matter how many times I blink, how wide I stretch my pupils, how near or distant I focus my gaze: My baby boy looks like a little old Chinese man. [...] He started life logically, a miniature Morton Sass. [...] Moses has taken on a decidedly Chinese cast" (184). When his second son Ira is born, Sterling is disappointed that the baby looks like a Lung, but a month later, he has "metamorphosed from Lung to Sass. No sign of Lung chromosomes remained. Natural selection. We had finally done something good together. The result was perfect Ira" (217). The Darwinian language insinuates that the Lung chromosomes are degenerate and should be discontinued.

In Social Darwinism, which applies physical characteristics to socioeconomic and moral ones, class is part of the language of natural selection. At its height in the United States, Jane Addams pointed out that the often insurmountable barrier between the poor and the rich was due to such ideology: "It had been believed that poverty was synonymous with vice and laziness, and that the prosperous man was the righteous man" (14–15). Such a belief continues in our age. Sterling's dismay at Moses' physiognomic transformation derives from his anxiety about ethnicity as much as about class. In his mind the Lung chromosomes not only determine their carrier's racial characteristics but also his or her class position. Through Moses' appetite for Chinese food, Sterling comes to realize with anguish that Moses not only looks like the Lungs but also acts like the lower class too.

> Moses loves rice, and he will eat everything Zsa Zsa puts in front of him,
> no matter how Chinese; he loves even the funkiest of her concoctions, the
> meanest specimens of a base cuisine, elemental forms born of lean times and
> coarse palates, sodium-rich, designed for the simple purpose of helping ease
> the grains of rice [...] past the tongue: salted fish, shrimp paste, black beans,
> preserved turnip. (220–221)

Moses' relish for "the meanest specimens of a base cuisine" alarms Sterling. He didn't marry into a white and wealthy family to produce such a son. Contrary to Social Darwinist notions of genetic degeneracy and natural selection, the Lung genes dominate the Sass genes in Moses.

It is sadly ironic that Sterling, all his life running away from his parents, his ethnicity, and his class, ends up fathering another unwanted self in Moses. To Genius and Zsa Zsa, however, Moses is the son they have long lost. He loves them, their food, their stories, and "picks up the Chinese effortlessly" (222). Louie's characterization of Moses serves as a brilliant allegory of the return of the repressed in Sterling—his own son turning out to desire exactly what he has disavowed. Revealingly, Sterling grumbles to himself that "his appetite for their food and language are registered as trespasses Moses has perpetrated against me" (222). His ambivalent relationship with Moses is worsened when they move to San Francisco, far away from Genius and Zsa Zsa. Moses misses his grandparents—their cooking and their stories. He tapes on his headboard "a Xerox of a photo of six Chinese whom [Sterling] dubbed 'the ancestors'" (298). Upon close examination, Sterling understands why Moses treasures this picture: "Genius's face blooming on the face of one of the elders, the gentleman in wire-rimmed glasses, and Moses' in the bespectacled boy over his right shoulder" (299). He is deeply disturbed by this discovery: "Genius and Moses, like father and son, skipping my generation, as if I didn't exist" (299). At a subconscious level, Sterling knows the depth of his self-loathing and self-effacement, and that is why Moses' resemblance to and love for his grandfather exasperate him so. He is determined to keep Ira from becoming another Moses: "This is why Ira is so important; I won't let this happen again; I will see to it that Ira remains pure" (222–223). Ira's purity is no more or no less than his white looks, seemingly unadulterated by the Lung blood.

The births of Moses and Ira are episodes crucial to Sterling's character development, for the children allow him to exteriorize the battle of desire and disavowal raging inside him, with Moses representing his Chinese self and Ira the assimilated self that permits no preservation of the former. As symbolic acts these episodes represent the social and historical contradiction inherent in American democracy, the contradiction between the American ideal of egalitarianism and racial and economic injustices. The author's choice of killing Ira in a car accident brings about a huge hole in Sterling's psyche that ironically and painfully makes him whole at the end. Ira's death is a kind of exorcism that returns Sterling to his people. Only after Ira's death does Sterling see for the first time Ira's face "alive in Genius" (324). At the Chinese cemetery where Ira is being buried, Sterling finally comes to fully understand how lost he has been.

> Will the ancestors recognize Ira as one of theirs without Genius at his side or there to welcome him? And will those same ancestors claim me, after my breakneck dash from them and into the arms of any willing American girl who would have me—my desperate attempt to overcome the unremarkableness of being a Lung, and create a family more to my liking? I embraced school because school wasn't home, European cuisine because Escoffier wasn't home, Bliss because she wasn't home. My sons were the blades of scissors that were supposed to snip me permanently, and genetically, free from home, from past and present, from here and over there. (With Ira [. . .] I thought I had succeeded in erasing every trace of myself, committed genealogical suicide.) (323)

Ira's death enables Sterling to live, to live as the son of Genius with dignity and wholeness. Food reference appears at this critical moment as a site of struggle; food sends Ira's spirit off to the world beyond. It is also food that celebrates a lost son's return and tests his loyalty to his culture. Beside Ira's grave Genius and Zsa Zsa unpack and spread the food:

> Thick slabs of boiled pork belly, strips of glistening *cha-siu,* a hunk of roast pig with crispy skin the same hue as the dirt. Four pounds of meat. Oranges, sweet tricornered muffins, sponge cakes. And a giant whole chicken at least five pounds, all appendages attached [...]. [...] At the foot of the grave they've arranged a picnic buffet. Tinfoil trays full of food.

Sterling's initial reaction is repulsion and fear. He shudders at "the thought of Zsa Zsa and Genius down on hands and knees urging Morton Sass to the brink of the grave to dine" (326). When Bliss expresses her outrage over the pork, Sterling replies defiantly, "Ira's Chinese too, you know" (327). His defense of the Chinese ritual leads him to participate in it. "I close my eyes and bow from the waist, a stiff, slight tilt forward. The greasy smoke [incense] burns high in my nose, lifting off the top of my head. I feel free of the others" (328). No longer caring what the Sass family thinks of his Chineseness, he kneels by the grave, "surrounded by the smells of the roasted meat, the incense, the citrus oils" and tries "to dig the delicate, spider-thin sticks into the hard yellow dirt" (328). It is the same ritual bidding farewell to Ira that ushers Sterling into a new life.

In performing the Chinese burial ritual, Sterling reclaims his self and reenters his community. At his last TV cooking show, he wakes up from his act and feels deeply ashamed. "[T]his time I hear myself as I never have. I hear myself as Moses must, as Genius, as Yuk, I hope, never will. [...] If Ira had grown up and gotten a faceful of my act, I would have died" (331). Halfway into the show, he drops the Hop Sing accent and the comical act. He looks straight into the camera and says, "Salt was invented by the Chinese. [...] *We* flooded fields with seawater, and after its evaporation, *we* harvested the remaining crystals from the soil" (332–333, emphasis mine). His claiming of the collective identity signifies his reentrance into the Chinese community. "I hear myself say 'we,' as if I were there with the ancestors, among the world's first Lungs" (333). He remembers the Chinese saying about cleansing and purifying oneself with salt after one has come into close contact with death to ward off the "bad wind." "I feel it now, a tingling sensation, like teeth grazing my skin. I pour the salt in my hand, then rub my palms together. The salt falls through my hands. I know what I'm doing is not nearly enough" (333). As Ira symbolizes Sterling's assimilated self, so does his physical proximity to Ira at death symbolize the approach of his own living death. The ritual of purification with salt, which he has mocked in the past as superstition, now cleanses him and removes the peril of self-destruction.

As Sterling succeeds in rediscovering his roots, Genius dies, having completed his fatherhood and his own American journey. His death awakens in Sterling both remorse and comfort.

> [H]e was trying to be a father to me. I cried, big noisy tears, because he had
> to endure me, my meanness, because too late I missed him. From the dirt and
> dust of these feelings I realized Genius had gone to follow Ira, to make sure
> he was taken care of, to protect and guide him, to show him the tricks of the
> trade, the ring around the neck, how to exploit another's appetite in order to
> satisfy one's own. (360)

After leaving the hospital, Sterling feels compelled to see Moses, whose connection to Genius is stronger than his own. Louie again resorts to food for the articulation of the complicated emotions in Sterling regarding his love-hate relationship with his father and son. He brings Moses an artichoke and explains, "You pull off a scale, she loves me, pull off a scale, she loves me not. You take away all the tough stuff, the prickles and pokey parts, and every time, inside, you find a heart" (361). The metaphor of the artichoke speaks about Sterling's relationship with his father more than that with his son. With Genius dead and Moses standing in for him, Sterling can finally say to himself that he and his father have loved each other despite their mutual disappointment in each other.

Sterling's sorrow over Genius' passing and his remorse at the shame he has felt over his parents' immigrant life and class status now become condensed in his relationship with Moses, and it is through his interaction with his son that he comes to find final identification with his father, and this identification operates once again through food references. At Genius' funeral, Sterling holds Moses tight, "as if he were Ira and Genius rolled into one, because he is, and by my holding on they won't get away" (370). It is at this moment that the author deploys food as a site to construct ethnic identification, an ethnicity that frustrates any notion of authenticity. In the kitchen of the funeral home, Sterling tries to find a snack for himself and Moses. After Moses rejects a variety of choices, Sterling suddenly remembers what Genius used to make for him when he was a schoolchild—"the concoction of saltine crackers, sweet condensed milk, and boiled water" (371). It has been a long time since Sterling has tasted this snack, but he remembers it as "comfort food, warming and soothing. The mere thought of a bowl of Genius's cracker stew evokes good, safe, happy times" (371). Not until this moment has Sterling ever revealed any memory of a happy time with his father. He asks Moses to help make this snack. When done, Moses doesn't seem impressed. "It's Chinese," Sterling tells him to coax him to give it a try (372). Then he turns to us, readers:

Trust me. If you can only know what I know. Let the steam caress your face, smell the roasted sweetness, the milk's own sugar, and feel the glow of well-being radiating from within. I don't blame Moses his skepticism, because until this moment I wouldn't have believed either. But I'm not making these feelings up, they are as real as the food is pure: just flour, water, sugar, milk, and salt. (372)

The evocation of the maternal in the imageries of milk, warmth, sugar, and sweetness points to the reconstructed father-son relationship and helps Sterling build a loving relationship with Moses. "It really is Chinese, you know," he tries to convince his son. "Ah-Yeah used to make it for me. It's a special recipe he brought from China. And think about it, you and I just whipped this up together" (372). Moses now believes it and claps his hands, "We just cooked Chinese food!" (372). This is an epiphany to Moses, because he has never associated Chinese food with Sterling. "That's right. The real thing!" Sterling reassures. "Moses opens his mouth, and lets me feed him" (372).

This final scene completes the journey Louie has designed for his protagonist, moving from his abduction by the ideology of assimilation and class unconsciousness to his homecoming, with the entire journey immersed in food tropes. At the end, by making and eating his father's cracker stew with Moses, he finally establishes the link that has been absent between Genius and Moses. Interestingly, Genius' concoction is neither Chinese nor French; it is his invention out of the circumstances of an immigrant bachelor living in poverty. Sterling, by proclaiming it Chinese and "the real thing," affirms his ethnicity without appealing to authenticity. Louie's refusal to authenticate Sterling's ethnic identity through "authentic" Chinese cuisine resists essentializing ethnicity and proposes that ethnicity is a construct that a particular group performs. With the novel's conclusion, Louie suggests that we construct our ethnicity based on private and familial history and practices. Sterling is Chinese insofar as he recognizes himself as the son of his father, and only when he becomes Chinese in this sense is he able to pass down his ethnicity to his son.

"What I do with my hands"

Chinese American men's historical engagement in food service and laundry has decidedly cast them as effeminate in the conventional gender schema. Louie's choice of these two gendered occupations for father and son sets the stage for the dramatization of their emasculation by racial and economic exploitation, and this dramatization often centers on food references. Like class and ethnicity, class and gender are inextricably interlocked in *Barbarians*, which ascribes much of these men's feelings of powerlessness and inchoate anger to their experience of class and gender oppression.

Gendered occupation is a notion carried over from the social analysis of the nineteenth and twentieth centuries, Baxter and Western point out, which "was underwritten by a master concept of 'industrial society,' or 'industrial capitalism.' Economic activity was based on the production of goods, not services" (1). Despite the increasing professionalization and service orientation of the working class in the United States today, the popular image of the working class nevertheless remains masculine, reinforcing a macho culture among working-class men. Food and laundry services continue to be perceived and experienced as women's work, secondary to industrial and construction work in its wage-earning potential and its demand for physical toughness. The gendering of occupation was even more relevant in the late 1970s in which *Barbarians* is set than now.

Almost as soon as the book opens, Louie begins to tackle Sterling's gender complex with dark humor. Through Sterling's interaction with the butcher over a capon, a "castrated rooster," Louie demonstrates his protagonist's heightened sense of inadequacy about his masculinity (5). "Think about it," Sterling says to Fuchs, "*Snip!* And as if that's not bad enough, they throw him back in with the others to plump, big and fat, and he struts around like cocks do, big man in barnyard, only the hens are snickering behind his back" (5). Initially this seems to insinuate Fuchs, a Jewish man, but several sentences later, it becomes clear that it is Sterling himself who becomes the target of such insinuation. He recalls seeing Renee Richards, the transgendered tennis pro, in a newspaper photo. "I was immediately drawn to her looks, found her rather sexy even, that is, until I read the accompanying article detailing her surgical transformation. 'Can't tell a she from a he?' I scolded myself. 'What kind of man are you?'" (6). This homophobic self-castigation is followed by the scene of preparing the castrated bird that further illuminates his feeling of gender ambivalence. "I rub the mustard onto the capon's skin, with its largish pores and nipple-like bumps; the mustard's whole seeds, tiny orbs rolling between my palm and the lubricated skin, produce a highly erotic sensation" (11). A few pages later, subliminally identifying with the capon, he accuses himself of being a chicken: "I'm the chicken around here. Too chicken to insist that Lisa Lee stay; too chicken to tell Bliss not to come" (17).

Sterling's gender insecurity is not solely determined by his occupation; French cuisine, after all, is a male-dominated world. Furthermore, cooking shows such as *Emeril Live* and *Iron Chef* feature masculine performance. In Sterling's case his vocation is compounded by his ethnicity, and the prevailing stereotype of Asian American men as undersexed produces his experience of diminished masculinity and agency. With his gender imaginary structured by American hegemonic representations of masculinity as white, heterosexual, and propertied, Sterling cannot help but look up to models of manhood that instill in him only self-loathing. In front of his bathroom mirror, he holds up a photo of Robert Redford, the American epitome of manhood, to his face and "gauged the extent of my deficiencies" (18). Gazing at a replica of Michelangelo's *David* at the club, Sterling measures himself against the ideal of masculine beauty: "[W]here does that leave me?" he wonders (43). Louie shows us a truthful but bleak picture about the fact that in Sterling's world there is no model of masculinity that resembles him.

Brilliantly, Louie later has Sterling deconstruct *David* by classing the figure as a laborer. "All day I have thought about the David's hands. They are huge [...]. Michelangelo isn't selling beauty, but deeds. [...] The David is a monument to work, what's accomplished with one's hands. That's all I want people to consider when they see Sterling Lung: what I do with my hands" (53). This transcoding of masculine beauty, a rare moment in the Sterling character, challenges racial/ethnic gendering in the effort to unify all working-class men under the icon of masculine hands. Janet Zandy writes, "Hands are maps to history and culture [...]. Hands are class and cultural markers" (*Hands* xi, 1). Although rarely studied, "hands are everywhere in working-class literature,"[9] and hands "signify power relationships of control" (1, xi). Sterling's observation of the *David*'s huge hands suggests his gender and economic identification with the working class, particularly men whose hands control materials and create wealth. This identification, however, at the same time frustrates his desire to control his destiny as well as the products of his labor, because the metonymy of hands reduces human beings to working parts, divorces mind from body, and empties ontology from the laborer. For Sterling, this very tension in the signifier of hands, figuring for the paradox of ownership and dispossession, finds an expression in his gender anxiety located in another body part.

And it is his ponytail. Louie aptly utilizes it as a device to yield multiple meanings to explore the intersections among gender, ethnicity, and class. To his parents Sterling's ponytail is a source of shame because it is culturally associated with both femininity and subjugation. (The Manchurian reign exacted death from any man who lost his queue.) Sterling thinks that because of his ponytail "Genius has no problem calling me his fourth daughter" (40). To the ladies in the club, who find his presence both unthreatening and amusing, it becomes an emblem of Sterling's servile/feminine position among them. Libby Drake, for example, "touches my shoulder, then caresses my ponytail, her fingers running through my hair like a litter of nesting mice" (40). Millie Boggs jokes that "my ponytail would make a 'delicious whip,' as she gave it a playful tug. [...] I can't stand Sharon Fox, who grabs hold and says, 'Giddyup!'" (40). Sterling's ponytail becomes a site where gender, class, and ethnicity interlock to demonstrate an asymmetrical power relationship between him and the rich white ladies. One cannot ignore that his ethnicity plays a significant role in his emasculation, for it is difficult to imagine the same women fondling a black male cook, for instance. To Bliss, however, Sterling's ponytail is the source of attraction; "she has said that she will terminate our relationship if ever I cut my hair. [...] She says this is the way Chinese men have traditionally worn their hair" (40). For her the ponytail becomes a phallic symbol of an exotic manhood that brings excitement into her life. Thus centered on the ponytail is a nexus of meanings contingent on class, ethnicity, and gender.

Sterling's feminization attributable to ethnic stereotypes and his occupation is by no means absolute; his gender imaginary shifts and varies depending on different power and gender dynamics. Although the ladies in the club dominate and harass him, he still retains an illusion of autonomy and control, for in his fantasy these women are his to please, and their teasing and petting ironically reinforce this fantasy. "In this house of women [...] I am the engine that makes things go. [...] They have to eat, and that's why they come daily. And praise my cooking, squeeze my arm, caress my hair, pat my cheeks, pinch my rump" (31). Sterling fantasizes himself to be the only man in a house/harem of women who don't restrain themselves in front of him from "their talk of sweets and diets, gynecological procedures and dinner parties, cosmetics and brassieres" (31). Ironically, this scene evokes the picture of a eunuch serving and guarding the emperor's concubines more than that of a highly virile man pleasuring multiple female subjects, but in his fantasy Sterling congratulates himself for having arrived and sexualizes his relationship with these women via food to conjure up a sense of masculine power. Libby Drake is described to be "as lustrous as a polished apple" (37) and as wearing a "massive braid that resembles a lobster tail" (39). "Her legs gleam in the sun, as my hand [...] lift[s] the tomato, which yields to me its loving weight, its thin-skinned plumpness that molds to the curve of my hand. It is the perfect thing to squeeze" (38). By juxtaposing women to food, Sterling manages to exercise the male privilege of objectifying and consuming them.[10] Sterling's participation in this discourse compensates for the feeling of powerlessness toward rich white men.

His experience in the club illustrates the interrelationship between class power and racial and gender hierarchies. The ladies in the club, empowered by their racial and class privileges, feel entitled to direct and humiliate their male Chinese American chef, but as soon as rich white men enter the scene, the dynamics of power change. At Sterling's first culinary event for male guests in the club, both he and Libby Drake feel as though they had been suddenly dispossessed. "I feel so small tonight," Libby tells Sterling, "with men in my club" (39). Her remark offends Sterling. "Aren't I a man?" he muses (39). On the other hand, however, Sterling himself never thinks of the gardener as a man either: "Except for the gardener—he doesn't really count—Drake is the first man I've seen at the club" (37–38). What constitutes a "real" man is contingent on his class and ethnicity. Sterling fails to realize that because of their position as domestic servants and their status as racial minorities, neither he nor the gardener counts as a man.

It is with conspicuous wealth that the "real" masculine presence arrives at the club. Looking out of the kitchen window Sterling observes, "More guests converge on the club, arriving in their Simonized Steel tons, two hundred horses under the hood, commanded by manicured hands, designer-framed eyes, and thin-soled Italian shoes" (38). In this brief depiction is apparent the model of property-based masculinity that is central to the hegemony of capitalism, presenting the businessman as a new model of masculinity. This new model is no longer about physical power; rather it valorizes wealth, unscrupulous competition, and bottomless greed, a hegemonic masculinity that is culturally privileged and has power over other less culturally sanctioned masculinities. Sterling's desire to identify with this very model only engenders a deeper feeling of deficiency. "My eyes flit to the men. I struggle to get a fix on them. I feel like a boy again, trying to take my father in, his great intimidating size, overlaid with the constant accusation" (42). Reminded of his father, who has constantly chastised him (at least as he remembers), "You're useless" (42), Sterling returns to his boyhood fraught with resentment and unfulfilled longings. Now, watching these rich men consuming the feast he has prepared that is "so labor intensive, costly in time and energy," he comes to identify for the first time with his father as a fellow man living at the mercy of other men (38–39).

> My eyes can't hold these men, because they wear suits that fit; because their
> cars guzzle gas and they don't care; because their women paint their nails, sign
> my paycheck, pet my hair; because their shirts [...] are synthetic, the wash-'n'-
> wear fabric that's killing the Chinese hand-laundry business, and bringing my
> father to his starch-stiff knees. (42)

Palpable with rage at this realization, Sterling comes to an embryonic awareness of class solidarity in which he joins his father in recognizing the economic injustice in their world.

In both Genius' and Sterling's world, class exploitation often comes hand in hand with ethnic and gender othering. The white male guests at the club, deeply rooted in America's history of legal exclusion of people of color from citizenship (e.g., the Naturalization Act of 1790 granting citizenship to "any free white person"), insist on treating Asian Americans as perpetual foreigners. Drake persists in practicing his awkward Mandarin on their "Chinese chef" and in asking where he is from, refusing to believe that Sterling is from Long Island, New York (47). When the dinner conversation moves to the subject of the Chinese "Ping-Pong diplomacy," one man comments, "It's suited for the whole race of them. Those petite paddles and little balls are perfect for their little hands." Another joins in, "Ping-Pong doesn't require strength" (49). To legitimate such racial emasculation Drake resorts to pseudo science:

> "The physiological differences are the product of Darwinian adaptations. [...] Chinese culture doesn't value the individual. That's why you always hear them talking about 'the people' or 'the masses.' [...] They put three or four of their men on a job that one average American can do by himself. For this reason the Chinese have no evolutionary imperative to develop bigger, stronger bodies." (49–50)

These racist remarks are made within Sterling's earshot as he brings their coffee and buses their dirty dishes. Racism, almost always collaborating with sexism, homophobia, and class oppression, so degrades the humanity of the Other that the victim becomes paralyzed with fear and resentment. Pinioned by his class position, Sterling has no choice but to swallow the racist poison as he swallows the cold leftovers of the fancy dinner he has cooked for others.

Class powerlessness engendered by class unconsciousness and subscription to the myth of the American Dream drives the oppressed into masochism, with the oppressed reviling themselves as solely responsible for their misfortune and misery. In Sterling's case, his class powerlessness compounded by racial emasculation brings about a compensatory pathological fantasy of mastery, a revenge that is both impotent and melancholic. Inside the big white house empty of the rich women, Sterling conjures up the illusion of ownership and power that arouses him. On the bed of its master bedroom,

> I feel myself harden, my prick hooking on a spring, and I begin moving my hips, back and forth, slowly. I think of Libby Drake's rich bosom, Sally Hayes's pouty lips, Millicent Boggs's long calves, Dottie Cone's painted toenails; then I summon up every one of my parents' customers I had a crush on, women who lived in houses as nice as this, who spent their days making their faces and bodies beautiful for men. (31–32)

Class envy and class revenge are at the heart of his sexual fantasy in which a reversal of the real-life asymmetrical power relation takes place. The more sexual the fantasy becomes, the angrier and more violent his acts, as if masculinity could be experienced only through violence. He fantasizes:

I fuck the rug some more, then the brass bedpost, the armoire, the back of the overstuffed chair; eventually I fuck the entire bedroom. Still unsatisfied, I fuck the runner in the dark hallway, the moldings, the telephone and its stand just outside the bathroom. I fuck the banister, the stairs, the dining room table, where the ladies are most intimately acquainted with me. I leave droplets of myself everywhere, the sticky residue of my love [...]. I fuck the front door like crazy, then the shabby mat at the threshold. When they enter the house their well-heeled feet must cross this very spot. I roll onto my hip, yank the elastic band down, setting myself free, and let loose instantly, long body-shaking shots that seem to originate in my brain. (32)

What deserves a pause here is the fact that Sterling not only imagines "fucking" the rich white women who treat him like a maid but also "fucking" their properties that give them the power to dominate him, pointing our attention to the intersection between class and gender.

Sterling's father, Genius, has none of his son's illusions. In his old age he faces his abject position without self-loathing. "What is he, in this country, but work?" he understands. "Without it, he's worthless, he is even more a nobody than he already is: he goes from laundryman to Chinaman" (232). The apparent anger and resignation in his realization reject the promise of the American Dream and rip apart the romantic camouflage of poverty as dignity. The young Genius, however, has also dreamed of Americanization and success. Lured by the promise of the Gold Mountain, he enters America under a purchased identity, suffers detention at Angel Island, and works ten hours a day in the laundry, making barely enough money to feed himself and to support his family in China. Yet he dreams about "driving a car, in his suit and hat, honking the horn as he drove past," and this dream walks into his life in the shape of a blond woman named Lucy. Her hair is sunshine, and her dress delicious—a "dress with eggs" (242). Genius sets out the beautiful Japanese tea set meant to be a gift to his wife in China to catch the dream. Lucy drinks the tea and pilfers a cup upon each visit until the whole set is in her possession. A curious relationship begins to develop, with Genius sewing her dress and feeding her with his best food. Lucy, a working-class girl abused from time to time by men, comes to acquire through her whiteness a position of power over Genius. Through food and eating, Louie vividly pictures their lopsided relationship. "She asked for a fork and, with it, piled her bowl of rice high with the meat. He resisted thinking she was greedy" (251). Genius tries to seduce her with food, "whiskey in a shot glass, then coconut candies and fruit jellies in rice paper" (252). After she eats her fill, she points at the can of roasted chicken on the shelf that he plans to send to China and takes it home.

Genius begins to visit her at her house on Mondays, a long bus ride from his laundry store. "Often he brought a bag of groceries, roast pork, soy sauce chicken, bok choy, things he purchased on his Sunday excursions to Chinatown. Before long she started telling him to buy her soap, beer, Quick Soup, Colgate toothpaste. He might cook for her, wash and iron her clothes" (257). He has become not only a provider but also a servant. "It was work on top of work" (257). In his mind Lucy is his American wife whose wants and needs are his responsibility, a white wife lording over him in a way that he would never tolerate of his Chinese wife. Between them is a gender-role reversal enabled by racial hierarchy. "He was awed at the size of his nonexistence. How he was nowhere, barely noticed in the solid world [...]. Governments did not know him, his own daughter did not know him, his own wife addressed him by another's name, his presumptive wife hardly felt his presence" (261). Now the only thing that makes him go to visit her is the junk car in her yard. He takes apart and reassembles the engine and becomes ecstatic over its signs of life. One day on his way home, a group of white men beat him up and call him "Jap! Jap! Jap!" (263). A few years later, Lucy shows up at the laundry and briefly steals Baby Sterling.

This American history of Genius can be interpreted as an allegory of the bittersweet relationship between America and the Chinese immigrants. Lucy's initial interest in Genius is a metonymy of American fascination with the Chinese as the exotic Other upon their first arrival at San Francisco. America first found the Chinese useful in various services and industries, particularly in the construction of the transcontinental railways, just as Lucy keeps Genius around as long as he is useful to her. Lucy's relationship with Genius allegorizes race-, class-, and gender-based power relationships holding between Chinese immigrants and America, nonreciprocal ones in which America gains socioeconomic as well as psychological advantages over the Chinese. In this encounter the Chinese were changed forever by their American experience. They became feminized in that they were deprived of socioeconomic and political power, many were forced to live as bachelors because of the Page Law and antimiscegenation laws,[11] many had no choice but to make their living by serving the whites, and many hopelessly longed for white women.[12] Mirroring this larger social phenomenon are Genius' long years of loneliness and the short episode with Lucy that poisons his relationship with his wife after she finally joins him in America. Lucy's brief abduction of Baby Sterling symbolically sets off his estrangement from his parents and ancestral culture.

Genius' loss of his son to assimilation is also metonymical of the difficult relationship between many Asian American men and their fathers. Fatherhood is a central motif in *Barbarians* with strong connections to the themes of race, class, and gender. In Asian American literature, particularly by male authors, fatherhood is in crisis. Under the coercion of assimilation, many Asian American men experience agonizing ambivalence toward their immigrant fathers, whose authority has been usurped by other male figures, American or Americanized, who seem to be more American, more affluent, and more authoritative than their own fathers. In Frank Chin's *Chickencoop Chinaman,* the Chinese American filmmaker, Tam Lum, desperately seeks a father figure in the black boxer, Ovaltine Jack Dancer. His denial of "Chinatown Kid" as his father—"He wasn't my father. He was...he was our dishwasher"—is fraught with race, class, and gender shame (45). Chang-Rae Lee in *Native Speaker* portrays a Korean American man, Henry Park, who is embarrassed with the ways of his immigrant father and finds a suitable alternative father figure in the Korean American politician John Kwang, who appears to be thoroughly assimilated, envisioning himself as mayor of New York City. Sterling's reluctant love for Genius and resentful acceptance of Morton Sass as an alternative father figure vividly dramatize the painful psychological complex of Asian American fatherhood.

To Sterling, though, Genius occupies a contradictory position as both a masculine and an emasculated figure. On the one hand he admires and envies his father's "dark, ponderous prick," which he regrets that he fails to inherit (111). In the incident of hauling the old refrigerator, Genius' response to the racist remark by other drivers turns him into a superhero in Sterling's eyes. Unlike his son, who is so diffident that he agrees with the racists that "there was something unerringly Chinese about hauling this useless machine," Genius "stuck his [...] head out the window, bracing himself with his Lucky Strike hand, and shouted, 'Fuck you!' without a trace of accent, and flipped them off with his free hand" (81). Sterling remembers, "At that moment Pop was Superman. If he'd gotten hold of the thugs' car he would have torn loose the hood and tossed the engine into their laps" (81). On the other hand, Sterling is ashamed of his father for his "stupid smile, eyes cast down, head bowed and bobbing, the obsequious professionalism," which he hates but believes he has inherited (344–345). Genius' sucking up to his customers renders him feminine and repulsive in his son's eyes precisely because Sterling loathes himself for living daily the life of powerlessness. His own docility and model-minority complex become painfully humiliating when rendered patent in his father.

When he marries Bliss, Sterling imagines that he has traded Morton Sass for Genius. He believes that Sass' whiteness and money have the transformative power to de-ethnicize, up-class, and masculinize him, and his union with a white woman is the crown for successful assimilation. However, he cannot help feeling fake, as if he were hiding something upon whose discovery he would come to ruin. One cannot help hearing the echo from Louie's collection of short stories, *Pangs of Love,* in which dark comedies present male Chinese

American yuppies afflicted with anxiety, displacement, and alienation. Sau-ling Wong comments on these characters, "Fluency in the hegemonic culture [...] is no guarantee of authority. When assumed by someone with the 'wrong' skin and hair color, it is mere impersonation, mimicry, occupation of a subject position that is not yours, or can be yours only through acts of fakery" ("Chinese/Asian American Men in the 1990s" 185). Louie in *Barbarians* stages a homoerotic comedy of errors in the men's room at Sterling's wedding that vividly demonstrates Wong's sharp observation. Morton Sass says, "Now, Sterling, I want you to show me what you got." Sterling nervously thinks,

> He wants to see your sex. Wants to see if you measure up. He's going to
> whip out his prodigious horse and you your wee birdie. Assert his dominant
> position in the family. More than ever, you wish your real father had passed on
> some of his size.
>   "Give me your best shot," your father-in-law says. [...]
>   You're not sure you're willing to do this. You were right the first time,
> his purpose isn't biblical but urological. [...] That's what this is, a test of your
> worthiness, your virility, and it's going to take quite a shot, slightly uphill,
> across a span no sperm under normal reproductive conditions would ever
> have to cover. (161–162)

Sterling is relieved to realize what Sass wishes for is no more than the conventional act of male bonding. "Come on, show me your knockout punch," Sass commands (162). Sterling takes the invitation, unleashing the long repressed anger and frustration at the white male world. "You feel you had wanted to hit him your entire life. When you're through, your hand is on fire" (163). His anger toward the world of injustice can only take such symbolic form of aggression contained by the façade of male comradery.

With the legacy of the problematic Asian American fatherhood, Sterling is most susceptible to pressures about his own authority in front of his sons. Sass strategically uses this issue in coercing Sterling to quit his job at the club to be the sole owner of the latter's labor and product, the TV cooking show. Sterling resists Sass' coercion in an attempt to maintain his sense of autonomy. "You can't play houseboy the rest of your life," Sass reasons with him. "What will Moses think of you? [...] He sees it on your face. In your body. Your posture. His little brain is soaking you up. He's forming opinions about you that will turn your heart to chopped liver one day" (188). Sterling wavers, imagining what Moses sees and trying to remember how he as an infant had seen his father. His resentment of Sass at this point is suggested by a food analogy. Sass' "elbows planted on the desktop, chin perched on his hands, one layered on top of the other, like cuts of pork" (188–189). Sass, a tough businessman, never gives up on a profitable idea. He pokes where it most hurts in Sterling—the truth that he really has no autonomy at all: "You've got too many bosses. A bunch of females telling you what to do. You think Moses doesn't see that? This one wants something, that one wants something. Every want-something is like a blow to your head. The kid sees that. Punch-drunk daddy. It's all over you" (189). Sterling is so devastated by the image Sass paints of him that he cannot meet the old man's gaze. "Too intense, too harsh, and to stare back I might lose myself, be immolated like bugs in fire" (189). What Sterling experiences in this encounter with his rich white father figure is as emasculating as his encounter with the male guests dining at the club. On both occasions, the assault of emasculation against Sterling is performed through class and ethnicity, reducing him to a sexless and powerless child. "I'm a little boy craning his neck, shattering his eyes on gold-robed authority" (189).

Keenly aware of the fragility of his own authority with a racially mixed son, Sterling fears and hates Sass for the possibility of having his own fatherhood usurped by the very man who has replaced his own father. He reacts strongly to Sass' possessive remark, "my little Moses": "Sweat boils on my brow. I'm startled by his claim on the little boy's body. He is my son. He is my blood. I ball my hands into fists. I salivate remembering the impact my flesh made against his flesh" (188). In the meantime he knows very well that if a war broke out between them, he would be the one vanquished. This intense hatred of Sass, however, is ironically contained by his masochistic, identificatory desire for the same man. Having lost respect for his own father, Sterling ties his sense of manhood to the new father figure, whose approval and love are paradoxically sought after and resented. On Father's Day he and Bliss visit her family. "A celebration of me and Morton Sass! The two 'dads,' as we were called by Selma Sass. I loved how she lumped us together. I brought steaks from Fuchs's, and the two dads grilled, like real men" (194). Louie's irony is hard to miss: Sterling's gender security is dependent on the very man who dominates him and threatens his fatherhood. Sass occupies such a position of power solely because he is white and rich.

Genius' brief but tortured relationship with Lucy, Sterling's abduction, and his difficult father role toward Moses all serve as allegories of Asian American history saturated with race, class, and gender injustices. With the minor character Yuk, however, the political unconscious in *Barbarians* presents another allegory projecting its utopian impulse to resolve the irreconcilable conflicts in Asian American history. Food references play a significant role in this allegory. Yet this resolution is fraught with class and ethnic crises as well. Near the end of the novel, Louie shifts Sterling's emotional tie from Bliss to Yuk, subtly suggesting that Sterling will eventually make good his parents' promise to Yuk. At the narrative level, this suggestion entails Sterling's character growth, from someone who holds "no romantic interest" in Chinese women to someone who feels "the bright yearning" for Yuk (7, 364). At the level of the political unconscious, however, Yuk allegorizes a borderless existence that seems to undermine demarcations along the lines of class, nationality, and ethnicity, and this borderless existence figures for globalization.

Yuk, from Hong Kong (before its return to China in 1997), is a woman without a country. As a flight attendant she travels between continents and speaks different languages. She is not only deeply ingrained in traditional Chinese culture but also familiar with American pop culture. Her ease in border crossing is best portrayed in her relationship to food. She is a culinary cosmopolitan, lover of Chinese cuisine and connoisseur of Western fare. Interestingly, Louie has her introduce steak, Texas toast, and Sizzler restaurants to Genius and Zsa Zsa, who have lived in the states for decades (73, 75). Ironically, it is she who Americanizes the old couple better than America. To Ira's grave she brings the funeral food from Chinatown, culturally correct to the last detail. Her ease in border crossing makes Sterling's American life seem old-world, his awkward attempts at assimilation pathetic.

In the matter of class, Sterling assigns Yuk the position of a peasant even before their meeting—"a barefoot girl with oily scalp and barbarian tongue" who is trying to secure a green card through an American marriage (74). He is deeply ashamed when he finds out that the *David* statue at the club has been made in her uncle's factory in Hong Kong and that she has traveled extensively in Europe. As a gift she presents him with two moon rocks (91). Louie's choice of this particular gift is wonderfully sarcastic. On the one hand, it points to the absurdity of global circulation of commodities and of the commodification of anything imaginable. On the other, Yuk chooses moon rocks because the globalizing pop culture of America deludes her into wondering "what to get for man who is from the land of everything" (92). Yuk's character undermines the divide between the First World and Third World by the fact that she is more affluent than Sterling in both cultural and economic capital. Contrary to Sterling's presumption that he has to rescue Yuk from a backward life, she has transformed the lives of the Lungs with her beauty, worldliness, and confidence.

Yuk as a political allegory for globalization projects a utopia of a diasporic Asia that maintains the integrity of traditional cultures even as it gains fluency in Western culture, and this diasporic identity sustains its consistency without alienation. As her name, meaning "jade," symbolizes riches and strength, so does the character Yuk allegorize the sophistication and strength of the diasporic. Such a utopian vision becomes possible, however, only at the suppression of Asia's colonial history and its present postcolonial condition. Asia's becoming increasingly diasporic is a consequence of colonial violence and neocolonial exploitation by transnational corporations that create both a small elite and a large working class in a diasporic subject's native land. Many critics of globalization have argued that the global market has worsened poverty, increased national and international inequalities, and deepened the ethnic and religious divide.[13] In addition, some of the intraethnic exploitation occurs in the diasporic Asia that moves fluidly between nations. Yuk, as the allegory of a new breed of hybrid Asians, arouses no more than a utopian impulse that critiques the American history of racializing, emasculating, and impoverishing Asian immigrants.

Such an American history is incarnated in the characters of Genius and Sterling, who represent an Asian America that has undergone humiliation in its early phase and alienation in its recent one. Their stories serve as an allegory of race, class, and gender conflicts in the social life of America. Genius' tortured and lopsided relationship with Lucy typifies that of Asian immigrants with America in which nation building rested on gross economic exploitation of Asian immigrants. Lucy's kidnap of Sterling likewise stands for assimilation's abduction of Asian Americans, an abduction that attempts to turn them into seekers of the American Dream at the cost of ethnic and gender dignity. Sterling's difficult relationships with his parents and son Moses lay bare the consequence of this abduction. Louie's novel marvelously presents these nuggets of truth embodied in his characters, who are fashioned by his apt culinary tropes and references to delineate the nexus of race, class, and gender motifs.

Diasporic Asia, a direct product of global capitalism, has altered the Asian American community in many ways. One of them is that questions about its ethnicity are no longer easy to answer because many diasporic Asians do not identify themselves with nation-states, which Louie exemplifies well in Yuk. It seems that the identification between Asian Americans and diasporic Asians is least problematic in their common or proximate culinary practices. The next chapter examines how Asian food references ethnicize Li-Young Lee in his poetry despite his disavowal of an ethnic identity and his insistence on diaspora and transcendence.

4

Diaspora, Transcendentalism, and Ethnic Gastronomy in the Works of Li-Young Lee

In an aluminum bowl marked with scratches and dents from years of use, he kneaded the whole wheat dough with the vigor of a man about to commence a long awaited journey home. The final products were dark golden brown discs of fried dough filled with a spicy lentil mixture. Scented with cumin and asafetida, Darwanji's dal puris held the promise of a long journey, the romance of the railways, and the pleasure of returning home.

—Sharmila Sen, "Looking for Doubles in the Caribbean"

Li-Young Lee is an ethnic Chinese without an upbringing in an ancestral culture, without a grounding knowledge of the Chinese language, and without the community of a Chinatown or a suburban Chinese American community. His condition of exile, however, has proved to be immensely productive of emotional intensity and imagination, and his poetics derives largely from his ontological condition as an exile, driven by the desire to transcend time and space by appealing to the metaphysical at the exclusion of the cultural and material. As if no material or cultural location were sufficient for his poetics and identity, he formulates a transcendentalism—one that has a strong affinity with the ideas of its American father, Ralph Waldo Emerson—in which the poet's true self becomes God or the "universe mind" unfettered by cultural or ethnic allegiances (Marshall 134). As such the poet has no dialogue, as Lee claims, with his sociocultural composition (Marshall 132). His polemical disavowals of ethnic identification on the ground of transcendentalism, however, are in dialectic tension with his frequent use of ethnic signifiers in his poetry and memoir.

This tension in Lee raises the question that Stuart Hall asks of a Caribbean filmmaker: "From where does he/she speak?" ("Cultural Identity and Diaspora" 392). Quite different from the popular idea of an intuitive knowledge of the self, Hall proposes that one's cultural identity is constructed through his or her semantic practices, and semantic practices are never stable and finished. He suggests,

> Perhaps instead of thinking of identity as an already accomplished fact, which the new cultural practices then represent, we should think, instead, of identity as a "production" which is never complete, always in process, and always constituted within, not outside, representation. This view problematises the very authority and authenticity to which the term "cultural identity" lays claim. (392)

The tension lying between Lee's quest for the Absolute and the necessity to speak from a material place constitutes a dynamic realm in which he operates as a diasporic Asian American transcendentalist poet, multiple selves that Lee attempts to unify with the lexicon of American transcendentalism. He would disagree with Hall, who argues, "We all write and speak from a particular place and time, from a history and a culture which is specific" (392). It goes without saying that Lee cannot escape relying on cultural, material places from which to speak, but it is not easy to locate the place that is central to his poetics. In this chapter I argue that food serves as a central place from which Lee speaks, a locus that constructs and defines his sense of reality.[1] It is the references to food and eating that enable his articulation of the universe mind and his identity as an exilic and transcendent poet. By centering on alimentary imageries and motifs, I also show that his ethnic self and the transcendental self are not mutually exclusive, as he tries to argue.

Food and the Ethics and Aesthetics of Exile

"Diaspora" and "exile" are two terms that have gained much purchase in postcolonial theory and U.S. ethnic studies, and they are often used interchangeably. Despite this practice, however, there is a subtle difference between the two terms. In Lee's case, I believe that his family history and poetic sensibility make him an exile more than a diasporan. According to John Durham Peters, "In Jewish thinking, *exile* and *diaspora* are sometimes synonymous. The Hebrew terms *galut* and *golah* can be translated as both" (20). In spite of their historical affinities, these two terms do differ. Peters explains that

> in recent usage *diaspora* often lacks the pathos of *exile*, a term that is never without a deep sense of woe. Like exile, diaspora can be elective or imposed; perhaps the historical lack of zeal for returning to Jerusalem on the part of some Jews, grown comfortable in the diaspora, lifts the burden of homesickness from the notion of diaspora. [...] The key contrast with exile lies in diaspora's

> emphasis on lateral and decentered relationships among the dispersed. *Exile*
> suggests pining for home; *diaspora* suggests networks among compatriots.
> Exile may be solitary, but diaspora is always collective. (20)

Peters' observation is insightful into the solitary and woeful existence of the exile in differentiation from the collective nature of diaspora. He fails, however, to foreground the fact that colonialism and globalization have given rise to a different ethos or pathos of migration from those experienced by the dispersed Jewish community. In recent history both diaspora and exile entail a process of forceful removal from home. Migration in search of safety and of economic and educational betterment is by no means a voluntary choice. It is colonialism's devastation of the spirit, the land, the cultures, and the histories of many non-European peoples that has offered more despair than hope, more suffering than well-being, and more abuse than power. Likewise, globalization has exacerbated the unequal distribution of resources, education, and power in the world. And the militarist neocolonialism in Afghanistan and Iraq makes daily life hellish for the locals. These are among the forces that push people out of their homes in search of better and safer lives.

Exile in the sense of estrangement or alienation from home is not solely reserved for immigrants. Internal exile, due to alienating forces of race, gender, class, sexuality, and religion, is becoming a powerful discourse. Peters says it well: "Inasmuch as the world is cruel and its history one of oppression, we will always need a discourse of exile. [...] Exile is an idiom available for the uprooted and abused, an insurgent rhetoric that can comfort the captives or petition the captors" (36). The discourse of exile, useful as it is in critiquing inhumane conditions, is as limiting as its offshoot, the discourse of identity politics. The nostalgia in exile for the one true home appeals to the desire for the fixity of identity and belonging, a fantasy that arises from the human condition of incompleteness.[2]

Yet exile can be an attitude quite free from woeful nostalgia. Edward Said has offered a model of the exilic intellectual, à la Adorno, Swift, and Naipaul, who is blessed with a double perspective, disallegiance, and ironic distance. Said describes this figure of the intellectual as "a shipwrecked person who learns how to live in a certain sense *with* the land, not *on* it" (*Reader* 378). To live with the land is to be open to strangeness, which one doesn't attempt to dominate and domesticate. To live with the land is also to carry home in memory, to not lose hope, the sense of wonder, and critical acuity. This intellectual in exile does not hopelessly seek belonging, either in the impossible return to the "true" home or by giving in to the assimilatory impulse of the new locale. Rather, he or she experiences "the fate [of exile] not as a deprivation and as something to be bewailed, but as a sort of freedom" (380). Such an exile is free from the fantasy about true arrival or return and assimilation. Thus, an exilic displacement renders one a marginal person, "undomesticated" and "unusually responsive to the traveler rather than to the potentate, to the provisional and risky rather than to the habitual, to innovation and experiment rather than the authoritatively given *status quo*. The *exilic* intellectual does not respond to the logic of the conventional but to the audacity of daring, and to representing change, to moving on, not standing still" (380–381).

Lee is such an exilic intellectual in that what fuels his poetic engine is not a nostalgic, despairing search for an origin as the ground for self-definition. Rather, it is his recurrent conceit of "the winged seed" that serves as a self-representation, one that generates poetic and critical energy, and this conceit has everything to do with food. Interestingly, "diaspora" is composed of "dia" (through, throughout) and "spora" (spore, sperm), a notion suggesting a strong affinity to Lee's "winged seed."[3] Contrary to its connotation of ungroundedness, however, the seed trope turns out to be deeply grounded in Asian history. He has taken the seed trope from "the garden of nutmeg" in Song of Songs, which his father evoked in a Thanksgiving message.

> East of you or me, he [father] claimed, east of even the last man from China, lived a sentient perfume, an inbreathing and uttering seed, our original agent. [...] it is the mother of spices; the song of songs [...] both the late wine and our original milk, it is a fecund nard. And there go forth from this vital seed figures distilled a day, or a year, or a century [...]. An ark, all fragrance, is our trove, the Seed, stringent past jasmine. "We are embalmed in a shabby human closet," he said. "Get out! Get to the garden of nutmeg." (*The Winged Seed* 90)

Born out of the allegory of the garden of nutmeg, the seed trope surrounds itself with food references, patently olfactory in this sermon. The pungent fragrances of nutmeg, mace, cardamom, cumin, pepper, fennel, aniseed, and the like perfume ointment, heal the body, flavor wines, preserve and season meats, vegetables, and fruits. In the West spices have been vital to medicine, cosmetics, cuisine, and religious and official ceremonials ever since the conquest of Alexander forced the East into contact with the Hellenic world.

The history of the spice trade is a portal into the violent history of colonialism. Lee's seed trope carries with it the memory of that history. The garden of nutmeg is said to originate from "east of even the last man from China." This rhetorical gesture is not an expression of ethnic pride but a reminder of the actual spice traffic and its attendant violence. His father's sermon impregnating "the Seed" "with the suggestion of movement points not only to the complex beginning of the Old Testament but also to the colonial destruction of the spice gardens in the Orient. In reading the same sermon, Walter Hesford points out that "[t]he preacher's words evoke the sensuous garden of the Song [...] to create spice perfumed gardens, to transfer us to another time and place, another way of being" (41). In this complacent tone, Hesford aligns the readers with the Western subject who glorifies such transportation to another time and place, forgetting that it is not so much the passion to know others as the greed for the lucrative spice trade that lured European adventurers to the East Indies.

The Spice Islands, part of today's Indonesia, became irresistible to the Occidental world as early as the beginning of the 1500s.[4] One can say that the dangerous voyages from Europe to the Spice Islands were the precursor to the Western colonization of Asia. Giles Milton writes, "Nutmeg [...] was the most coveted luxury in seventeenth-century Europe, a spice held to have such powerful medicinal properties that men would risk their lives to acquire it" (3). At the beginning of the spice trade, "ten pounds of nutmeg cost less than one English penny." In London it was sold at "a mark-up of a staggering 60,000 percent. A small sackful was enough to set a man up for life, buying him a gabled dwelling in Holborn and a servant to attend to his needs" (6). The ruthless, sometimes bloody, competition among the Portuguese, the Spanish, the Dutch, and the English traders escalated the price of spices and resulted in rampant violence against each other as well as the islanders. Writing about the Dutch ship *Mauritius*, which set sail in the spring of 1595 for the Spice Islands, Milton recounts what happened upon its landing. "Angered by the escalating price of spices," the crew of the ship went on a rampage. "What followed was an orgy of destruction that was to set the pattern for the Dutch presence in the East Indies. The town was bombarded with cannon fire and prisoners were sentenced to death" (61). In the context of British history, it is the spice trade that called for the formation of the East India Company, which played a tremendous role in the opium trade and in the process of colonizing Asia, particularly South Asia.[5]

In historical reality the garden of nutmeg helped initiate European colonialism in Asia, whose present-day consequence is the demographic movement westward, thus creating the ever-increasing population of the diaspora. In mythological reality the garden of nutmeg represents the Garden of Eden, from which all humans are exiled. The senior Lee's desperate cry at the end of his sermon—"Get out! Get to the garden of nutmeg"—speaks of the powerful longing for home in both senses (home on earth and home in heaven), which can be sustained and gratified only by turning to religion, myth, and lore. Lee's choice of the seed trope thus aptly allegorizes his and his father's lives, which are filled with longing, movement, and search. One might argue that the senior Lee's exile from China and Indonesia has little relationship to European colonialism. Although not a direct catalyst for his exile, colonial legacy bears a heavy responsibility in China's antagonism toward the West, an antagonism that resulted in a series of political movements purging Western capitalist ideologies, of which the Lees were among the casualties. In the case of Sukarno's regime, it was the anti-West campaign that resulted in the imprisonment and exile of the senior Lee, whose only "guilt" was having taught Shakespeare and Kierkegaard. In the seed conceit Lee represents his father's as well as his own wandering in the postcolonial world—the seed is "born flying," "to begin its longest journey to find its birthplace, that place of eternal unrest. From unrest to unrest it [is] moving. And without so much as a map to guide it, and without so much as a light" (*Seed* 92). Having been transported to unknown places, the seed knows no destination but only the journey itself.

Lee's conception of himself as a winged seed and his poetry as winged seeds is a precious inheritance from his father, who had given up a series of identities before he brought his family to the United States. As John C. Hawley notes, the senior Lee "had to invent himself throughout his adult life"—from Mao Zedong's private physician to a philosopher, a doctor, and a vice president of a university in Indonesia, an evangelical preacher in Hong Kong, and finally a Presbyterian minister in Pennsylvania (192). The senior Lee's ability to adapt and reinvent himself anywhere he happened to be finds an apt expression in the trope of the winged seed. "Seed," a notion endowed with the powerful evocation of the cycle of life, takes on extraordinary meanings in his life rifted by several lives and deaths. Lee writes in his memoir, "I remember, as long as I knew him, my father carried at all times in his right suit-pocket a scarce handful of seeds. *Remembrance*, was his sole answer when I asked him why" (*Seed* 33). The poet adopts the seed trope as a traveling and protean identity for himself. "I was one of those seeds," he writes, "my father kept in the pocket of his suit" (*Seed* 56). To be a winged seed entails movement, possibility, and hybridization. Despite its destiny of constant movement, it carries hope, promises new flowering, and secures regeneration in a distant land. Lee captures the connotation of this trope in a powerful image of dandelion seeds. "I could witness hundreds of dandelion seeds float slowly over the valley, each carrying a spark of the late sun, each turned to gold by what it bore from one side of the river to the other" (*Seed* 36). This image of dandelion seeds as Lee's self-representation suggests that he carries within himself the seed that is his father, and from it comes his renewing sense of self, his elegant songs, and his own fatherhood.

Lee's seed trope bearing the memory of the colonial beginnings fraught with grand dreams, plunder, and violence sets out to be a political trope, lending itself to Said's conceptualization of the intellectual in exile. The seed trope, as a self-definition, points to both the politics that necessitates exile and the politics that operates the exile's positioning in a new place. Lee imagines the seed to have come from violence while meditating about his father. "Did he say seed is told, kept cold, scored with a pocketknife, and then left out to die, in order to come into further seed, speaking the father seed, leading to seed [...] a road we sow ahead of our arrival?" (*Seed* 46–47). Despite its violent beginning, the seed multiplies itself and sows a path into the future. In this lyrical imagining of the seed, he discloses the exile's violent partition from home and kinsmen, promises memory and father's legacy, and offers a utopian impulse. For in the seed "may be growing the flower that will overthrow all governments of crows or senators. [...] This seed revises all existing boundaries to proclaim the dimensions of an ungrasped hour. This seed carries news of a new continent and our first citizenship" (*Seed* 36). Here Lee's notion of citizenship challenges the ordinary meaning of a national, political identity and envisions the "first citizenship" of a utopian world that has revised "all existing boundaries" for the better. In such "a new continent," such categories as exiles, insiders, outsiders, nationals, refugees, immigrants, or illegal immigrants would cease to exist. Impelled by this utopian telos, his seed/exile can never wallow in what Said calls "an uncritical gregariousness" ("The Mind in Winter" 54). Although an American citizen, Lee has never stopped feeling like an outsider and examining America with a clear eye. His poem "The City in Which I Love You" presents a picture of the American street to be as chaotic and dangerous as any of Jakarta, from where his family escaped.

> Past the guarded schoolyards, the boarded-up churches, swastikaed
> synagogues, defended houses of worship, past
> newspapered windows of tenements, among the violated,
> the prosecuted citizenry, throughout this
> storied, buttressed, scavenged, policed
> city I call home, in which I am a guest. (*City* 51)

Compact in this sharp imagery are stories of crime, racism, poverty, and inhumanity that are commonplace in urban America.

Lee incarnates Said's model of the intellectual in exile whose trove is "dislocation and disconnectedness," which Lee considers to be his "spiritual reality" (Moyers 268). Poignant in his imaginary identification with "the winged seed" is the poet's self-assignment as an intellectual in exile—"a seed that had no place to rest, a seed which, born flying, flew" (*Seed* 91). In his exilic displacement, therefore, he does not lament the loss of home (which never existed) but rather celebrates the potentiality of life and renewal made doubly precious and sweet by the poignant connotation of death in both the metaphor of seed and the omnipresent reference to his father's passing.

If there is any sense of origin in Lee's poetic sensibility, it is the "scarce handful of seeds" of memory about China passed on to him through his parents' stories and cooking. For the Chinese diaspora, the origin of ethnic identity, after more than a century and a half of emigration and immigration, displacement, and dismemberment, is a place to which one can never return. The "original" China is no longer there; it too has been transformed. China, to the Chinese diaspora, belongs to what Said calls an "imaginative geography and history" that helps "the mind to intensify its own sense of itself by dramatizing the difference between what is close to it and what is far away. [...] It has acquired an imaginative or figurative value we can name and feel" (*Orientalism* 55). To this real/unreal China, which is a necessary part of the Chinese American imaginary, we cannot literally go home again. In turn, "home becomes meaningful," as Jianguo Chen suggests, "only when exile begins and exile constitutes an essential component of homing, forever searching for a new sense of home—a home in the making" (79). When one lives at home, home is rarely the object of desire. On the contrary, home is often claustrophobic for the young, the restless, and the female. As Carol Boyce Davis points out, "[m]igration creates the desire for home [...]. Home can only have meaning once one experiences a level of displacement from it" (113). The desire for home generates its re-vision and idealization, motivating an endless search for and invention of the origin.

The re-vision of home for the Chinese diaspora (or for any other ethnic group) relies heavily on the discursive pleasure of storytelling and the nondiscursive pleasure of food. This truth is amply evident in Asian American literature and film. With the removal from geographical sites such as China, Taiwan, Hong Kong, and Singapore, the overseas Chinese vest their homesickness in the maintenance of rituals and festivals, both of which depend on storytelling and food rituals. In *The Joy Luck Club*, Amy Tan portrays such a community, epitomized by the mahjong table, whose occupants are engaged in forging a home through stories and food, through secret rivalry in culinary skills, and through food-dominated celebrations of festivals, birthdays, weddings, and friendship. In some cases such as Lee's, however, those in exile don't have access to a community; the closest is the extended or nuclear family. Foodways nevertheless continue to be the bloodline that keeps alive ethnic identity and the bittersweet longing for home. Yet the foodways also set the exile apart as an "alien," an abject and threatening presence in the midst of "natives."

After three years of wandering in Asia and the United States, the Lees settled in East Vandergrift, Pennsylvania, in 1964, when Lee's father became the minister of its all-white Presbyterian congregation. The town's inhospitality is best encapsulated by the oxymoronic name it gave him, "their heathen minister," and the Lees' feeling of alienation was deepened by the beginning of another war against Asians (*Seed* 82). Lee's memoir reveals his experience of painful displacement that often centers on food. In the provincial eyes of the town, the Chinese foodways set the Lees apart as heathen, uncivilized, and abhorrent. The town's abjection of what is foreign turns on food. Lee recalls a childhood made lonely by things other children said about his family's culinary habits. "They say you keep snakes and grasshoppers in a bushel on your back porch and eat them. They say you don't have manners, you lift your plates to your mouths and push the food in with sticks" (*Seed* 86). Food is the matter that most frustrates the culturally conditioned human impulse to separate the inside from the outside, because food is the most frequent medium in the necessary but potentially dangerous traffic between them. Humans as omnivores always oscillate between "the two poles of neophobia (prudence, fear of the unknown, resistance to change) and neophilia (the tendency to explore, the need for change, novelty, variety)"; the tension between the familiar and the foreign often causes "fundamental anxiety in man's relationship to his foods, resulting not only from the need to distrust new or unknown foods, but also and more importantly from the tensions between the two contradictory and equally constraining imperatives of the omnivore's double bind" (Fischler 278). The people of East Vandergrift revealed their fascination with and fear of the seemingly strange foodways of the Chinese in verbalizing and sensationalizing them. Never mind that the Lees didn't eat the things of which they were accused;[6] the fantasy that they did disgusted and thrilled the townspeople. As they denigrated the Chinese foodways, they probably shuddered and perspired in imagining what it would be like to eat snakes and grasshoppers and to eat them with sticks.

Julia Kristeva believes that "[f]ood loathing is perhaps the most elementary and most archaic form of abjection" (*Powers* 2). Although she speaks of food loathing in the context of the primordial impulse (of a child) to establish self in separation from other (mother), her objective in theorizing abjection is to implicate the social. In our attempt to establish ourselves in differentiation from others, we often abide by a system of purity and pollution in evaluating foodways. Our food not only tastes better but is also healthier and cleaner than others'. When we have unwittingly taken in what we consider to be filthy food, we purify ourselves by vomiting, by abjecting ourselves. Mary Douglas argues that dirt is not absolute and dirt is nothing but disorder. "Dirt is the by-product of a systematic ordering and classification of matter, in so far as ordering involves rejecting inappropriate elements" (35). Our system of ordering food matter socializes our taste buds and metabolisms, which, in turn, stand in the front line of demarcating the border between us and them, between Self and Other. Such demarcation is never simply a line drawn between good and bad cuisine or even clean and filthy food. It always informs the construction of a moral judgment of a particular culture. Those who eat filthy food are believed to indulge in filthy ways. The questions Lee had to face about the disgusting things his family supposedly ate were humiliating precisely because of the association of diet with morality, an association even a child makes without understanding.

Lee and his family are no exceptions in their encounter with the food-ways of East Vandergrift. He remembers that as a child he felt strange in "a world which found my family strange, with our accented speech and permanent bewilderment at meatloaf" (*Seed* 69). The Lees' bewilderment at meatloaf encapsulates their feelings of displacement and alienation. While othering via culinary differences seems to be a very human act, we must take into account the power relations in a given situation. The Lees, being the single family of "foreigners" in town, did not possess the power to humiliate or abject. Their visceral and moral sense of difference via food practices thus couldn't result in actions that affected others. Through their disgust with the Lees' eating habits, the people of East Vandergrift succeeded in subjecting the extreme minority to public humiliation. Although Lee does not explicitly reveal the pain caused by the questions put to him regarding his family's eating habits, we can sense the trauma in his repeated line, "I'd heard worse" (*Seed* 86). Such accusatory questions had the power to damage the young and vulnerable psyches of Li-Young and his siblings.

In contrast to their humiliation by the townspeople over Chinese food, Lee depicts the warmth and love expressed through familiar food in his family, defiantly singling out foods that might frighten most white Americans. In one lyrical moment, Lee writes about his trading with his mother.

> *What else have you to trade?* I answered, *This fish head. Good*, she answers, *I'll give it back to you the way you like it, with ginger, miso, green onion, the eyes steamed to succulent jelly. Plus the rich brain*, she said, *You may eat the rich brain*. I thank her. *For you*, I say, *I will fry the tail*. (*Seed* 96)

Lee makes no compromise with the reading public's discomfort with such food, subverting the tourist attitude toward ethnic, culinary markers.[7] He shows proudly that packed in the small, delicate parts of the fish are a mother's love and good wishes, for many Chinese share the belief that parts of animals nourish and strengthen the analogical parts of their eaters. Relish for such foods is culturally specific, as Lee points out: "It's clear I got my appetite from my father, my taste for brains and eyes" (*Seed* 96). In writing about Lee's long poem "The Cleaving," Jeffrey Partridge regards Lee's eating of fish heads as a subversive act. "This ravishing enjoyment is an act of defiance in Bakhtin's sense of the carnivalesque—an overturning of hegemonic and hierarchical order, a response to the age-old argument that Chinese eating habits mark them as barbaric and inhumane" (112).

For the exile, his or her culture's foodways must function as a cushion from displacement and homelessness, as comfort food that momentarily transports the exile to the ever-elusive home. It is often through the palate and nose that the exile awakens the memories of his or her home and loved ones. Lee evokes the pathos of the exiled with the single sharp image of "the black cooking pot" that his family "carried through seven countries" during their wanderings (*Seed* 88). This image recalls the seed trope (e.g., a seedpod like a chestnut or watermelon seed). This image, also suggesting a snail, which carries its home on its back, vividly captures the state of being of the exile: home is on the road, as protean as imaginary. In turn, home cooking carries heavy value for those it feeds—the value of belonging and togetherness.

In an alien environment, the aroma of home cooking arouses a deeply entangled feeling of nostalgia and belonging. In his imagination Lee takes flights of stairs in search of memory and finds food for thought. "On the fifth I smell fried salted fish [...] I jump to the sixth, where my grandmother is stirring a soup of ginger, young hen, lemon grass, and tom yum, standing over a fire-blackened pot and crying, *Memory is salt. Don't forget me*" (*Seed* 136). This lemony, spicy soup unique to Southeast Asian cuisine not only reminds him of the comfort of home but conveys the injunction of memory for those in exile. The multiple meanings of salt unite the themes of food and home, food and love, food and the survival of the exile. "Memory is salt," Lee's grandmother instructs. Without it elements of food don't come together to make a savory dish. Without it family or community cannot stay whole under the stress of transplantation. Exiles are haunted by the urge to look back, as Rushdie puts it, "even at the risk of being mutated into pillars of salt" (10).

Salt, with its connotations of sorrow and flavor, is a long-standing mythological trope expressive of the intertwining pangs of homelessness and the relish of remembrance. The biblical tale of Lot's wife turning into a pillar of salt for looking back, besides showing the consequence of failing to obey God, may also suggest the arrested state of the exile when one turns one's gaze *only* upon the past—looking at it as a factual past, as though that past were unmediated by memory, narrative, fantasy, and myth filtered and constructed by the present. Speaking of the Indian writers in exile, Rushdie writes, "[O]ur physical alienation from India almost inevitably means that we will not be capable of reclaiming precisely the thing that was lost; that we will [...] create fictions, not actual cities or villages, but invisible ones, imaginary homelands, Indias of the mind" (10). In theorizing identity as an endless production, Stuart Hall resonates with Rushdie and believes that "our relationship to it [the past], like the child's relationship to the mother, is always already 'after the break'" ("Cultural Identity" 395). We can never return to our past as if we had never left.

The cultural identity of an exile is a constellation of narrative acts enunciating the past as well as the present.

If salt is memory, as Lee has his grandmother say, then his prizing of salt can be interpreted as his valorization of memory in the invention of home and community. To him neither is stable or fixed. One must imagine it, create it, and sustain it with memory. As salt makes cuisine possible, so does memory make possible a past cathected with love and longing. Thus his emphasis on memory indicates his belief that the past is never directly accessible to us; rather, our narratives conjure up the memory about our past. To demonstrate this point, he singles out cooks as individuals who understand best the function of salt/memory. He writes, "Only the baker knows that bread is a form of our deepest human wish, a shape of love [...]. [...] Love is a massive compass and several gravity, numen manifest in what can be eaten. Know how bread is knit by salt. For tears alone are active seed, leavening perishing forms, apparent at an imperishable wheel of hunger" (137). If bread is love and salt memory, it is memory that creates and sustains love. Lee's notion of love clearly exceeds romantic love. He explains in an interview, "Romantic love interests me only slightly. More than anything, a kind of universal love—divine love [...] are what interest me" (James Lee 274). Bread, a universal food with variations in shapes, textures, and tastes, symbolizes the love that transcends the individual or family. "We are bread," he proclaims (*Seed* 138); therefore, we are love; we are the bread that Christ broke among his disciples as an offering of divine love. Aside from the religious connotation, he also offers the wisdom of an experienced chef. As bread is knit by salt to bring out its sweetness, sugar and salt or love and sorrow are agents for mutual fulfillment. In other words, sugar cannot bring forth gratifying sweetness without the complement of salt. This trope of bread making enacts the aesthetics of the exile: the sweetness of home is made possible through feelings of sorrow and displacement, and the plenitude of home is made imaginable through feelings of lack and loss.

The pathos in this entangled cluster of imageries—salt, bread, tears, memory, and love—is not only among the most palpable aesthetics of the exile but also his or her ethics. Tears over the traumatic dispersal from home intensify the victims' capacity to love. As though having been dispossessed, the exile gains a greater capacity to give and a deeper understanding of human vulnerability. Lee recalls an incident that exhibits his family's reaction to those who suffer a similar predicament. Shortly after their arrival in the United States, they met a young woman with a naked baby wrapped in newspaper on the train from Seattle to Chicago. "The child's sallow, puny body was smeared with newspaper ink. The mother, dirty, gaunt, looked wild" (*Seed* 15). Lee's family "had been living on butter cookies" and "had two tins of them" to share among the parents and four children. "Butter cookies and the sixty dollars in my mother's purse were to see us through the next few days until my father found work" (*Seed* 15). Despite the threat of her family's starvation, Mrs. Lee offered the mother and baby "the unopened tin" of cookies along with her sweater. When the young woman didn't know what to do with the cookies, Mrs. Lee went over and began to "chew up a biscuit and, all the while humming to the child, and lightly rocking, pass the spit-brightened, masticated paste of her mouth into his" (*Seed* 16). This temporary relief from hunger put both mother and baby to sleep. Similarly, Lee uses food to portray his father's compassion for those ignored by East Vandergrift—"'the shut-ins,' [...] mainly old, infirm, crazy, or dying" (*Seed* 67). To them he and his father would deliver hot dinners once a week. With these stories, Lee shows that dispossession and exile have given his family sensitivity to others' pain, and alacrity to offer assistance.

The love in Lee's family for each other in the face of misunderstanding and alienation is also expressed through the references to food. In his short poem "Early in the Morning," which recalls the love between his parents, Lee infuses the text with the aroma of Chinese breakfast cooking. "While the long grain is softening/in the water, gurgling/over a low stove flame, before/the salted Winter Vegetable is sliced/for breakfast/my mother glides an ivory comb/through her hair" (*Rose* 25). The olfactory images of soft rice and pickled greens set the tone and scent of the familial morning ritual that is both ethnically specific and universally recognizable as tranquility and love. Accompanying the aroma of a simple Chinese breakfast is the picture of his mother gliding "an ivory comb/through her hair" as his father looks on and "listens for/the music of comb/against hair" (25). In this ordinary but intimate setting, he paints the picture of his father relishing the simple pleasure of watching his wife comb her hair, a pleasure made precious by his experience of imprisonment and his declining health because of it. His father likes his mother to wear a bun on the back of her head. "He says it is kempt./But I know/it is because of the way/my mother's hair falls/when he pulls the pins out./Easily, like the curtains/when they untie them in the evening" (25). With the unlikely juxtaposition to breakfast cooking, Lee subtly suggests the eroticism of his parents in the brief but dramatic imagery of hair falling like curtains closing at night. In this short poem, he constructs a cycle of an ordinary day in his family, beginning with breakfast preparation "before the birds" and ending with the falling of his mother's hair in the privacy of his parents' bedroom (25). Her hair described as "heavy/and black as calligrapher's ink" evokes an intertextuality with his other poems in which we see the father write and paint with brush and ink, projecting the poet's solace in the love between his parents.

"Eating Alone" and "Eating Together" pair well for their alimentary imageries and their intensity of the poet's longing for his deceased father. "Eating

Alone" "centers thematically on the inevitable and often lonely movement of life toward death" (Moeser 118). Lee's depiction of nature's cycle focuses on the winter garden. "I've pulled the last of the year's young onions./The garden is bare now. The ground is cold,/brown and old" (*Rose* 33). Remembrance of his father walking in the very garden rushes in and brings forth the image of his father holding up a windfall pear for his son to observe. "I still see him bend that way—left hand braced/on knee, creaky—to lift and hold to my/eye a rotten pear. In it, a hornet/spun crazily, glazed in slow, glistening juice" (33). The complex impression—the aging father's creaky joints paired with the rotten pear drowning a hornet in its juice—builds upon the tone of loneliness and grief in the first stanza. Vivid in this picture is the poet's meditation on life's inevitable journey toward death. The speaker's longing for his deceased father is given a ghostly shape in the third stanza. "It was my father I saw this morning/waving to me from the trees. I almost/called to him, until I came close enough/to see the shovel, leaning where I had/left it, in the flickering, deep green shade" (33). The father's ghost accompanies the speaker and refreshes every memory of him. No description of sadness is directly offered here. Rather the poem continues to the last stanza to picture a Chinese meal that switches the image of the cold, dying garden to that of a warm, aromatic kitchen. "White rice steaming, almost done. Sweet green peas/fried in onions. Shrimp braised in sesame/oil and garlic. And my own loneliness./What more could I, a young man, want" (33). Lee's deep sorrow over his father's absence is powerfully suggested in the vividly inviting food, which now he must eat by himself. Despite the sorrow associated with his father's absence, there is a quiet feeling of comfort in the last stanza, the comfort of a delicious, home-cooked meal. Among the ingredients in the braised shrimp he adds "my own loneliness" to convert it into nourishment. The loving details of the menu and the meal's preparation also evoke a strong sense of family, a family in which the speaker has learned the art of Chinese cuisine. The last rhetorical question suggests his acceptance of his father's passing. Daniel Moeser interprets, "The lack of a question mark at the end of the poem shows that the speaker is making a statement of hopefulness and contentment" (119). It is almost as if Lee suggests that his skills in Chinese cooking can rescue him from loneliness and sorrow, or at least the food helps make loneliness bearable.

"Eating Together" celebrates the togetherness of family by means of a Chinese lunch and laments the absence of the father. "In the steamer is the trout/seasoned with slivers of ginger/two sprigs of green onion, and sesame oil./We shall eat it with rice for lunch,/brothers, sister, my mother" (*Rose* 49). This Chinese meal serves as a metaphor for the uniquely ethnic way of being. Tight family and leisured eating, valued in the Chinese culture, differ from the mainstream American life in which fast foods, microwaved dinners, and soggy sandwiches dominate many people's diet. Partridge notes, "In the community of family, the poet is not lonely, and neither is his father" (113). Lee offers another uniquely ethnic picture—the manner in which his mother eats the fish. "[M]y mother/who will taste the sweetest meat of the head, holding it between her fingers/deftly, the way my father did weeks ago" (49).[8] With ease he slides from the image of his mother holding the fish head between her fingers to the memory of his father. Their shared relish in the sweet meat in the fish cheeks marks the singularity of this family displaced in a culture that regards such a delicacy as nonfood. This image of eating a fish head also accentuates the absence of the father, for he did the same thing with his fish head only "weeks ago" (49). But now he is gone, "lonely for no one" (49). It is the living that are lonely for their lost loved ones, and eating together and eating home cooking are how we shore up against that loneliness.

Metaphysics via Food

Most critics classify Lee as an Asian American poet and choose to focus on his experience as an émigré and his double identity as a Chinese in exile and an American in citizenship. For example, Judith Kitchen in *The Georgia Review* attributes Lee's poetry in *The City in Which I Love You* to his unique subject position as "a Chinese American trying to make sense of both his heritage and his inheritance" (160). Yibing Huang, writing for *Amerasia Journal*, assesses Lee's book of prose poetry, *The Winged Seed*, as "a typical fable of Asian American experience, of how tradition and the parents' generation are always, in consciousness or the unconscious, linked with pain and burden" (190). Lee expresses his strong objection to this classification in an interview with Tod Marshall.

> I have no dialogue with cultural existence. Culture made that up—Asian American, African-American, whatever. I have no interest in that. I have an interest in spiritual lineage to poetry—through Eliot, Donne, Lorca, Tu Fu, Neruda, David the Psalmist. [...] Somehow an artist has to discover a dialogue that is so essential to his being, to his self, that it is no longer cultural or canonical, but a dialogue with his truest self. His most naked spirit. (132)

Lee believes that poetry in dialogue with the cultural is a "lower form of art" (131). It is like poetry "built on sand; it looks solid, but it isn't because it speaks from a self that is grounded in things" (133) and things disappear. True poetry, he claims, sheds the poet's false (cultural) identity. In the same vein, Helen Vendler proposes that the "lyric desires for a stripping-away of the details associated with a socially specified self in order to reach its desired all-purpose abstraction" (*Soul Says* 2–3). "If the normal home of selfhood is the novel," she asserts in valorizing poetry, "then the home of 'soul' is the lyric, where the human being becomes a set of warring passions independent of time and space" (5).[9] Lee would wholeheartedly agree with Vendler that the soul is home to poetry. But would Vendler, who has more power than any U.S. critic to make or break a poet, regard Lee as such a poet? Probably not. In her review of Bill Moyers' *The Language of Life,* which contains Moyers' interview with Lee, Vendler mocks it as "laughably politically correct, summoning up an anxious roll call of representatives from what academics call the 'marginalized' and the 'Other.'" She remarks that Moyers' book "is a misrepresentation of the achievement of contemporary American poetry to concentrate so tediously on 'the Other'" ("Poetry for the People" 14–15). Although her disparaging comments are directed at Bill Moyers, it is not difficult to detect her contemptuous tone regarding the poetry by the marginal and the Other.

Ironically, discredited by critics such as Vendler as hotcakes of multiculturalism, Lee nevertheless maintains his polemical appeal to the naked self and demonstrates his ambivalence toward his ethnicity. This ambivalence, however, has little to do with culturally enforced self-loathing. His objection to the reviewers' classification is rooted in his desire to transcend all cultural representations. For him, cultural identities are works of the rational mind, and true poetry works against it. He remarks in an interview,

> I've noticed that we can't be free of stereotypes as long as we're thinking
> with our rational mind. So it was important for me to take a breath and then
> go under [...] to try to escape all stereotypical views of what an Asian is
> in America, what an immigrant is [...]. The only way I could escape those
> stereotypes was to defy my own rational thinking. (James Lee 275)

Rejection of his Asian American identity, for Lee, does not purport a willing surrender to the ideology of assimilation. Rather than becoming an American, he desires the "state of nobodyhood." His response to his ontological condition as an exile taking the form of cultural transcendence aims to counter the stereotypes of Asians in U.S. popular culture. He explains in the same interview,

> The culture we live in offers or imposes versions of "somebodyhoods" that are
> really shallow and false. [...] If I can attain a state of "nobodyhood," which is
> the same thing as the state of "everybodyhood," that's much richer and more
> full of potential than some false, made up, Hollywood magazine, university, or
> cultural version of "somebodyhood." (J. Lee 275–276)

The seeming paradox of nobody being everybody is central to his transcendentalism, which strives to achieve the state of the naked self in relationship to God.

Diaspora, for Lee, is not a uniquely ethnic condition; rather it is a human condition, a view derived from Genesis in which human history begins in dual exile from the Garden of Eden and the presence of God. "It is arrogant of the dominant culture," he comments, "to think it's not part of a diaspora." He regards himself as exilic in this sense. "The difficulty is that the earth is not my home" (J. Lee 279). Although his concept of diaspora is Christian, it is rooted in his existential condition as an exile and in his father's theology necessitated by his experience of imprisonment and exile. The latter's influence on his son is unfathomable, and one can say without risk of exaggeration that most of Lee's writings are trained to the remembrance of his father. In "My Father, in Heaven, Is Reading Out Loud," he captures brilliantly the symbiosis between them, even beyond the grave.

> Because my father walked the earth with a grave
> determined rhythm, my shoulders ached
> from his gaze. Because my father's shoulders
> ached from the pulling of oars, my life now moves
> with a powerful back-and-forth rhythm:
> nostalgia, speculation. (*The City in Which I Love You* 39)

Lee's metaphysics is not only an answer to his ontological condition as an exile but also functions as an umbilical cord linking him and his deceased father.

The senior Lee's fascination with and eventual conversion to Christianity can be traced back to his initial exile from communist China and his exile again from Indonesia. Hesford documents that Lee's father was "converted to Christianity while a prisoner in Indonesia" (40). Wandering from country to country, from continent to continent, the senior Lee found communities among Chinese Christians, exiled or not, who sublimate alienation to divine deliverance. Lee's parents used to stand in front of other Chinese refugees and immigrants and speak "about the mysterious hand of God which had preserved us and protected us throughout our trials in Indonesia" (*Seed* 130). He recalls that once a year his family would meet four hundred other members of "the Ambassador Temple in a Maryland wood, where they witnessed, sang, prayed, preached, danced in the aisles, got slain in the spirit, rolled on the floor, and got generally all over holy, shouting hallelujah!" (*Seed* 130). Such religious orgies offer the diasporic Chinese badly needed catharsis and serve to exorcise the demon of banishment. In religion they find solace and in each other a sense of home. In the lives of the Lees, the pangs of exile and constant movement have necessitated Christianity's vital place. Homelessness is a human condition in the Christian theology; it is the life humans are doomed to lead on earth. As I suggest above, such religious fervor would probably not have touched Lee had his parents not been exiled from China and Indonesia successively. As a consequence, Lee's affinity to the universalistic concept of humankind overrides his affinity to Asia.

Few of Lee's critics take into account his transcendentalist yearnings as part of his social living. They either want to rescue him from ethnic determinism or fault him for not being sufficiently ethnic. Xiaojing Zhou argues against the tendency of some critics to interpret Lee's poetry by emphasizing his Chinese ethnicity. By reducing his art to expressions of his ethnicity, Zhou points out, critics minimize "the rich cross-cultural sources of influence on Lee's work and of the creative experiment in his poetry." On the strength of Hans-Georg Gadamer's notion of "horizon," Zhou theorizes that "one's heritage is not possessed once for all, nor is it necessarily inherited through ethnic lineage. Rather, it is changed and renewed with the changing conditions of human life and human consciousness" ("Inheritance and Invention," 114, 115). Lee's rich inheritance harnessing different cultures and histories leads to an expansion of his horizon, a position that, according to Bakhtin, promises creativity. In his essay on Lee's "Persimmons," Steven G. Yao remarks that many of Lee's critics (including Zhou) "have relied on an overly simplistic model for cross-cultural literary production" (3). In a close reading of Lee's most anthologized poem, Yao makes the case that "Lee achieves only a superficial integration, or 'hybridization,' of Chinese and American culture" and "'grafting' offers a more exact term than hybridity for understanding Lee's accomplishment in "Persimmons" (19–20). To him Lee is more American than Asian American because Lee's knowledge of China is so meager that the Chinese culture he represents offers only a "voyeuristic appeal" (6).

Both Zhou's and Yao's efforts to free Lee from interpretive limitations, however, only partially meet Lee's own self-portrait as a poet on a quest for the Absolute. To be Asian, American, or Asian American occupies little space in his self-representation. His metaphysical schema aims to rid him of such labels: "My true self is universe or God. I assume that my true nature is God. I assume that I am God in my true nature" (Marshall 134). What he claims to be true of himself he attributes to all true poets. "When I read poetry, I feel I'm in the presence of universe mind; that is, a mind I would describe as a 360-degree seeing; it is manifold in consciousness" (Marshall 130).

Lee's transcendentalism bears a strong resemblance to Emerson's, whose famous declaration goes, "[A]ll mean egotism vanishes, I become a transparent eyeball; I am nothing; I see all" (Ziff 39). Lee's "360-degree seeing" and Emerson's "transparent eyeball" offer a political liberal license to all "true" poets, as Lee deems them, and true poets possess the naked self that is the universe mind or God, free from cultural and social constraints and therefore free from the blind spots that all people have as social individuals constituted by race, class, gender, religion, and language. In his statement "I am born into the great, the universal mind. I, the imperfect, adore my own Perfect" (Ziff 240), Emerson anticipates Lee's self-anointment as God in his true nature, a god that is twin to Emerson's "Oversoul, within which every man's particular being is contained and made one with all others" (Ziff 206). The concept of self in both men's articulations of the transcendent, therefore, is seated in essentialism. Harold Bloom in his usual abstruse eloquence describes Emersonism as the American Religion. "*Self*-reliance, in Emerson [...] is the religion that celebrates and reveres what in the self is before the Creation, a whatness which from the perspective of religious orthodoxy can only be the primal Abyss" (146).

As an American transcendentalist, Lee is situated within the American poetic tradition of the sublime. His appeal to that which is other to the social is an appeal to what Vendler calls "the grand, the sublime, and the unnameable" (*Part of Nature* 2). Departing from European Romanticism, the object of the sublime in American poetry is much more than nature itself; it is nation, technology, and power that have been elevated to sublimity.[10] Many of the major interpreters of American poetry, such as Bloom and Vendler, regard the American sublime as a sensibility that defines American poetry as much as the American spirit. Nativist in sentiment, their assessment of American poetry would probably annoy Lee, if not affront him, for he refuses to be a grateful guest in this country by critiquing it and by considering it "a country/wholly unfound to himself" (*Book of My Nights* 6).

Rob Wilson, interrogating the nationalist implication in the American sublime, puts forth his thesis that "[a]s a poetic genre, the American sublime helped to produce the subject and site of American subjection as sublime" (3). Or in my blunt paraphrase, the American poetic expression of the sublime is a performance of a distinctively American subject substantiated through the subjugation of land and its first peoples. Centering on "the material sublime" in American poetry, Wilson points out that the will to American sublimity finds its representation in a "landscape of immensity and wildness" that serves as the "Americanized self's inalienable ground" (3, 5). Although Lee does not participate in the representation of such an American material sublime, he is nevertheless part of this American poetic tradition in which wild immensity, be it nature, force, or rhetoric, predictably accompanies self-deification and hyperbolic imagination. In "Degrees of Blue," he evokes the sublime through the grand language of power:

How is he going to explain
the moon taken hostage, the sea
risen to fill up all the mirrors?
How is he going to explain the branches
beginning to grow from his ribs and throat,
the cries and trills starting in his own mouth?
And now that ancient sorrow between his hips,
his body's ripe listening
the planet
knowing itself at last. (*Book* 31)

In this vast field of vision traversing the private, the historical, and the planetary, Lee centers himself as the knower and seer. His rhetorical will to power and his self-deification place him squarely within what Wilson calls the American "collective will-to-sublimity" (6). Lee's disavowal of all that is cultural cannot hide his American roots even when his disavowal is sublimated into a metaphysical form of mysticism.

Lee is, of course, fully aware of the self's submergence in the diurnal mass. To him, precisely because most of us most of the time are socially anchored, we become "entangled with a phantom" (Marshall 134). Like Heraclitus and many Buddhist and Western process philosophers, Lee (whose undergraduate study was in biochemistry) tells us that material objects in fact have no materiality. "Modern physicists are proving what the ancient mystics have always known: that matter is 99.9999% space" (Marshall 133). Everything we see, touch, and hold onto is fading away. "So where is ground?" Lee asks (Marshall 133). In "Arise, Go Down," he writes, "[s]eeing how one cancels the other. / I've become a scholar of cancellations. [...] to see in each and / every flower the world cancelling itself" (*City* 37–38). This knowledge of "the world cancelling itself" renders illusory all that is worldly. His poetry, he tells us, is born out of his frustration because he cannot continuously live the life of the universe mind. It is writing poetry that keeps him living "in constant remembrance of who I am. That I am not this. I am not this stuff that is fading away" (Marshall 134).

One can read this as Lee's opposition to the reification of existing social and cultural practices while finding his own poetic voice, which resonates with Martin Heidegger's claim that new social and cultural worlds can come to be if we cease trying to control socially constituted objects and if instead we permit a poetic world-making process to work through us (17–87). The new emerging, of course, will still be social and historical. In much less grandiose language, Gadamer makes a comparable claim when he tells us that something new can be created if we, with our cultural prejudgments, risk those prejudgments by entering into open dialogue with people and texts with other often incommensurate prejudgments (345–350). Lee's desire to enter into dialogue with all other poets present and past is interestingly similar to Gadamer's position, although he in his desire to possess a 360-degree consciousness may be forgetting that prejudgments and cultural worlds are often incommensurate and that the creative result of dialogue will remain socially and culturally specific.

Situated in the Christian tradition, Lee's appeal to that which is Other to the social takes on the absolutist lexicon of God and the universe mind. His attempt to go beyond the social and the rational finds good company in Asian philosophies and religions as well as contemporary Western thinkers. In Daoism it is the transcendent Dao that is Other to the social prioritized by Confucianism, and in Buddhism it is nothingness that defies the material and the cultural. Lacan theorizes the Real that is not codifiable by the social. For Kristeva it is the Semiotic that operates in constant tension with the Symbolic. All of the above positions claim that there is something more "real" than the reality of socially constituted objects and subjects. Henry Ruf sums this up well: "There is an irremovable 'Real' that our entire conscious and unconscious symbolic apparatus cannot account for or control" (209). Lee's appeal to God is his way to name the unnameable, the Lacanian Real that is Other to social rationality. When he disavows his ethnic identity, he is really attempting to resist absolutizing social and cultural identities. The flaw in his metaphysics, however, lies in his belief that the material, social world hinders his union with the universe mind. In contrast, the transcendent Dao offers the way socially constituted people are to live with creative quietude in the situations where they find themselves. Likewise, the Real for Lacan reveals the symbolic world's inability to avoid radical instability in its effort to control enjoyment. In neither case is a transcendent, socially naked person being postulated. This is why Žižek à la Lacan argues that one cannot approach the Real without going through cultural and material specificities.[11] The movement of the universe mind always brings one back to the cultural and material. Ethnic identification and Lee's transcendent self are not mutually exclusive.

If we look at more of his poems, it becomes apparent that Lee speaks from a social or ethnic self to reach the transcendent, and his semantic/semiotic place from which to speak is Asian food. Fruit is the unifying imagery in "Persimmons" and becomes the locus from which he articulates an immigrant's analysis of his own experience between two cultures and his critique of the intolerance of the mainstream culture. The adult speaker returns to his childhood memory keyed up by two words, "persimmon" and "precision." Yao points out that "[t]he system of Chinese phonotactics does not include the complex syllable onset of the *pre-* at the beginning of the word *precision* as an allowable sequence" (7). The young Lee, speaking Bahasa Indonesia and Mandarin Chinese, encounters the difficulty of reproducing the sequence of sounds that distinguishes the first syllable of "persimmon" from that of "precision." The poem begins by picturing a classroom situation where the immigrant child is punished for making this phonetic error. "In sixth grade Mrs. Walker/slapped the back of my head/and made me stand in the corner/for not knowing the difference/between *persimmon* and *precision*" (*Rose* 17). Lee makes it apparent that the child knows the difference in meaning between these two words—"How to choose/persimmons. This is precision" (17). He then describes precisely how to choose, peel, and eat the perfect persimmon.

> Ripe ones are soft and brown-spotted.
> Sniff the bottoms. The sweet one
> will be fragrant. How to eat:
> put the knife away, lay down newspaper.
> Peel the skin tenderly, not to tear the meat.
> Chew the skin, suck it,
> and swallow. Now, eat
> the meat of the fruit,
> so sweet,
> all of it, to the heart. (17)

The speaker's sophisticated knowledge in the selection and consumption of persimmons counters the common, racist assumption that broken or accented speech signifies underdeveloped intellect. As a child, Lee came to understand this prejudice with immense pain and humiliation. He recalls,

> When I was six and learning to speak English, I talked with an accent [...].
> [...] I noticed early that all accents were not heard alike by the dominant
> population of American English speakers. Instead, each foreigner's spoken
> English [...] fell on a coloring ear, which bent the listener's eye and,
> consequently, the speaker's countenance; it was a kind of narrowing, and
> unconscious on the part of the listener, who listens in judgment, judging
> the speaker even before the meaning or its soundness were attended to. [...]
> The result was that while in Chinese, with my family, I rattled like any good
> loose child [...] and spoke my broken English without embarrassment [...],
> in public school or any other place where fluent English was current, I was
> dumb. Perceived as feeble-minded, I was [...] spoken to very loudly, as though
> the problem were deafness. (*Seed* 76–78)

His early experience of physical punishment and social isolation over his phonetic difficulty in English resulted in self-disgust. He remembers "how I used to hold a hand very casually over my mouth when I talked, hoping to hide the alien thing. And I grew to hate its ugliness more than anyone" (*Seed* 78).

The sharp irony in "Persimmons" points to two situations. First, Mrs. Walker humiliates the immigrant child "for not knowing the difference" between two English words, "thereby marking herself as someone grossly insensitive to the very category of 'difference,' as a poor teacher [...] who both fails to recognize and neglects to practice the import of her own lesson" (Yao 8). Second, Mrs. Walker demonstrates her ignorance by committing the errors of selecting a green persimmon, calling it a "Chinese apple," and cutting it up with a knife. Lee's critique of the mainstream's ignorance and arrogance, embodied in this sixth-grade teacher, centers on this particular Asian fruit. In introducing an exotic fruit to her students, Mrs. Walker offers misinformation and humiliates the immigrant child. Even though the child declines his share of "the Chinese apple," knowing the sour and astringent taste of an unripe persimmon, he is not spared when his classmates scrunch up their faces and turn to stare at him, silently accusing the Chinese of being foolish people who eat such terrible-tasting apples.

Centered upon the same fruit is also the contrast between the cruelty of the American society, whose microcosmos is Mrs. Walker's classroom, and the love and comfort inside the immigrant home. The image of a persimmon round as the moon and warm as the sun, central to the aesthetics and ethics of this poem, counters the earlier scene of punishment and humiliation in the classroom. In the sixth stanza, the centerpiece, Lee de-exoticizes the fruit by giving it a private value. "My mother said every persimmon has a sun/inside, something golden, glowing,/warm as my face" (18). These three lines evoke an intimate image of a mother cupping her son's face in her hands and trying to heal his injured psyche. Persimmons capture all that is golden, warm, sweet, tender, and gratifying in such a moment. In the eighth stanza, Lee brings into the folds of the persimmon trope his relationship with his dying father.

> Finally understanding
> he was going blind,
> my father sat up all one night
> waiting for a song, a ghost.
> I gave him the persimmons,
> swelled, heavy as sadness,
> and sweet as love. (18)

These are the two persimmons the speaker has put on his bedroom windowsill to ripen, "where each morning a cardinal/sang, *The sun, the sun*" (18).

Lee associates persimmons with heart—"so sweet,/all of it, to the heart"—employing it as an objective correlative for his heavy heart and deep sorrow over his father's illness. The symbol of persimmons vividly sets the contrast between a culture, ignorant of its ripe connotations, that punishes a child for mispronouncing words and the immigrant home where love cancels fear and pain. Persimmons thus figure for the rich, full warmth of his parents' love, which he finds lacking in American culture. And love and tenderness are the spirit of Lee's songs that bring him closer to God or the universe mind.

For Lee divine love includes profane love. Mining the riches of Song of Songs, he rescues the sensual and the erotic, and unifies the sacred with the profane.[12] In "This Room and Everything in It," he invokes Song of Songs to describe his love for his wife, blurring the line between the erotic and the divine. Again food is the site where such blurring takes place.

> Your scent
> that scent
> of spice and a wound,
> I'll let stand for mystery.
>
> Your sunken belly
> is the daily cup
> of milk I drank
> as a boy before morning prayer. (*City* 49)

In "Persimmons" the loving details surrounding the fruit are highly charged with eroticism. Returning to the second stanza, in which the speaker displays his knowledge on selecting and eating this fruit, we see how erotically suggestive his vocabulary is: "sniff," "soft," "sweet," "the bottoms," "lay," "skin," "suck," "swallow," "eat," "meat," and "heart" (*Rose* 17). Yao elegantly terms this moment "an erotics of consumption" (9). Persimmons thus eroticized lead the reader into the third stanza, in which Donna appears as the speaker's object of desire. "Donna undresses, her stomach is white" (17). With the time frame shifted away from the traumatic classroom scene, this stanza presents the speaker as an adult lover: "we lie naked,/face-up, face-down. [...]/I part her legs" (17). Donna's attraction to the speaker is made clear through the association with persimmons—"she is beautiful as the moon"—resonant to the seventh stanza in which the speaker's mother compares a persimmon to the sun, punning for son. As the fruit emblematizes the speaker, "golden, glowing,/warm as my face" (18), so is Donna implicitly linked to the fruit by Lee's simile of "the moon," round and "beautiful," gravitating and gravitated toward the sun/son. The fruit symbolic of the sun masculinizes the speaker, the son, while it is simultaneously symbolic of the feminine moon that assists the display of the speaker's manhood as sexual agency—"I part her legs."

The speaker's attraction to a white woman and his romancing of her via a few words of Chinese are an issue to some critics. Yao interprets the figure of Donna as "the ultimate object and symbol of assimilationist desire" (9–10). Tim Engles asserts that Lee himself suggests that "the speaker's attraction to white America has involved a prostitution of sorts of his heritage" (191). While the assessment of this issue lies outside the domain of this chapter, it raises a related question of Lee's relationship to his ethnicity in "Persimmons." The large, orange-colored persimmon comes from grafting a branch of the Asian specimen onto a native plant rootstock to achieve hardiness. Its duality allegorizes a new identity of Asian immigrants in the United States. Yao strongly argues against the postcolonial lexicon of hybridity in assessing the aesthetics as well as the ethnic identity of "Persimmons."[13]

While appreciative of Yao's erudition of Chinese and Western languages and lyricisms that establishes the fine distinction between "hybridity" and "grafting," I think that ethnicity as mediated by persimmons is a matter of nondiscursive engagement, a gustatory *jouissance* and a bodily memory, rather than a matter of cultural and linguistic asymmetry. It is true that "Persimmons" begins by marking the speaker's ethnicity along the line of linguistic displacement. Yet Lee's opposition to the cultural insensitivity in the episode of Mrs. Walker's pedagogical error relies strongly on nonlinguistic acts.[14] Following the physical punishment and humiliation occasioned by the speaker's mispronunciations, the second stanza exhibits his precise and confident knowledge on how to choose and eat persimmons. "Peel the skin tenderly, not to tear the meat./Chew the skin, suck it,/and swallow" (17). Lee seems to establish the speaker's ethnic authenticity via his relationship with persimmons. His knowhow in enjoying this fruit testifies to his Asianness, as though it were an innate knowledge, a bodily memory. This seemingly biologist approach to ethnicity is not necessarily guilty of essentialism. Enjoyment, though a bodily activity, is culturally specific. The people in East Vandergrift enjoy meatloaf while the Lees enjoy fish heads, neither understanding the other's gustatory passion. The speaker's loving account of the fruit, erotically tactile, evokes sensations more than beliefs. This nondiscursive ethnic identification evinces how culture inscribes even our taste buds and metabolism.

In the eighth stanza of "Persimmons," Lee shows how the speaker forges his ethnic identity by introducing the father, the paternal heritage. He gives his father the two persimmons he has been ripening on the windowsill, "swelled, heavy as sadness,/and sweet as love" (18). His love for persimmons, which comes from his parents, now transfers his love to them. The poeticism of the persimmons relies on tactile and olfactory imagery, suggesting the association of heart and feeling with persimmons. In the last stanza, the speaker finds three of his father's paintings in the cellar, one of which bears two persimmons, so vivid that "they want to drop from the cloth" (19). When told of the paintings, the father says,

I painted them hundreds of times
eyes closed. These I painted blind.
Some things never leave a person:
scent of the hair of one you love,
the texture of persimmons,
in your palm, the ripe weight. (19)

The father's lines show that his connection to Chinese tradition continues despite his loss of perception. The countless repetitions have ingrained the art of representing persimmons in the body: "the feel of the wolftail on the silk,/the strength, the tense/precision in the wrist. [...] the texture of persimmons,/in your palm, the ripe weight" (19). The father's story seems to tell us that it is the somatic that continues one's connection to one's ancestral culture. His emotional reflection on things that one never forgets "despite any form of geographical, linguistic or even sensory displacement" offers a consolation to the son that his link to his parents and their culture leaves imprints in his body, despite his fading skill in Chinese and feelings of disconnection (Yao 18). It is significant that "Persimmons" concludes with the father's speech, offering the resolution that the value of persimmons is measured by weight—the weight of memory, of loss of memory, and the weight of cultural inscription in one's body.

Most pertinent to ethnicity is one of Lee's best long poems, "The Cleaving." Food and eating are central to its themes and aesthetics. Only after the indulgence in the carnal does he arrive at a meditation on the transcendent. Only after the montage of ethnic markers—Chinese cuisine and physical features—is he able to empty out ethnicity. "The Cleaving," set in a Chinatown, begins with the speaker's identification with the man working in "the Hon Kee Grocery" (*City* 77). "He gossips like my grandmother, this man/with my face" (77). Emanating from the first few lines is a sense of belonging: "I could stand/amused all afternoon/in the Hon Kee Grocery" (77). What amuses the speaker is not the exotic, which attracts tourists to Chinatown, but the familiar sights, smells, and tastes associated with home. The following lines present an aromatic and alimentary image of meats hung inside the grocery.

[R]oast pork cut
from a hog hung
by nose and shoulders,

her entire skin burnt
crisp, flesh I know
to be sweet,
her shining
face grinning
up at ducks
dangling single file,
each pierced by black
hooks through breast, bill,
and steaming from a hole
stitched shut at the ass. (*City* 77)

Lee depicts this scene with such ease that the seeming violence is muted by humor and appetite. The details about roast pork and ducks serving as markers of his ethnic subjectivity—"flesh I know / to be sweet"—seem to appeal to the sensory, the bodily. Significantly, the line break occurs at "know," not "flesh," to underscore that the speaker's ethnicity is based on intellectual as well as visceral knowledge.

Such union of the mind and the body when constructing the speaker's ethnic self enjoys a high moment in the fourth stanza, describing roast ducks.

The head, flung from the body,
opens down the middle where the butcher
cleanly halved it between
the eyes, and I
see, foetal-crouched
inside the skull, the homunculus,
gray brain grainy
to eat. [...]
The butcher sees me eye this delicacy.
With a finger, he picks it
out of the skull-cradle
and offers it to me.
I take it gingerly between my fingers
and suck it down.
I eat my man. (79–80)

On the surface this moment describes the fellowship between two Chinese men expressed in their mutual enjoyment of duck brains. The particular association of duck brains with "man" and "foetal-crouched [...] homunculus," however, has far-reaching significance in ethnicizing the speaker. Lee alludes to the

Chinese legend of Yue Fei, a general during the Song dynasty, who defeated foreign invaders but was unjustly punished by the emperor under the advice of a corrupt courtier. Afterward, everywhere the courtier went, people spat and threw stones at him. Hated and chased by people, he could find no better refuge than inside a chicken's skull. Since then the Chinese eat fowls' brains with glee.[15] Lee's allusion to this legend serves to wed the mind (which is familiar with the Chinese cultural tradition) with the body (which relishes hardcore Chinese cuisine) to give an impression[16] of the speaker's ethnic authenticity. Lee has expressed a sense of helpless regret, such as in "Persimmons," that he has lost the Chinese language, and the reference to the legend of Yue Fei provides a measure of redemption in establishing himself as a cultural insider.

Lee's evocation of this legend through duck brains not only defines the speaker's ethnicity but also initiates the unifying trope of eating in this poem. Much like the function of persimmons, the imagery of eating weaves together several strands of otherwise disparate motifs in this poem. From duck brains, Lee moves on to eating nonfood matter such as people, their actions, their manners, and their history. The trope of eating figures for appropriation, incorporation, and assimilation, all that we take in through our senses and becomes us.

> What is it in me will not let
> the world be, would eat
> not just this fish,
> but the one who killed it,
> the butcher who cleaned it.
> I would eat the way he
> reaches into the plastic tubs
> and pulls out a fish, clubs it, takes it
> to the sink, guts it, drops it on the weighing pan.
> I would eat that thrash
> and plunge of the watery body
> in the water, that liquid violence
> between the man's hands,
> I would eat
> the gutless twitching on the scales,
> three pounds of dumb
> nerve and pulse, I would eat it all
> to utter it. (82–83)

The prominence of orality here connotes the poet's voracious desire to understand the world, as he appropriately explains, "my reading a kind of eating, my eating/a kind of reading" (82), for eating is a kind of assimilation that translates the foreign into the familiar or converts the threatening into the nourishing. Lee humorously resolves "the omnivore's paradox" (the tension between neophobia and neophilia) by an infantile delight in tasting and testing everything he lays his eyes on (Fischler 278). Only through introducing the outside into the inside can one understand the concerned matter. As a poet Lee believes that he must "eat it all/to utter it."

This understanding of one's relationship to others and their worlds brings us back to Gadamer, whose hermeneutics promotes fusion of the horizons of understanding through genuine dialogues. I have argued elsewhere that "all interpretations of texts are done by readers who come to the text with prejudgments which determine the readers' horizons of understanding" (Xu, "Making Use of European Theory" 49). In a dialogic encounter with a text, a culture, or even an individual, one risks the stability of one's own prejudgment by opening oneself up to a different "prejudice," creatively appropriating what is foreign to one's mental landscape. Such risks, Gadamer promises us, often result in creative infusions of the radically new. Lee's eating trope certainly suggests the kind of risks involved in introducing into the Self what is Other. This act of seeming assimilation, however, does not produce homogeny by effacing differences as some of Gadamer's critics charge.[17]

"The Cleaving" is by far the strongest Asian American poem in Lee's oeuvre. Hesford goes so far as to assert that "[i]n the central 'City' the poet denies his Asian past and identity to cleave to his American beloved; in the concluding 'Cleaving' he cleaves to his Asian past and Chinese-American identity" (53). The celebratory embrace of his ethnicity takes the form of gleeful indulgence in Chinese cuisine and appetite—the appetite that establishes him to be a big eater of not only food but also his race: "I would devour this race to sing it" (83). Eating his race to sing it entails the incorporation of Asian American history, which is fraught with injustice and sacrifice. Deploying "death" as a metonymy for this history, he sings,

> [...] I would eat,
> [...] the standing deaths
> at the counters, in the aisles,
> the walking deaths in the streets,
> the death-far-from-home, the death-
> in-a-strange-land, these Chinatown
> deaths, these American deaths. (83)

His eating and singing of this history serve as an elegy for all the Asian Americans who died after eating much bitterness. By eating their misery and deaths, he endeavors to understand and place himself within Asian American history.

The trope of eating suggests two diametrically opposed meanings. On the one hand, it stands for the poet's eager absorption of all that is around him in order to turn daily life into poetry. On the other, it figures for the poet's attack on his adversary, in this case racial hostility. In psychoanalytical theory, orality is associated with both pleasure and aggression. Although orality is mostly discussed vis-à-vis infants, Freud and Lacan never disassociate infant modality from adults. Indeed, when Lacan theorizes the Real that is constantly threatening the stability of the Symbolic, he makes it clear that the primordial underlies as well as frustrates the social. Lee's imagery of orality integrates into the self what is pleasant and vanquishes what is hostile. In response to Emerson's offensive remark about the Chinese, Lee interposes both implications of the eating trope.

> I would devour this race to sing it,
> this race that according to Emerson
> *managed to preserve to a hair*
> *for three or four thousand years*
> *the ugliest features in the world.*
> I would eat these features, eat
> the last three or four thousand years, every hair.
> And I would eat Emerson, his transparent soul, his
> soporific transcendence. (83)

The racial othering by Emerson is particularly alienating.[18] Although Lee has never acknowledged Emerson's influence, the two men's transcendentalisms, as I have discussed, bear a strong resemblance. Thus, it may strike one as curious that Lee belittles Emerson's transcendentalism as "soporific" in order to cut down the virility of the master's (father's) influence, reducing it to an old man's ramble—an oedipal antagonism Lee displays via aggressive orality.[19] The poet, therefore, avenges himself and the Chinese by subjecting Emerson and his racist remark to the trope of eating, and with the same trope he simultaneously embraces his people and their four thousand years of history.

Partridge is correct in pointing out that "[w]hile eating Emerson seems overtly and violently to disassociate the speaker from Emerson and his influence, as a 'food' substance Emerson also becomes a nutrient for the speaker's poetic utterance" (114). The one "who eats is at one with what is eaten" (Partridge 118). Eating (*chi*) in Chinese has the connotation of assaulting or overcoming, such as in chess, where one "eats" the opponent's pieces, and it is overcoming through incorporation. In *The Woman Warrior*, Maxine Hong Kingston tells the story of her mother, who overcomes the sitting ghost by catching it, cooking it, and eating it (78–88). She is now better off for having eaten the ghost. Lee situates himself in the Chinese semantic tradition of eating oppositions and joins the battle against racial injustice in the American literary tradition while allowing himself to be nourished by that very tradition. Or borrowing Sau-ling Wong's words, Lee belongs to "the company of fabulous Chinese heroes who overcome ghosts, monsters, and assorted evils by devouring them" (25). In this poem, the eating trope creates a cross-cultural site in which Lee performs his Chinese American self.

As soon as the ethnic self is constructed, Lee proceeds to empty it out by moving his motif of eating to that of death and by meditating on the nothingness of this material world in order to "witness the spirit, the invisible, the law" (Marshall 141). The poem's metaphysical moment, therefore, is made possible only through the extravagant display of food, its killing, cutting, cleaning, cooking, and eating, much of which is culturally specific. Continuing the trope of eating, he writes,

> Bodies eating bodies, heads eating heads,
> we are nothing eating nothing,
> and though we feast,
> are filled, overfilled,
> we go famished.
> We gang the doors of death.
> That is, our deaths are fed
> that we may continue our daily dying,
> Our bodies going
> down, while the plates-soon-empty
> are passed around, that true
> direction of our true prayers, [...]
> As we eat we're eaten. (85)

The references of eating, being eaten, and dying configure to voice his metaphysics that materials fade away and only the pure consciousness of the universe mind lasts. Only after he establishes the trope of eating is he able to cancel out materiality and cultural/ethnic identification in favor of transcendentalism.

In the poem's conclusion, Lee returns to the theme of ethnicity. Only this time it becomes expanded by his metaphysical meditation to include a diverse cluster of ethnic markers that may or may not be Asian, only to be rid of them all. Urged on by his reflection on death/change, Lee loosens the rein on his utopian impulse to de-ethnicize, de-gender the butcher by exploding his ethnic identity to such an extent that its overflowing labels come to mean nothing. What remains after such an explosion of signifiers is the singularity of his face.

The terror the butcher
scripts in the unhealed
air, the sorrow of his Shang
dynasty face,
African face with slit eyes. He is
my sister, this
beautiful Bedouin, this Shulamite,
keeper of Sabbaths, diviner
of holy texts, this dark
dancer, this Jew, this Asian, this one
with the Cambodian face, Vietnamese face, this Chinese
I daily face,
this immigrant,
this man with my own face. (86–87)

The butcher, after passing through these conventional ethnic markers, in the last line simply becomes "this man with my own face," embodying all, therefore emptied of all ethnicities. Simultaneously, Lee also purges the butcher's gender by referring to him as "my sister." The butcher thus becomes the transcendent self embodying all ethnicities and genders, and therefore is tied down by none.

In settling for the final identification of the butcher to be "this man with my own face," Lee also postulates that the specificity of an individual cannot be reduced to his or her socially constituted identities. Although this ethnic specificity is other than any of the social masks people wear, still they always wear social masks. The I-Thou encounter, which Gadamer regards to be the necessary presupposition of all discourse, must transcend socially constructed categories (321–322). Emmanuel Levinas argues that interpersonal ethical relationships have priority over each individual's social identity. We are different because of a singularity that, in such encounters, calls for a responsibility to the other that cannot be passed off to anyone else (116–125). The other to whom one is responsible always remains an embodied, socially constituted person. Xiaojing Zhou aptly employs Levinas' ethics of alterity in explicating several of Lee's poems and contends that "Lee's corporeal aesthetics dismantles the binary construct of the self and its other through articulation of an alternative lyric subject" ("'Your otherness is perfect as my death'" 305). "Face," the last word in "The Cleaving," captures this ethical relationship best. It is the face-to-face encounter that is central to our relationship with others, and in such an encounter uniqueness overwhelms sameness and the universality of uniqueness overwhelms difference. Correspondent to Levinas' notion of human singularity, both English and Chinese semantic traditions are rich in connotations of "face," such as "saving face," "having big face," "losing face," "giving face," "facing up." With "face" denoting respect, dignity, courage, and honor, Chinese- and English-speaking cultures certainly mark the face-to-face encounter as an ethical moment.[20]

Lee's interpersonal ethics originates from his transcendentalist impulse to render cultural differentiation meaningless. Yet it is precisely his cultural difference that makes him a fascinating poet. His disavowal of ethnic identification in order to be regarded as a transcendentalist poet, a soul speaking from nowhere as Vendler insists, creates a dynamic tension in his poetry (*Soul Says* 5). On the one hand, Lee's poetry works its way exactly through Asian diasporic signifiers, and on the other, his wish to be stripped of all cultural identifications and politics ironically places him squarely within American transcendentalist and sublimic tradition, a culture irrevocably tied to the U.S. history of imperialism, as Wilson explicates convincingly. His poetic journey toward the transcendent turns out to be a cornucopia of cultural particularities such as Asian food. His wonderful poetry reveals profoundly his strong affiliations with both Asian and American cultures, neither of which is free from political implications. It is his poetry that best argues against his own position and demonstrates that it is not necessary to postulate a universe mind in order not to reify the social.

The undeniable connection between food and body is the fundamental ground for studying food as the porous border of embodied subjectivity that lives, among other things, a social, cultural, economic, gendered, exilic, and sexual life. So far I have considered how food bears upon ethnicity, gender, class, and diasporic existence. The subject of the final chapter is food and sexuality, a long-standing relationship few people question since it is frequently depicted in literature and film. In reading Monique Truong's *Book of Salt* together with Mei Ng's *Eating Chinese Food Naked*, I explore how subversive sexualities dramatized via food portray a desiring subjectivity that is fully immersed in ethnicity, class, gender, and exile.

5

Sexuality, Colonialism, and Ethnicity in Monique Truong's *The Book of Salt* and Mei Ng's *Eating Chinese Food Naked*

"Here, my ramekin," he'd order, "lick this!" And he'd drop his white pants, invariably covered in flour so that a small cloud of white dust enveloped him, giving the illusion that he was some sort of genie rising out of the white-tiled kitchen floor. He would pour some delicious elixir from a small silver pipkin over his penis and well, it was difficult to deny him.

—Marianna Beck, "Only Food"

The common thesis in these novels by Monique Truong and Mei Ng reiterates the inextricable involvement of food and sexuality. Both novels delineate via food and sex a desiring subjectivity that is deeply immersed in ethnicity, coloniality, diaspora, class, gender, and space. In *The Book of Salt* (2003), Truong juxtaposes two cases of diasporic gay existence in Paris in the 1920s and 1930s, one of Gertrude Stein and Alice B. Toklas, and the other of Bình, their Vietnamese cook, both of which unfold chiefly via culinary tropes to reveal the truth that the ability to practice sexual transgression heavily depends on one's race and class. While *Salt* portrays three characters whose sexuality is as subversive as it is stable, in that the hetero/homo divide remains fixed, Ng's *Eating Chinese Food Naked* (1998) presents a contemporary character whose sexuality evolves from hetero- to bisexuality, a fluid identity that critiques the rigidity of the hetero/homo bifurcation. Matching *Salt* in its political dimension, *Eating* operates in a nexus of sex, food, and ethnicity, in which Ng frames the search of her protagonist, Ruby Lee, for sexual identity. It is also through similar alimentary imageries and tropes that Ng dramatizes the tensions between the ethnic, domestic space and the cosmopolitan space of streets, diners, and cafes—tensions that interlock motifs of food, ethnicity, and sexuality in this novel. The four-pronged language of food, ethnicity, space, and sexuality constructs Ruby's movement from a hetero with a subconscious desire for women to a queer consciousness that disobeys the either/or demand.[1]

The Sources of *Salt*

Fittingly, *Salt* tells the stories of three diasporic lives having crossed oceans to arrive in France—lives submerged in cooking, dining, and desiring. Keeping the rhythm of the sea—the ebbs and flows of memories—*Salt* lures the reader into these three lives to taste their salt—salt of "kitchen, sweat, tears or the sea" (*Salt* 5). Set in Paris between the late 1920s and 1934,[2] the tale travels along two interconnected story lines—one of Gertrude Stein and Alice B. Toklas and the other of their Vietnamese cook Bình, all three having traveled across the sea to find fame or livelihood. Truong's fictional Stein and Toklas are largely based on the historical figures at their residence of 27 rue de Fleurus, one of the most celebrated salons in Paris during their time. Truong's imagination of Bình seems inspired by the account of the two "Indo-Chinese" cooks in *The Alice B. Toklas Cook Book* (1954) and in Stein's *Everybody's Autobiography* (1937). In the midst of describing numerous cooks in their employment, Toklas briefly mentions Trac and Nguyen among several nameless "Indo-Chinese" cooks. Trac came into the Steins' household through a newspaper advertisement. Toklas remembers him as "a person with neat little movements and a frank smile. He spoke French with a vocabulary of a couple of dozen words" (186). Toklas' detail on how Trac communicated by negation supplies Truong with interesting materials, such as Trac "would say, not a cherry, when he spoke of strawberry. A lobster was a small crawfish, and a pineapple was a pear not a pear" (186). When Trac married and left, Nguyen replaced him. Toklas tells us that Nguyen was "a servant in the household of the French Governor-General of Indo-China, who brought him to France" (187). Truong's Bình character derives yet departs from these two models. Bình is a servant in the kitchen of the French governor-general in Saigon but gets fired and banished after his affair with Chef Blériot becomes exposed. Bình is a fabulous cook who drinks to forget his sorrow, just as did Nguyen, Toklas remembers, who "would drink gently and harmlessly, for he cooked marvelously" (187). Toklas' mentioning of Trac's sea travel as a cook from Marseilles to his home and back again corresponds to Bình's experience of sailing from Saigon to Marseilles and then to Paris.

Truong is accurate in describing Stein's and Toklas' arrogance, ignorance of the culture from which Bình comes, and condescension toward him. Colonial attitudes are amply evident in their narratives. For instance, without bothering to learn where her cooks came from and how different their culture was from other Asian ones, Toklas simply describes both Trac and Nguyen as "Chinese cooks" and their cuisine Chinese (188), not discriminating between Indochinese and Chinese cultures. Echoing the colonial discourse that polarizes the native into the noble, childlike savage or the menacing and corrupting villain, Toklas describes Trac as full of "childish joy" when she taught him several desserts, and the other Indochinese as full of vices (187).

> We had a succession of them [Indochinese servants]. Each one in turn was either a gambler, which made him morose when he lost (and he always lost, for he did not work when he won), or he drank, which was unthinkable in our little home, or he loved women and would become dishonest, or he was a drug addict and he would not be able to work. (187)

The gentility and moral purity of "our little home" are clearly threatened by the bad elements working in their kitchen.

In *Everybody's Autobiography*, Stein briefly describes "an Indo-Chinaman," explaining that she and Alice prefer Indo-Chinamen because "[t]hey are French but not so absorbing not so yet being Frenchmen," which can be interpreted to mean that they are convenient because they cook French but demand much less attention than the "real" French (125). The split between being and not yet being French signifies the colonial ambivalence that Homi Bhabha describes as "the disturbing distance in-between [the Colonialist Self and the Colonized Other] that constitutes the figure of colonial otherness," and this colonial otherness envelops both the colonized and the colonizing (45). Participating in the colonial discourse, Stein is as ambivalent as the French toward the Indochinese. Caught between disdain and paternalism, she describes her Vietnamese cook in a jesting, belittling manner: as the historical Stein describes Trac to be "little that is he is a little man" (Stein 125), so does Truong's fictional Stein call Bình "Thin Bin" (Truong 32). Although based upon these two cooks minimally present in Stein's and Toklas' writings, Truong's Bình occupies the central consciousness of the novel, unfolding two worlds in which his joy of cooking makes tolerable his pain in being a marginal man in matters of race, class, and sexuality.

"I kneel down to see what he hungers for"

Truong's sensual description of food and its preparation infuses the relationships between cooks and diners with erotic possibilities. By employing abundant culinary descriptions highly suggestive of sexuality, she constructs three desiring subjects whose different backgrounds in race and class determine their profoundly different emotional states. In *Salt* the two sets of erotic and culinary relationships are Bình and his American lover, Marcus Lattimore, and the Steins, as their friends call them. Lattimore is one of the young men who gather Saturday evenings at Stein's salon. The mutual attraction between Bình and Lattimore results in the former's employment by the latter on Sundays,

Bình's only day off from the Steins. The first meal Bình cooks for Lattimore is figs stewed with duck, so exquisitely described that its sexual connotation can hardly be missed. This dish consists of "Twenty-four figs, so ripe that their skins are split, a bottle of dry port wine. One duck. Twelve hours" (75). The number of the figs stands, in Bình's fantasy, for the only day of the week when he and Lattimore have each other, ripe with desire as figs ripened to split, to relish without rush and disturbance.

He plans a meal for such an occasion to maximize pleasure and satisfaction. "The figs and the port I will place in an earthenware jug 'to get to know each other'" (76).

> Twelve hours will be sufficient for a long and productive meeting. By then the figs will be plump with wine, and the wine will be glistening with the honey flowing from the fruit. The port is then ready to be poured onto the duck, which should sit in a clay dish. [...] The duck is then placed in a hot oven for one hour and basted, every ten minutes or so, with spoonfuls of port that have grown heavy with drippings and concentrated sugars. Before the wine reduces to nothingness, the figs are added, and just enough stock to evaporate and moisten the heat in the final moments of cooking. (77)

With ambiguous diction like "productive meeting," "heavy with drippings," and "moisten the heat," Truong's language is impeccable in staging Bình's erotic fantasy framed by a culinary drama. But reality disappoints. The first thing Lattimore tells him when they meet is that in the future Bình has to let himself in (implying that he spends Saturday nights elsewhere) and that "dinner should begin no later than eight" (78). Lattimore's "terse" tone sets the distance between master and servant. In planning the dessert, Bình reflects on the kind of lover Lattimore is (78). "A soufflé is most definitely out of the question. Too temperamental, a lover who dictates his own terms" (79).

No longer sure if there is any possibility for intimacy between them, Bình begins to imagine Lattimore's involvement with someone else, and such imagination moves fluidly between cuisine and sex.

> Then, once the duck has been served, I will leave your garret for the night, for a café and a glass or two of something strong. Very strong, and you and your someone else will be alone at last. My departure will signal that intimacy has joined the party. [...] you two can now dispense with the forks, knives, and spoons. Your hands will tear at an animal whose joints will know no resistance. The sight of flesh surrendering, so willing a participant in its own transgression, will intoxicate you. Tiny seeds from heart-pregnant figs will insinuate themselves underneath your nails. You will be sure to notice and

try to suck them out. You will begin with each other's fingers. You will end on
your knees. (80)

Since Bình now believes that his fabulous dishes will only enable someone
else to love and enjoy Lattimore, he begins to evoke the element of violence
inherent in the discourse of cuisine to vengefully mix pain with pleasure. The
tearing of flesh is as sexual as metaphorical of his painful humiliation. Only
after Bình finishes preparing the elaborate dishes and steels himself to leave,
however, does he find out that no one else is coming to dinner. He and Lattimore "celebrated Sunday by drinking wine from each other's lip. [...] Pleasure
for pleasure is an even exchange. Lust for lust is a balanced scale" (83). From
here on Lattimore becomes Sweet Sunday Man, who misnames Bình "Bee."
Bình sums up their relationship this way: "I cook for him, and he feeds me.
That is the nature of our relationship" (213). To frame this statement in the
consistent sexual undertone, one could interpret the nature of their relationship as "I cook for him, and he penetrates me." This sexual role-playing is
consistent with Bình's role as the submissive partner to the French chef, Blériot,
in Vietnam (52–53).

Their asymmetrical relationship is further demonstrated in terms of Sweet
Sunday Man's culinary demands and Bình's creativity in meeting them. Revealing his ignorance in matters of the kitchen and his custom of being served by
others, Lattimore asks for foods that are out of season, such as "[r]ipe figs when
there is frost on the ground, lamb when all the trees have already lost their
leaves, artichokes when the summer sun is fast asleep" (236). For Bình, who is
unaccustomed to making choices over what he cooks or with whom he has sex,
the only form of agency is creative compliance. To keep his lover happy, Bình
must improvise.

> I have simmered strings of dried figs in bergamot tea. I have braised mutton
> with bouquets of herbs tied in ribbons of lemon rinds until their middle-aged
> sinews remember spring. As for the artichokes, I have discarded all the glass
> jars of graying hearts afloat in their vinegared baths that I found hiding inside
> his kitchen cabinets. Sometimes [...] it is better to crave. (236–237)

Compared to Bình's earlier meditation on figs stewed with duck, this culinary
description exudes labor and frustration. At the end it is as if Bình were offering
himself a lesson that sometimes "it is better to crave," for gratification demands
a price he cannot afford.

Soon into their Sunday relationship, Bình realizes that Sweet Sunday Man's
real interest lies in Gertrude Stein, her work, her travel, and her guests. Bình at
first thinks of his lover's interest advantageously.

The honey that he craves is the story that he knows only I can tell. Last week when I told him about the cupboard and what my Mesdames have stored inside, his breath left him. Sweet Sunday Man wanted to know the exact number of notebooks. He wanted to know the order of the typewritten pages. He wanted to know the exact words that GertrudeStein had written and that Miss Toklas had dutifully typed. (149–150)

In time Bình finds out that Lattimore not only wants the details but also wants him to steal one of Stein's notebooks, his reason being "she is the twentieth century [...]. What she keeps and what she does not will tell you about the future" (209). Bình begs, "Ask me something else," for "what you ask of me, I cannot do to my Madame and Madame. The infidelity, the betrayal, the savagery of it, even I am not capable of it" (211, 212). When Lattimore coaxes Bình by offering a gesture of love and intimacy—a photograph of both of them—knowing how empty Bình's emotional life is, Bình becomes helpless, reversing the position of power he used to fantasize in the metaphor of honey and bee: "Sweet Sunday Man is a honey talker, and I am his Bee" (212). What makes him decide to take the notebook later, however, is not Lattimore's bait of a photograph; rather, he takes it because he sees his name, "Bin," Stein's misnomer for him, "written again and again and again" in the pages (214). He is angered by Stein's use of him: "I did not give you my permission, Madame, to treat me in this way. I am here to feed you, not to serve as your fodder" (215). Bình takes the notebook to Lattimore, with the rationale that "[t]his notebook may belong to my Madame, but the story, it belongs to me" (215). Nothing prepares Bình for the consequence of his act. He returns to Lattimore's residence a week after he offers him the notebook only to find the place vacant, repainted for a new tenant. A note folded together with the receipt for the photograph says, "Bee, thank you for *The Book of Salt*. Stein captured you, perfectly" (238). Chilled by the realization, Bình thinks coldly, "He did a meticulous, well-thought-out job until the very end" (238). Once again he is manipulated and used by a lover.

Truong's choice of Bình's sexuality is significant. His queerness is constructed as a critical terrain upon which are mobilized overlapping differentiations, such as race, class, and coloniality. In turn his queerness gains its meaning and discursive consistency precisely through these elements. Richard Fung points out that "[r]ace is a factor in even our most intimate relationships" (116). Bình and Lattimore's relationship is one of power in which factors of race and class preclude any possibility of reversibility of roles. The poor Vietnamese serves mainly as an instrument with which the wealthy American achieves pleasure, alimentary and sexual. The clichéd scenario of an "Oriental" houseboy serving his master, however, is complicated by the fact that Lattimore is black passing as white. His mother's blood has exiled him from America. With her money, which she has earned from his white father by being silent, Lattimore is able to receive a good education and to live in Paris hobnobbing with world-renowned artists and compatriots. Truong makes Lattimore less a villain than he could be by having him reveal his history to Bình, exposing his vulnerability to his lover. Upon learning of Lattimore's secret, Bình admires and envies his self-invention. "Sweet Sunday Man, I marvel at the way that you can change from room to room. I envy the way that you carry yourself when you are in the studio, surrounded by the men who think of you as one of their own. [...] I see your stance, its mimicked ease and its adopted entitlements" (151). Bình's envious marvel at his lover's successful passing only deepens his own pain and feeling of alienation. He reflects,

> [M]ine marks me, announces my weakness, displays it as yellow skin. It flagrantly tells my story [...] to passersby curious enough to cast their eyes my way. It stunts their creativity, dictates to them the limited list of whom I could be. Foreigner, *asiatique,* and this being Mother France, I must be Indochinese. They do not care to discern any further, ignoring the question of whether I hail from Vietnam, Cambodia, or Laos. Indochina, indeed. We all belong to the same owner, the same Monsieur and Madame. [...] To them, my body offers an exacting, predetermined life story. (152)

Evident in Bình's melancholia is the shorthand to the colonial subjectivity that renders itself salient through self-objectification. His anguish echoes Fanon's widely quoted line, "What else could it be for me but an amputation, an excision, a hemorrhage that spattered my whole body with black blood?" (*Black Skin, White Masks* 112). Bình's melancholia stemming from epidermal over-determinism brings to light the instability of the colonial discourse. Contrary to its ideology of ontological differences among the races, the colonial discourse relies heavily on the metonymic trope of the epidermal surface. And when that surface fools the eye, the trope of darkness, standing for degeneration, inferiority, and immorality, collapses.

In contrasting his fate with his lover's, Bình highlights the economic layer in the racial/colonial discourse. There is no arguing that Lattimore's money makes possible his escape from discrimination and his life in Paris of leisure and dignity as a (white) man. Bình, however, bears the unshakable yoke of poverty in addition to that of race. The stratification among the colonized is made particularly apparent in Mother France, where poverty disallows Bình from assuming any identity other than that of a domestic servant. In a series of negations, he arrives at the singular identity he is allowed to assume.

My eyes, the passersby are quick to notice, do not shine with the brilliance of a foreign student. I have all my limbs so I am not one of the soldiers imported from their colonies to fight their Grande Guerre. No gamblers and whores joined me at the hip so I am not the young Emperor or Prince of an old and mortified land. Within the few seconds that they have [...] they conclude that I am a laborer, the only real option left. (152)

Bình seems to be particularly disturbed by the absence of depth, of mystery, and therefore of intrigue in his identity in the eyes of the French. Such absences are not due to any lack in his identity, but rather to its wealth of racial and class signifiers. Unlike Lattimore, who is "a blank sheet of paper" in Paris, whose enigma lies precisely in its emptiness, Bình carries his country, his race, his class and servitude in his body—an antitext that yields one fixed meaning (151). For Bình this antitext is antihuman. When a man is robbed of mystery and unpredictability, he is no longer a man. Thus, Bình muses nostalgically that in "a busy Saigon marketplace [...] I was just a man," whose identity is indeterminable "at a passing glance" as "a student, a gardener, a poet, a chef, a prince, a porter, a doctor, a scholar" (152). What Bình says suggests that it is the fantasy of becoming that nourishes the subject and underwrites humanness.

The fantasy of becoming plays a major role in enabling Lattimore to live in Paris as a man of society. His self-introduction as an iridologist, trained to predict future illnesses by reading irises, and as a writer opens the doors of such people as the prince of Cambodia, the emperor of Vietnam, Gertrude Stein, and others. His popularity in the circle of exiles depends on the secret he keeps. Then why does he offer that secret to his Sunday cook/lover? Is it a gesture of trust or an act of bribery? Or is it his arrogance that Bình does not have enough French and credibility to share his secret with anyone that matters? Truong's narrative offers no definitive answer to these questions, but she makes two moves with the Stein character that maneuver the reader's sympathy toward Lattimore. The first is Stein's curiosity about Lattimore's race; she quizzes Bình, "Thin Bin, is Lattimore a Negro?" (157). Truong's juxtaposition of Lattimore to Stein vis-à-vis Bình indicts both for using Bình to spy on each, but Stein's racial curiosity makes her more despicable than does Lattimore's curiosity for Stein's work in progress. As though this particular detail were insufficient in steering the reader toward this judgment, Truong designs another racial moment for the Stein character. In her conversation with her lover about Robeson, Stein can hardly disguise her racism. "I asked him why he insisted on singing Negro spirituals when he could be performing requiems and oratorios. Do you know what that curiosity in a suit said? In that basso profundo voice of his, he replied, 'The spirituals, theys a belong to me, Missa Stein'" (188). Such details demonstrate that even in the liberal-minded Stein, racial discrimination remains a powerful force. Race, thus, along with food and sexuality, structures the characters' identities and relationships in *Salt*.

Just as between Bình and Lattimore, Truong also creates a gastronomy-structured relationship between Alice Toklas and Gertrude Stein that is highly suggestive of eroticism. For six days of the week Alice serves her lover's culinary needs by choosing menus and directing Bình. On Sundays, when Bình cooks for Lattimore, Alice goes to the kitchen and "gets butter and flour underneath her fingernails, breathes in the smell of cinnamon, burns her tongue, and is comforted" (26). Truong describes Alice as a traveler in the kitchen, infusing American dishes with places they have been to, or in Truong's words, "Her menus can map the world" (27). A good balance between adventure and sensuality is her signature; for instance, she "puts absinthe in her salad dressing and rose petals in her vinegar" (27). The result is a feast of seduction, and the mere fact of her having handled the food is sufficient to excite her lover.

> GertrudeStein thinks it is unfathomably erotic that the food she is about to eat has been washed, pared, kneaded, touched, by the hands of her lover. She is overwhelmed by desire when she finds the faint impressions of Miss Toklas' fingerprints decorating the crimped edges of a pie crust. Miss Toklas believes that these nights are her rewards. (27)

Truong's erotic language of cooking and eating not only constructs the desiring subject but also normalizes the homosexual relationship. The Steins' sexuality is described as so normal that it no longer signifies transgression. Remarkably different from her presentation of Bình's queerness, which gains its critical energy through factors of race, class, and coloniality, the Steins are complacent, conforming, socially accepted in their same-sex arrangement. Their relationship indeed largely mirrors that of a white and propertied heterosexual couple in the early twentieth century.[3] Without ever entering their bedroom, Truong's novel conjures up the erotic and sexual in the lives of these two women through the highly suggestive language of food. Alice is described as emitting "the sounds of lovemaking when she is among the tomatoes" in their Bilignin garden and weeping "with the juices of the first strawberry full in her mouth" (138). Alice serves Gertrude "the omelet" (Bình has made), "the curved edges still humming heat [...], a song of a temptation" (154). "Miss Toklas believes that with every meal she serves a part of herself, an exquisite metaphor garnishing every plate" (155).

The heterosexual domestic drama plays out in this lesbian relationship in the culinary site that reveals tenderness as well as pedestrian tensions in marriage. In her wifely capacity, Alice loves her "Hubbie" by banishing cream and lard from their diet six months before Gertrude goes to lecture in America to ensure her good appearance. Along with fatty food, salt, alcohol, and cigarettes are also banned. While helplessly submitting herself to such a regime, Stein, however, exacts revenge by not eating meals until they are tepid, knowing gleefully how important it is to Alice to eat while the food is hot. Each lover asserts her will over the other in feeding, eating, withholding food, or refusing to eat. Their union so much resembles a heterosexual marriage that their friends think of Alice as a Stein.

Food and Blood

Compared to the Steins' life, however, Bình's is anything but normal and pedestrian. In depicting the complex psychic drama of this Vietnamese chef, Truong relies heavily on culinary signifiers. Memories of life before exile are often evoked by kitchen activities, the partition between past and present rendered porous by food, smells, and tastes. Bình has been born to a father who is so successful in colonial mimicry that he has turned Catholicism into a profitable business and to a mother who has quietly endured poverty, abandonment, and abuse. Growing up in French Indochina, Bình has been coerced into accepting the myth of racial hierarchy, but his identification with the powerful and "beautiful" is mainly mediated through his older brother, Anh Minh, who plays the father figure in Bình's boyhood. Being abused frequently by their father ("the Old Man") because of his illegitimate birth, the boy attaches his love and admiration to his older brother partially because of the latter's "success" in the world of the French.

Anh Minh's identificatory relationship with the French is grounded in the kitchen of the governor-general. Bình recollects years later, "Anh Minh believed absolutely and passionately that the French language would save us, would welcome us into the fold, would reward us with kisses on both cheeks" (14). Saving Bình from their father's brutal abuse, Anh Minh obtains for his youngest brother the lowly position of a *garde-manger* in the household of the governor-general, where Anh Minh believes lies the future for both of them. He promises their father, "Even the lowest-paid helpers get two meals a day and a chance to wear the long white apron someday" (51). Anh Minh's mastery of French cuisine leads him into believing that he has become sufficiently French to assume the position of *chef de cuisine* after the old French chef has died; a taste of his "*omelette à la bourbonnaise, his coupe ambassadrice, his crème marquise* would convince Monsieur and Madame that there is no need to send for a chef from Paris" (14).

Anh Minh's disappointment offers Bình the first lesson on the fixity of colonial stratification. Now that the young chef Jean Blériot has arrived and Anh Minh remains an assistant in the kitchen, dignified by the Old Man as

"Minh the Sous Chef," Bình begins to see the dead end on his own path to glory. "[W]hat was I supposed to do? Twenty years old and still a *garde-manger*" (14). In Bình's eyes, Anh Minh has fallen as a father figure, made melancholic and pathetic by the colonial power structure. What Bình experiences through this loss is his own mourning for the lost object of identification. In psychoanalysis, mourning is healthy compared to melancholia, as Freud points out that after we lose our object-choice, mourning offers the assurance "that after a lapse of time, it will be overcome" (240). Bình's mourning for the loss of his object-choice (the assimilated Anh Minh) prepares for a new object-choice to displace the old.[4]

Bình's identification with his brother soon shifts to one with the new French chef, Blériot, whose beauty and youth enchant him. In the language of cuisine, Truong describes Bình's desire that "no man would admit to having"—"carving chunks of turnips into swans, the arc of their necks as delicate as Blériot's fingers, fingers that I wanted to taste" (15). Blériot picks Bình to be his translator at the market, and their mutual attraction becomes apparent "amidst the fruits of the sea" as Bình translates fish names. Seduction is like cooking. "For tenderness, we all know that braising is better than open flame" (62). Bình's transference to Blériot of his attachment to his brother is described as a trade. He thinks to himself, "My dear brother, I did not waste the time that you gave me. I traded it away for Blériot's lips counting down the notches of my spine, parting at the small of my back [...] as he brought us both heavenward without shame" (52–53).

Without being explicit, Truong nevertheless makes clear the sexual scene, in which Blériot is the dominant partner. Although Bình experiences ecstasy as the submissive partner, we don't know that he wouldn't enjoy more or equally being the dominant partner. But that is of course unthinkable between a white man and a "yellow" man in the colonial world of Vietnam. Their relationship soon becomes exposed, and predictably Blériot denies any such affair when confronted and lets Bình be fired for lying. The world as Bình knows it comes to an end when the Old Man severs their relationship and banishes him to the streets. Bình thus begins his exile as a sailor on a ship to France.

Though banished from his country, he can never banish the faithless French lover from his mind. Bình never gets over Blériot. In distinguishing mourning from melancholia, Freud describes the latter as pathological because the melancholic ego is unable to displace its object-choice and move on to a new object relationship. Consequently, "[t]he ego wishes to incorporate this object into itself, and the method by which it would do so, in this oral or cannibalistic state, is by devouring it" (Freud 250). Ironically, the ego's situation of being stuck and therefore impoverished also proves to be nourishing, for as Anne Anlin Cheng points out, "The melancholic eats the lost object—feeds on it" (8). But such consumption of the lost object necessitates self-denigration: as "the libido turns back on the ego, so do the feelings of guilt, rage, and punishment. [...] The melancholic's relationship to the object is now no longer just love or nostalgia but also profound resentment" (Cheng 8–9). Depending on the power positions of the melancholic, this psychic drama stages different social scenes. For the racially degraded and socially powerless Bình, resentment must be turned inward against himself, and it manifests itself as self-revilement.

What is peculiar with Bình lies in his self-punishment by resuscitating the corpse of his first lost object—the father, whose voice becomes the son's unceasing castigation and self-mockery: "Only a fool like you would believe that that French sodomite was going to save you. Out of love? Out of lust for your scrawny, worthless body?" (193). Every day he imagines the Old Man's tirade no matter where he is. "[T]he Old Man's anger has no respect for geography. Mountains, rivers, oceans, and seas, these things [...] have never kept him from homing in on me" (12). Although Bình argues fiercely to defend himself, he can never put an end to the Old Man's voice. In other words, he keeps alive the Old Man's voice to punish himself, thus further deepening his anger and self-hate. It "was my mistake," he acknowledges,

> from the very beginning, the fatal flaw in my design. I thought that I could suffocate the Old Man with shovelfuls of dirt and mud. [...] I should have thrown his body into the sea, expelled it and not me. My anger keeps me digging into the earth, pulling at its protective mantle, eager to see his body decaying deep inside. [...] This is as close to being immortal as the Old Man ever had the right to be, and I am the one, the only one who keeps him that way. (194–195)

Hatred, an eloquent expression of melancholia, tethers Bình to the Old Man in a bitter relationship of mutual consumption, with his melancholic ego devouring the lost object that consumes him.

How is it that the Old Man is dragged into Bình's melancholic landscape over the loss of Blériot? What does the Old Man have to do with the French chef? Why don't we simply regard the caustic voice of the Old Man as the evidence of Bình's melancholia toward his father alone? It is correct to assume that Bình has never gotten over his father, whom he has lost long before his death. As a child Bình desperately longs for paternal love and kindness, but in return he experiences mostly abuse and humiliation.

> "Look at Stupid over there [...]," the Old Man says, as he spits out the thin red juices flooding his lips. [...] He misses the spittoon. I jump up to wipe the floor clean. [...] He points his chin at me, offering me up to his cohorts

as he had my mother. The laughter is now high and pitched. I am standing in the middle of a room of men, all drunk on something cheap. I am looking at the Old Man as he is spitting more red in my direction. The warm liquid lands partly in the brass pot and partly on my bare feet. I am six years old, and I am looking up at this man's face. I smile at him because I, a child, cannot understand what he is saying to me. (45)

For a child coming to self-recognition, the father figure is vitally important, but this particular father instills in the child nothing but feelings of inadequacy and shame. Nevertheless, he remains the authority figure to the child, who consequently internalizes self-abjection and never acquires competence in distinguishing love from hate.

Why does the Old Man continue to grip Bình's psyche in his adulthood? In addition to the usual interpretation that because of his childhood experiences he has never developed a mature ego, I want to supplement by considering the factor of colonialism. The Old Man as a child is taken away from his parents and into the Catholic Church to be indoctrinated for the priesthood. Although he never becomes a priest, his conversion rate is higher than a priest's, because his gambling business is an ideal environment to make and save lost souls. The Old Man's assimilation into the colonial culture through religious conversion has established his (resented) authority among his people and his children, an authority that speaks in the dual voice of patriarchy and colonialism. Bình's racialization is partially attributable to his father's constant castigation of him for his "failure" and praise of Anh Minh for his "success" in serving the French. "Every day, I hear the Old Man's voice shouting at me from beneath the earth [. . .]. The moment that he took his blood from mine, separated it as if his were white and mine the yolk, I placed him there" (193). The egg metaphor suggests vividly the gravity of race in the father-son relationship. The Old Man's othering of the Other in order to preserve the delusion of having transcended his race has inevitably shaped Bình's aspiration and sense of worth. Unable to hate or forget the faithless French lover, Bình transfers his recent melancholia to the already melancholic relationship to the phantom of the Old Man, whose voice serves to condemn on behalf of the colonial power: "How dare you use the word of God to describe the things that you practice. [. . .] It sickens me to think about what you do, shaming my name" (193).

Bình's daily conjuring of his father's voice clearly bespeaks his own melancholic relation with the colonial power. Helplessly desiring to identify with the French despite their cruel rejections, he reviles himself both for being a "loser" and for longing to be accepted by the French, a soul-splitting ambivalence of psychic identification. In theorizing colonial ambivalence, Bhabha writes, "The very place of identification, caught in the tension of demand and desire, is a space of splitting. The fantasy of the native is precisely to occupy the master's place while keeping his place in the slave's *avenging* anger" (44). Such raveling of desire, anger, and hate in the racialized and colonized psyche produces a subjectivity that is melancholic and masochistic at the same time.

Truong weds food metaphors to the politics of language to describe the deep invasion of colonial power into Bình's subjectivity. "[T]here are some French words that I have picked up quickly, in fact, words that I cannot remember *not* knowing. As if I had been born with them in my mouth, as if they were the seeds of a sour fruit that someone else ate and then ungraciously stuffed its remains into my mouth" (11–12). Truong's brilliant metaphor offers a precise picture of the hideous coercion in the name of civilizing the Other. The seeds planted so "ungraciously" in the colonized sprout vines and branches to crowd out and suffocate indigenous cultural consciousness. In time these seeds are bound to bear "sour fruit" of racial grief. In another alimentary metaphor, Truong reiterates this point. This time it is Bình's relationship to Alice that is the colonial context.

> Believe me, it has not been easy for me to work for these two. Miss Toklas is a Madame who uses her palate to set the standard of perfection. In order to please her, her cook has to do the same, an extremely difficult feat. Her cook has to adopt her tongue, make room for it, which can only mean the removal of his own. (211)

In interlocking language and taste with the pun of "tongue," Truong reiterates my argument that food contributes to the constitution of subjectivity. Sovereignty is exercised through practicing one's foodways as well as one's language and doing it with confidence and joy. In Bình's case, however, the constant demand of colonial assimilation corrodes his agency, and the attempt to preserve his foodways is sometimes accompanied by humiliation. For the first dinner at the Steins, he decides to cook his mother's favorite: pineapple sliced "paper-thin" and sautéed "with shallots and slices of beef" (34). In requesting money for pineapples, he stumbles; instead of pineapple, he says "pear." "I lost [...] the French word for 'pineapple' the moment I opened my mouth. Departing at their will, the words of this language mock me with their impromptu absences. When I am alone, they offer themselves to me" (35). It is almost as if the French language has more "will" or agency than Bình does, toying with him and shaming him in public.

As an exile in the interior of his colonizers, a domestic chef for hire, and a sexual minority member, Bình has very limited space for the exercise of agency. Cooking seems to be the only site where he enjoys some self-determination and dignity.

Every kitchen is a homecoming, a respite, where I am the village elder, sage, and revered. Every kitchen is a familiar story that I can embellish with saffron, cardamom, bay laurel, and lavender. In their heat and in their steam, I allow myself to believe that it is the sheer speed of my hands, the flawless measurement of my eyes, the science of my tongue, that is rewarded. During these restorative intervals, I am no longer the mute who begs at this city's steps. Three times a day, *I orchestrate,* and they sit with slackened jaws, silenced. (19, emphasis mine)

Sometimes Bình's assertion of agency takes on the form of subversion in the kitchen, where he willfully commits errors or is negligent. He can conveniently forget "how long to braise the ribs of beef, whether chicken is best steamed over wine or broth, where to buy the sweetest trout" or "neglect the pinch of cumin [...] the scent of lime" (20). Even such limited agency in the kitchen comes with a price. To enter and stay in someone's kitchen, Bình must tell his stories to feed curiosity as well, a kind of prostitution of himself to eke out a living. His employers "are never satiated by my cooking. They are ravenous. [...] They have no true interest in where I have been or what I have seen. They crave the fruits of exile, the bitter juices, and the heavy hearts. They yearn for a taste of the pure, sea-salt sadness of the outcast whom they have brought into their homes" (19).

With his labor, his art, and his stories devoured by his employers, Bình becomes an allegory for the colonized vulnerable to the cannibalistic practices of colonialism—practices that nourish the Self by consuming the Other. Truong clinches this allegory with another kitchen episode, in which Stein and Toklas taste human blood in their food. Alarmed, Toklas reproaches, "Bin, have you been drinking?" and "Have I not given you enough time?" (70). One may argue that Stein and Toklas being Americans cannot represent the colonial power. But to do that one has to willfully ignore that the Steins, both real and fictional, comfortably identify with the French in their attitudes toward the "Indochinese" and that their power relation with Bình mirrors certain aspects of the relationship of the French with the colonized. The Steins' symbolic value for the coercive, exploitative, superior, and yet benevolent performance of colonialism upon the colonized (Bình) is one of the central themes in Truong's novel.

Bình is a cutter, spilling his blood in other people's meals. His racialized and exploited body experiences so strongly the loss of legitimacy that it takes pain and the sight of running blood to recognize its existence and evoke home. In studying Louis Chu and David Wong Louie, David Eng foregrounds male hysteria as a critical rubric. Eng supplements Freud's analysis of female hysteria grounded in the sexual body by considering the racialized body of men. He asks, "What exactly does hysteria imply socially and politically about male subjectivity?" (173). In speaking of the character of Ben Loy in Chu's novel *Eat a Bowl of Tea*, Eng remarks, "Male hysteria and racial hysteria are constitutive and intersecting discourses that mark his symbolic disenfranchisement from the normative national ideals of white masculinity" (181). Bình's habit of cutting may be interpreted as a hysterical expression of his disenfranchisement from the normative ideals of both white and Vietnamese masculinities. Interlocked with his sexual deviation from the norm is his racialization by the colonial regime that results in a deeply splitting ambivalence in his psychic identification. Contrary to Žižek's understanding that hysteria is "the effect and testimony of a failed interpellation," Bình's hysteria is the very effect and testimony of the success of colonial/racial interpellation (*The Sublime Object of Ideology* 113). Reduced to an arrested history and humanity, the colonized become ossified in their inferiority. As Bình understands it, a person cannot be truly human when denied the possibility of becoming, and he must mutilate himself frequently to be reminded that he is a sentient being, not an object.

Steven Levenkron suggests after studying clinical cases that most self-mutilators regard self-injury as "reward" because "pain was somehow connected to the idea of home and comfort" in the past. "If the familiar happens to be painful or harmful, that rarely stops someone from seeking it out" (27–28). Indeed, Bình sometimes cuts himself to remember his mother, who is the only love in his loveless world, and this comfort of recalling her love is associated with pain. Cutting and cooking are entangled in Bình's life, for his habit begins as an accident when he is nine: he is cutting scallions to help his mother make a soup. While listening to her humming, "I thread silver into my fingertips for the first time. [...] I am floating away, and a sea of red washes me back" (73). His mother stops cooking to apply lime juice to the wound as an antiseptic. The pain from the lime juice is so immense that Bình thinks his fingers are on fire (73). Yet this intense pain elicits Mother's care and love. "She sits down and wraps herself around me, pressing my stooped back into herself" (73). Mother's embrace, symbolic of the enclosure of womb, thus becomes associated in Bình's mind with cutting, with the safest place he knows: "I see there on my fingertips a landscape that would become as familiar to me as *the way home*" (73, my emphasis). Exiled overseas, without knowing if he would ever see his mother again, he cuts himself frequently to remember her.

Curiously, the language describing the habit also has a strong sexual undertone as though the remembrance of mother's love evokes remembrance of sexual love.

> In the beginning I preferred the blade to be newly sharpened, licked against a stone until sparks flew [...]. Now I know that such delicacy would only deny me that part that I savor most, the throbbing of flesh compromised, meeting

and mending. And sometimes when it is deep enough, there is an ache that fools my heart. Tricks it into a false memory of love lost to a wide, open sea. I say to myself, "Ah, this reminds me of you." (74)

Although immediately following the flashback of the kitchen accident at age nine, this quoted passage directs our attention to adult sexuality—"the throbbing of flesh compromised, meeting and mending." Who is the "you" that Bình refers to? Why is it "a *false* memory of love"? Is it possible that Bình is really thinking of Blériot, the French chef who has introduced him to homo-eroticism? Or is it Sweet Sunday Man, who has bedded Bình and also used him as a pawn in his game? Perhaps Bình's melancholia toward both lovers also manifests itself in self-mutilation, as though a knife entering his flesh is a simulation of their entering his body, leaving behind wounds that refuse to scar, but an experience of love nevertheless in his world. Pain, both physical and psychic, has simply become a necessary condition of intimacy.

Almost all of his human relationships being asymmetrical, with him serving as an instrument for others' pleasures, Bình can only momentarily overcome his profound sense of alienation with the act of self-mutilation. Whether as a lover or a chef, he is perpetually at other people's mercy. Despite a small measure of agency in the kitchen, he cannot help but perceive himself as no more than an object in other people's homes.

> My presence, just inside the entrance to my Mesdames' kitchen, ensures that all the cups are steaming and that the tea table stays covered with marzipan and butter-cream-frosted cakes. Always discreet, almost invisible, imagine that when the guests look my way they see, well, they see a floor lamp or a footstool. (148)

At times like this, the phantom of the Old Man reappears to ridicule Bình. "You're not nearly as bright or useful" (148). Such acts of self-abjection are often followed by cutting; as Bình remarks, "red on the blade of a knife" is a proof "that this body of mine harbors a life" (149). Invisibility thus becomes a condition of disembodiment and dismemberment, both real and symbolic, and this happens only when he enters the scene of racial hierarchy—the yellow race serving the whites—a scene that dominates his existence and consciousness.

The relationship between food and blood echoes that between food and murder. This relationship, a prominent motif in *Salt*, further substantiates Truong's allegorization of Bình as the racialized Other exploited and devoured by the colonial power. In the figure of pigeons, Truong constructs a traveling symbol standing for Bình, his mother, and the colonized Vietnam. Truong's reference to pigeons traces to *The Alice B. Toklas Cook Book,* in which Toklas recalls a French cook, Jeanne, teaching her how to smother pigeons. The scene in the market resonates with the pigeons' symbolic value in *Salt*. When Jeanne proceeded to demonstrate this practice, "the crowd of market women who gathered about her began screaming and gesticulating" (39). Facing these women's anger, Toklas retreated. But later, upon receiving the gift of "six white pigeons," Toklas did what Jeanne had shown her: "I carefully found the spot on poor innocent Dove's throat where I was to press and pressed" (39, 40). Toklas' elevation of the white pigeons to "innocent Dove" seems to inform Truong's symbolization of pigeons for the innocent, helpless, and powerless Vietnam embodied by Bình and his mother. In *Salt* Toklas orders pigeons for dinner one day and shows Bình how to smother them to ensure juicy tenderness: "If you cut off their necks, you will lose all the blood. Done *this* way, those birds will come out of the oven plumper and tastier than you can ever imagine. Exquisite!" (67–68). For Bình, who has cut many throats to feed others, this task is too murderous to be tasteful. Bình thinks silently, "I am fine when I have a knife in my hand, when it is the blade that delivers the *coup de grâce*" (69). Now his hands shake because "[t]he pigeon squirms under my fingers, its blood pumping hard, pressing through" (67), and Toklas instructs on the side, "Steady yourself. Stop shaking. Keep pressing down. Harder, that is right, harder" (67).

The association of pigeons with his mother begins in this scene as he remembers how he learned to kill chickens from his mother. "First, my mother would nick the skin until the blood flowed. If the knife was inserted deep enough, there is a red arc that falls neatly from the notch to the awaiting bowl" (68). Economy and mercy are the only principles for his mother in killing for food. Four pages later, Bình recalls the first time he cuts himself in his mother's kitchen, slicing scallions while his mother "is humming, and I think that I am hearing birds" (72). The association of his mother with both birds and killing birds renders the task of asphyxiating the pigeons deeply disturbing. Near the end of the novel, another scene involving pigeons folds back upon this association.

On a snowy February day, Bình sits on a bench in Jardin du Luxembourg, deeply depressed about the uncertainties lying ahead after the Steins sail for America. "Snow makes me want to sleep, not in my bed but on the corners of busy boulevards, in alleyways, underneath the awnings of crowded shops [...] when my body says, Please, no more" (217). Burdened by his death wish, Bình observes a troubling scene in which children are toying with an injured pigeon. "A pigeon, an ordinary, city-gray pigeon, stumbles between the girl's black boot and tries to spread its wings. [...] It lies there while the children become excited" (218). As he watches the pigeon's death struggle, he experiences intimations about his mother's dying. "I see you half a world away. I hear fever parting your lips. I feel your shiverings, colorless geckos running down your spine. I smell the night sweat that has bathed you clean" (220). Now the scene returns to the pigeon that refuses to die a "soft, concerted death," just as the pigeons in the Steins' kitchen squirm and linger under Bình's fingers (220). The finishing touch on the pigeon's symbolic value for his mother is the color of her *áo dài* (a traditional Vietnamese tunic for women). "I know you are in your best *áo dài*. [...] Gray is the color you wanted [...]. [...] I am holding your hand, leading you out of the front door of his house. You step out into the street, and you are a sudden crush of gray" (221). This picture of his mother echoes the scene of the dying pigeon in the park—"a flourish of white, a crush of gray" (218). Also, in his only letter to his brother, Anh Minh reports their mother's passing: "God has given Má wings" (230).

His mother, associated with the dying pigeon in the garden, with the pigeons slaughtered in the kitchen, is tightly linked to Bình, who entertains a death wish in his hallucinatory exit with her, leading her by the hand out of her husband's house where both of them have suffered abuse and humiliation: "We swore not to die on the kitchen floor. We swore not to die under the eaves of his [the Old Man's] house" (221). Powerfully juxtaposed to the pigeons that suffer bloodless deaths for human consumption, Bình commits symbolic suicides by bleeding himself into the dinners of his masters. Their consumption of his body aptly symbolizes the French colonizer's consumption of Vietnam—its resources and people. For Bình at the individual level, being the object of others' consumption—sexual, alimentary, and literary (Stein's use of him)—makes his hysterical habit all the more compelling.

Thus far the story of Bình is deeply tragic. I would be remiss if I didn't discuss the single uplifting moment in *Salt* that implies an anti-imperialist comradery over a fine dinner, and Bình shares this moment with none other than Ho Chi Minh himself. In chapter 9, Bình finds himself distraught with hunger and despair (in 1927 before his employment by the Steins). Truong suggests his contemplation of suicide as he stands on a bridge over the Seine, "on a day when this city had the foregone appearance of a memory, as if the present had refused to go to work that day and said that the past would have to do" (85). At this critical moment he meets a stranger on the bridge, a fellow countryman who addresses him as a friend. Although the stranger's identity is not directly offered until much later in the novel, Truong's details regarding this man are unmistakable to anyone who is familiar with the life of Ho Chi Minh. In their conversation, Bình finds out that this man has been a "[k]itchen boy, sailor, dishwasher, snow shoveler, furnace stoker, gardener, pie maker, photograph retoucher, fake Chinese souvenir painter" (89).[5] Ho did almost all these jobs in his early years overseas.[6] Bình also finds out that this man has been trained to make pastries (88)—a historical fact about Ho whose specifics historians debate.[7] The man on the bridge also reveals that he lives on rue des Gobelins, another historical fact about Ho.[8] In addition, he further reveals that he has worked on the ship

Latouche Tréville, which is documented as the ship on which Ho earned his passage from Saigon to Marseilles as a kitchen assistant. Bình recalls the story about a man named Ba sailing on the ship *Latouche Tréville* (90–91), and Ba was one of the aliases that Ho Chi Minh used (Nguyen Van Ba) when he was traveling to Paris.[9] Once in Paris, Ho changed his name to Nguyen Ai Quoc, which means Nguyen the Patriot. Truong refers back to this stranger near the end of the novel and offers his identity as "Nguyễn Ái Quốc" (246). It was with this very identity that Ho signed and presented the petition to the Paris Peace Conference in the summer of 1919 for the independence of Vietnam.

Truong presents Bình's meeting with Nguyen Ai Quoc as a lifesaving encounter that alters Bình's fate.[10] Food is central to this scene. To a starving and suicidal Bình, Nguyen Ai Quoc offers a delicious dinner at a Chinese restaurant, through which Bình tastes for the first time the fulfillment of fellowship. The meal consists of a pink pile of "the salt-and-pepper shrimp with the shells still on," "*[h]aricots verts* sautéed with garlic and ginger, [...] watercress wilted by a flash of heat," white rice, a bottle of good wine, and the dessert of an apple pie (96). Both delight each other with their fine palate "that had spent time in a professional kitchen" (97). "Morels?" Bình suggests. "Yes, he nodded." "An unexpected addition [...]. Rich with the must of forest decay, these mushrooms were hidden below the *haricots verts* until their aroma gave them away" (97). On the surface, their conversation and thoughts seem to center on food, but reading between the lines, we hear an undertone of nationalism and anti-imperialism. In savoring the watercress, both men stare at each other, as though they recognize some unexpected ingredient. Bình thinks, "Watercress is unmistakable, bitter in the mouth, cooling in the body, greens that any Vietnamese could identify with his eyes closed" (97). Watercress is a vegetable that evokes the diners' love of and longing for their homeland, a vegetable that conjures up the aroma and taste of the flooded land of Vietnam. At a symbolic level, this vegetable also stands for the people of Vietnam, who are misunderstood and overpowered by their colonizers. Bình's thoughts on watercress take this symbolic turn.

> The recipe is a deceptively simple one that calls for oil heated till it smokes, seasoned with nothing more than a generous sprinkling of salt and the blink of an eye. Any more contact with the heat, and the stalks turn themselves into ropes, tying themselves up in your mouth, making it impossible to swallow. (97)

Watercress, a delicate water vegetable, will rebel when overpowered by heat. No different from watercress, Vietnamese people will fight back when dominated by foreign powers, making the latter swallow the tough consequences of their actions. Anyone attempting to impose ways of life alien to Vietnam will have more than he can chew. This metaphoric connotation of watercress reminds the reader of the violent colonial attempts and failures by both the French and the Americans.

After watercress their conversation moves on to the salt in the dishes. Nguyen Ai Quoc mentions that it is "fleur de sel," "salt flowers" or "sea salt" (97–98). He explains to Bình the formation of sea salt by taking them "into a landscape of saltwater basins, rice-paddy-like when viewed from a distance" (98). "When seawater is evaporated by the sun in this way, it leaves behind its salt, in the same way that we will leave behind our bones" (98). Nguyen's remark is poignant of the aesthetics of the exiled and their woeful nostalgia for homeland. The images of rice paddies and the sea (the Pacific Ocean) transport both men home, sadly juxtaposed to the picture of bones bleached by the sun left behind on foreign soils. This cluster of images brilliantly conveys the pathos of the exiled men and of their inability to return home. Their dinner, however, suggests a more inviting metaphor for the existence of the exiled. The trans-cultural mixture of salt-and-pepper shrimp (Chinese), *haricots verts* (French green beans), watercress (Vietnamese), and apple pie (American) presents a kind of cultural exchange and collaboration that is powerfully oppositional to colonialism. Exiles like Nguyen and Bình understand the implications of travel: the importance of remembrance, the necessity to adapt, and the wealth of worldly ways. In answering Bình's question about the identity of the chef of this restaurant, Nguyen says,

> "First of all, friend, the chef here is Vietnamese. He's like me, thought that he would be a writer or a scholar someday, but after he traveled the world, life gave him something more practical to do. He now cooks here on the rue Descartes, but he will always be a traveler. He will always cook from all the places where he has been. It is his way of remembering the world." (99)

Equally displaced, this chef finds a new passion that sustains him as he travels from continent to continent. The original ambition to be a writer or scholar now becomes translated into being an artist, whose culinary memoirs are daily composed and ravishingly consumed.

Food, Sex, and Space

No reader of Mei Ng's novel *Eating Chinese Food Naked* can miss the tie between food and sex, as its title explicitly invites such a connection. But some may miss the title's other connotation about vulnerability and anxiety in practicing ethnic foodways. Implicit in this title is the intersection of sex, food, and ethnicity, in which Ng frames the search for sexual identity of her protagonist, Ruby Lee. It is often through culinary imageries and tropes that Ng stages tensions between sexuality in the ethnic, domestic space and sexuality in the urban space of streets, diners, and cafes. Ruby's journey from Manhattan to the Chinese laundry in Queens and back to Manhattan, punctuated and differentiated by food, signifies her movement from her heterosexuality troubled by a subconscious desire for women to a burgeoning queer, bisexual consciousness.

Eating begins when Ruby moves back to her parents' laundry in Queens after finishing her degree in women's studies at Columbia University. The main conflict of the narrative sets off to be her uncertainty about her future, but soon the reader realizes that deeper than that lies her uncertainty about her sexuality, which is underlined with an ethnic anxiety. And both uncertainties are articulated through food references in conjunction with spatial tension between the heterotopias of business and home that is the Chinese laundry and the urban space of anonymity and permissiveness in Queens and Manhattan. Resolutions to these conflicts also depend on culinary references and spatial movement.

The ethnic, domestic space in Ng's novel features various conflicts, between two immigrant parents, between parents and their American-born daughter, and within the daughter between love of and shame about her background. This domestic space often comes to life via food descriptions. Ng introduces these tensions at the very beginning of the novel in her description of the first dinner after Ruby's return. Ruby finds out for the first time that her parents no longer eat together: "her mother fixed a plate for herself and went down to the basement while her father ate in the kitchen by himself" (11). This detail sets the novel's forlorn tone and foreshadows familial frictions in which Ruby will find herself embroiled. It also serves as a metonymy for the separate lives her parents lead—their long history of estrangement and sexual incompatibility. Although Bell, Ruby's mother, is thrilled that "her baby had come back to her," she is tensely aware of the discord between them, for Ruby sits there "so stiffly, as if afraid of her own family" (11). With such brevity Ng succeeds in picturing Ruby's ambivalence toward home—one that is filled with ethnic and class tension as well as tenderness. In other words the Lees' ethnicity and class position structure their expressions of love and affection, as Ruby remembers that "[s]he and her mother had always loved each other through sacrifice and worry" (14). Not that being Chinese American entails the absence of joy and happiness; rather, their being immigrants and minority members in this country means economic disadvantage and vulnerability to racism and exploitation.

In the near absence of verbal or physical expressions of affection, the Lees communicate their love mainly through food. From a young age, Ruby is made aware of the difference between her family and her classmates' families. While other families kiss and hug, with parents sharing one bed, her family displays no outward expression of affection, with Bell and Franklin sleeping in separate rooms. Largely because of the lack of affection at home, adult Ruby desires but fears intimacy. Despite the lack of physical affection, however, she never doubts her parents' love for her, because through food her family has exhibited abundant love for each other. At the welcome-home dinner, Bell "picked out a choice morsel of chicken and placed it in her daughter's bowl" (11). Ruby's ambivalent emotions about her family are vividly portrayed by what follows.

> Ruby was so used to fending for herself that when the sweet white meat appeared in front of her, she nearly broke down and cried at the table. It didn't matter that she liked dark meat better. Her mother was chewing on a chicken foot. "You eat," Ruby said and tried to put some meat in her mother's bowl.
> Bell waved the foot in the air. "More sweet near the bone," she said.
> (11–12)

Bell's sacrifice moves as well as burdens Ruby, who wants to express her love for her mother while maintaining independence. The fact that Bell doesn't know Ruby's preference for dark meat reveals the distance widening between them since Ruby has left home for college. Now as an adult, Ruby notices that her "bowl is piled high with all the good bits, and there in her mother's bowl a heap of bones. But now that she's grown, for once in her life she would like to push away the full bowl and eat from the other, the one her mother guards with both hands" (14). Ng uses this image of Bell guarding her bowl with "a heap of bones" in it to suggest not only how sacrifices constitute Bell's identity but also the family dynamics resulting from her sacrifices. Ruby's guilt is palpable in her contemplation about why she has come to live with her parents. "The nagging feeling was stronger than ever [...] and it was then that she realized that it was her mother she had forgotten; it was her mother she had left behind and had finally come back to get" (16).

Now that Ruby is home, there is testing between mother and daughter about who they have become. Interestingly, Ng employs food in conducting such testing. While helping Bell with the dishes, Ruby notices and touches the "dried salted flounder hung on a string" (13). Bell comments, "Remember you used to love salty fish?" (13). Ruby quickly responds, "I still like it" (13). She accurately senses in Bell's voice something "that she needed to defend herself against, as if her mother were accusing her of something that had nothing to do with fish" (13). What Bell is really asking is whether college has educated Ruby out of the ethnic ways of life in favor of assimilation. Unlike Sterling Lung in *The Barbarians Are Coming*, Ruby is a character with political awareness of ethnic identification, although she experiences a certain degree of unease about her ethnic and class background. To impress upon her mother that she has not forgotten who she is, Ruby ventures to ask, "How do you make salty fish?" even though she knows she will never make it (13). Her interest in and appreciation of Chinese cuisine convinces Bell that Ruby hasn't been changed too much by her college education. To put Ruby at ease, Bell starts talking about how she used to make salty duck on the farm (13). Through such food references, mother and daughter communicate their mutual trust and reestablish their intimacy.

Food and ethnicity bear a visceral link that is more powerful than certain discursive performances, as I have demonstrated in chapter 1. Often when we think about the constitution of a subject, we tend to consider the social norms acting upon it from birth, norms that are maintained largely through discursivity. Food as a nondiscursive norm nevertheless cannot escape ideological and discursive manipulation. The discourse of racial superiority of whites often insinuates itself into ethnographical dietary interpretation that confirms the inferiority of nonwhite races. It is worth mentioning again what Den Fujita, McDonald's partner in Japan, said in 1987: "The reason Japanese people are so short and have yellow skin is because they have eaten nothing but fish and rice for 2,000 years. If we eat McDonald's hamburgers and potatoes for a thousand years, we will become taller, our skin will become white and our hair blond" (qtd. in Reiter 169). These racialized foodways play an essential role in legitimating transnational capitalism and globalization.

Although Ng's novel doesn't deal with transnational capitalism, it certainly points our attention to how racial hierarchy and capitalism work hand in hand in diminishing the normative power of ethnic foodways. As a teenager Ruby is often ashamed of the way her family eats. Ng pictures the instance in which the Lees make crabs in black bean sauce.

> Ruby watched the claws opening and closing, watched her father gather five legs in one hand and then push the shell away from the body. There was a cracking noise as the shell ripped away from the soft insides. The clear jelly heart still pulsed. He reached for the next crab. Bell chopped the crab into four pieces and still the heart pulsed. Ruby stirred garlic and scallion into the hot oil, then left the kitchen and practically ran around the corner to Jack's. She stood in front and ate a handful of Sno-Caps. [...] Ruby wished she had been born into a family that didn't kill its own food and didn't live behind the laundry and where the father and mother talked to each other once in a while. (41)

Granted that most American teenagers would be disgusted by witnessing the killing of their food, Ruby's disgust also comes from her family's class position and ethnicity. Killing one's own food, in the teenage Ruby's mind, is one of the things that separate immigrants from "regular" Americans, a practice belonging to an agrarian society and obsolete in advanced capitalism. In this transnational capitalist market, meats often appear in forms disassociated from their sources, and produce appears in markets remote from its origin. To overcome the disgust and shame over killing one's own food, Ruby rushes to the corner store, purchases Sno-Caps, and stuffs herself with them. It is as though payment for someone else's labor in making one's food restores the normalcy of the capitalist system of exchange and thus sweetens one's sense of belonging.

In addition to centering on issues of ethnicity and class within the domestic space of food, Ng explores Ruby's sexuality against the tension between the domestic space and the urban space. The domestic space, straddling the border between the public (laundry business) and the private, knows little intimacy and sexual freedom. There heterosexuality is offered to Ruby as a compulsory position but imparts to her the lesson of pain. Ruby's parents are long estranged, repelling each other in an unbreakable union of bitterness and sorrow. Ruby learns the lesson well and wants sex without marriage. She doesn't want her relationship with Nick to be more than sexual. While wandering in the city, she finds herself near Nick's apartment but decides against seeing him even though she is starved for sex. "It felt dangerous to see him while she was living at home—she might be tempted to stay with him; days and weeks and then years would pass without her noticing, and one morning she'd wake up and look out the window and there, surrounding the house, would be the dreaded white picket fence" (115). Ruby's fear of heterosexual monogamy and of the confinement of the domestic space propels her toward brief sexual encounters outside home. Living at home she feels sexually stifled, for there her desire is unspeakable, and any noise will arouse suspicion and guilt. Even after she moves out of her mother's bedroom into the basement, she still feels watched and chastised. Whenever she can, she walks the streets of Manhattan hoping to find a stranger to go home with. Ng offers an interesting fact to allegorize and naturalize Ruby's desire and behavior. One evening Ruby joins her father in watching a TV show about the hermit crab. "Strangely, these crabs lived in the forest and made their homes in trees. Thousands were scuttling out of the forest, across roads and highways, even, in their yearly exodus to the sea" (84). When they reach the sea, they mate. Like these hermit crabs, Ruby cannot engage in sexual activity at home. As she watches the show, "she was dying for a café where she might find some halfway decent person to go home with. That's what she needed to feel alive again" (84). Ng creates a comical moment here. Watching the hermit crabs mate, Franklin says, "I bet they're good eating. [...] I bet they're sweet" (84).

The association between food and sex is essential in delineating the character development of Ruby from someone confused about her sexuality to someone coming into full consciousness of her bisexuality. Initially, a subconscious preference for women frightens her. "Women were dangerous. Ruby knew a woman could break her heart just by looking at her" (87). At first she doesn't understand why she has returned home. "It was only partly that she didn't have money or a job or a house of her own. There was something else, something she couldn't quite place that had pulled her away from mornings where she would reach out and touch the hair of the one sleeping next to her" (24). Her restlessness and active sexuality are described through food metaphors. "Day after day, croissants and omelettes and pancakes with cream on top. One day the butteriness was too much for her stomach. No one could hold her down long enough to keep her from running" (24). Ruby runs from one sexual partner to another until she ends up home. It doesn't take long for her to realize that it is her mother that has pulled her home. In her relationship with Bell, Ruby's lesbian inclination finds a displaced but safe site for articulation. Her love and desire for Bell are often invested in food references too. Years ago when Bell had an operation, it was Ruby, only ten, who followed her mother's instructions and cooked for the family. "In the kitchen, Ruby had found a grace she didn't have with double Dutch or softball or flirting. Those things baffled her, but she had a way with ginger and black beans and garlic" (48). She kept cooking even after her mother recovered. After she finished cooking, Ruby would run to the factory to fetch her mother. "Bell was so proud she thought she would burst. It didn't matter so much then that her husband didn't say hello when she came home; at least she had her little girl" (49). Now at age twenty-two, Ruby imagines living with her mother in a "two-bedroom in Manhattan. With lots of windows and wood floor. [...] Maybe they would live up the block from a bakery where they could get apple turnovers for dessert" (19).

Just as the domestic space is given texture by the frugal practices of ethnic food, so is the urban space by rich pastries and desserts that suggest sexual freedom and liberal choices. "Apple turnover" is not an accidental signifier for intimacy or sexuality, since Ruby introduces herself to a potential sexual partner as "a coconut-custard kind of girl" (117). It is in Manhattan where Ruby associates desserts with sexual freedom and choices. Walking on Broadway, she stops at a bakery in which "she looked with longing at the little strawberry tarts and the apple turnovers and fancy cakes like Easter bonnets" (170). She envies "the people who walked right into the store and pointed confidently at something in the window and came out with a cardboard box that they held carelessly by the string" (171). With this cluster of images of food and city shoppers insinuating desire, sexuality, and its casual consumption/consummation, Ng suggests Ruby's longing for sexual freedom and envy of other people's certainty. She wishes that she knew what she wanted and could take what she desired. Is it her mother, Nick, men, or women that she wants?

Ruby loves and desires her mother, entertaining a fantasy of rescue that takes (elopes with) her mother away from her father to the paradise of Florida. She works as a temp to pay for the trip. Her fantasy reaches its climax in a dream where "she was having sex with her mother" (168). Ng treats such homosexual, incestuous fantasy as unproblematic by stating, "When Ruby was a kid, around the time when other little girls were being dandled on their daddy's knee [...] thinking about marrying him when they grew up, she was dreaming about marrying her mother and taking her away" (18). Ng's destabilizing of the taboo against incest reminds us of Foucault's remark in the context of the Western history of sexuality: "Incest was a popular practice [...] widely practiced among the populace, for a very long time. It was toward the end of the nineteenth century that various social pressures were directed against it" (154). Interestingly, when Ng must make Ruby aware of the social taboo against incest, she resorts to a food taboo to make the point. Ruby finds in a book on food rituals in which there was

> a tribe of people who grew yams and piled them up in the yard. When you visited your neighbor, you brought along a basket of yams [...], and when you left, they gave you some of their yams [...]. You weren't supposed to eat your own yams. Or your own dogs. Or your own sister or mother. Your own yams, your own sister, your own mother you may not eat. Other people's sisters, other people's mothers, you may eat. (168–169)

Framed against the arbitrariness of this particular food taboo, our incest taboo loses its rigidity as a law of nature. Ruby learns through this food taboo that it is a social demand that she transfer her desire for her mother to other women.

Ruby's love and desire for her mother are often described as conflicting with her need for freedom, for her mother is associated with the kitchen and the basement, a domestic space that makes Ruby restless. She longs for the urban space of anonymity where "diners with murals of the Acropolis splayed across their walls appealed to her in the early-morning hours [...] where she found herself sitting across from someone she might never have talked to if she hadn't fucked him" (86). To Ruby the space of the laundry/home, with its ethnic food and its customs and its poverty, is a different America from Broadway, so much so that she feels she can be "a regular American girl" only when she lives elsewhere (25). Her love and desire for her mother endure such spatial tension between the ethnic, domestic sphere and the city of casual contacts. Although ethnicity and poverty bother Ruby, these are not the only reasons that she longs for the urban space. For home, being the space saturated with demands and failures of heterosexuality, requires her to be complicit with her mother's suffering. She feels anger and shame when her silence condones her father's verbal abuse of her mother, and she feels guilt and shame when she opposes her father to protect her mother. On Broadway, however, she can look into people's eyes without shame. "Her eyes were full of tenderness and regret that she would never know their names or what was inside the packages they carried" (170). Almost always, food accompanies such street scenes, and the urban space is often associated with casual sex.

Ng has established the code that food is sex. Therefore, city, food, and sex form narrative nodes from which Ng's major motifs develop. When the narrative moves toward a resolution, Ng begins to utilize more heavily the intersection between food and sex. One major conflict must be resolved before Ruby can come to a full consciousness of her queerness: her relationship with Nick. By any standard Nick is a decent guy, but Ruby's fear of committing to monogamy constantly drives her into the arms of other men. Nick says again and again, "If only she wouldn't fuck other people, they would be happy together" (119). To Ruby, however, her affairs with men mean nothing, for "she loved Nick as much as she could love any man, but she had a feeling that if she ever met a woman, she would leave him for good" (120). Toward the middle of the novel, this conflict begins to move toward a resolution, for Ruby begins to see Nick's flaws, which are often food related. Ruby finally relents and lets Nick visit her at home. The scene at dinner offers Ruby the first sign that Nick is not the right person for her.

> Ruby had forgotten to tell Nick not to start eating until her father picked up his chopsticks. Nick reached across the table and helped himself to a plump morsel of chicken from the far side of the plate, the side right in front of her father. Ruby half waited for her father to rap Nick across the knuckles. No, no, Nick, Ruby said in her head, only pick in front of you, no matter what it is, even if it's the chicken head or chicken butt. (129)

Nick's poor table manners reveal him to be selfish. After this episode, Ruby moves into an all-women apartment building, the first subconscious choice to cut Nick off—subconscious because Ruby still consoles Nick that she is always at his place anyway. The last time they are together, again it is during a meal that she comes to realize their incompatibility. "She was talking and not eating. He was eating all the good meaty bits and leaving the bony parts for her. This made her quiet, and she felt sad suddenly that she loved a man who took the good bits for himself" (234). Ruby cannot help comparing Nick to her family, whose members demonstrate love through giving the best to others. In one of the dinner scenes, Bell "slipped a nice fat shrimp into Franklin's bowl. [...] Franklin picked up two pieces of the tender white breast and laid them in Ruby's bowl. 'One for your mother,' he said" (207). Their different table manners illuminate the different values inculcated by their families. Something as trivial as table manners reveals one's character, as Bell points out: "Not knowing how to eat was worse than going with another woman" (241). Although Ruby's disappointment in Nick's table manners plays a large role in her decision to stop seeing him, the more important reason arises later when he reveals his racism. Nick confesses that when he is angry he thinks, "Who is that ugly Chinese woman standing in my room? But now here you are and you're beautiful, I don't even notice your Chineseness" (236). His remark evokes in her a suppressed memory of racial trauma in elementary school. In the final scene between them, Ng uses the prop of food to signify Ruby's complete lack of sexual interest in Nick. "For the first time, the sight of his soft penis didn't seem to fit with the tins of dumplings, noodles, rice. It had just been in her mouth, but suddenly she didn't want it so near her food" (233). Food and sex, always working hand in hand in Ruby's apparatus of arousal, become disengaged at this final moment of their relationship.

When she comes to fully realize her queerness, it occurs at the narrative nexus of food, space, and sex. At a party in Manhattan, Ruby meets Hazel and becomes intensely attracted to her. "God, who knew that touching someone's hand could make her so wet" (231). Her desire for Hazel finds its expression in references to food. "She was seized with a sudden desire to shop at open markets for her, to buy only the most beautiful string beans and patty-pan squash and red bliss potatoes and herbs from Amish farmers. She also wanted to run out and buy some phyllo dough and wrap up something fancy in it and bake the whole thing until it was golden brown" (230). She tells Hazel proudly that she's going to attend a cooking school. To spin off from Bell's remark about the relationship between eating and being, we can venture to say that knowing how to cook, eat, and feed others is knowing how to love.

Now that Ruby finally comes to a self-understanding and sets off on the path of finding her happiness away from home, away from her mother, in the urban space of Manhattan, one may ask, What about Bell, whose life is more miserable without Ruby around? Ng's narrative offers both Bell and Franklin character development as well. Franklin at Bell's sixtieth birthday presents her with a pair of tickets to Florida. Bell herself begins to walk the streets of Queens as if her daughter's restlessness has infected her. Now she goes to American fast-food joints to drink tea and eat snacks, something she has never done before. Ruby is filled with love and comfort as she imagines her mother running in the sneakers that are her present to her.

> She'd run around the whole neighborhood, up and down every little side
> street. [...] she would keep on, past the junior high school, past the library
> and the supermarket, past the catering place and the hamburger joint and the
> bar with topless dancers. [...] She'd run past all the familiar streets, Main,
> Cedarhurst, Hollis, Union. She'd keep running, past streets she had never

seen before, past houses with people cooking and eating, talking and yelling, fighting and loving in dark rooms. She'd keep running, the sound of her own breathing in her ears, arms and legs pumping their long easy stride, taking her away to another place. (247)

Bell's journey outward into the urban space folds back upon Ruby's return home from college at the novel's beginning. Ruby describes her own journey with the same landmarks addressing the reader as though she were a tour guide for a trip from Manhattan to Queens.

> First you get on the R train and ride all the way out to the very last stop. Get off at Union Street. Go upstairs and take the bus, the Q44, the Q63, the Q29—or, if you're lucky, you can take the Q66 so that you don't have to walk down from Main Street. [...] You can walk down Cedarhurst Boulevard if you want an ice-cream sandwich from the German deli, or you can walk down the side streets, where there is shade and rows and rows of single-family houses. [...] When you hit Hollis Avenue, you can see how things have changed. There are new bodegas that have the same yellow-and-red awnings and men sitting outside on crates. [...] Next to the Shell Gas Station is the transmission place with the pack of rabid dogs that bark and jump and throw themselves against the fence when someone walks by. [...] Now you see people coming out of their cars carrying rifles in protective sheaths instead of bowling balls. In the middle of the block is Lee's Hand Laundry, where I grew up. (16–17)

Ruby's description of the journey suggests a spatial stratification that is ethnically and economically determined. Cedarhurst is a white, heterosexual ("grass plots [...] trimmed on Saturdays by husbands in their undershirts"), middle-class space; Hollis is an ethnic, poor, violent space (16–17).

Bell's movement outward traverses both of these spaces, the ethnic ghetto and the space of the supposed American Dream. This movement can be interpreted as Bell's practice of freedom and care for the self—an agency that undermines patriarchal oppression and ethnic fear of persecution, both of which are aptly symbolized by her husband, Franklin. It is Franklin who has stopped Bell from going to English classes for fear of losing her. "After he had shown her everything he could, he stopped wanting to go out. He started getting carsick, train-sick, bus-sick. He sold his Chevrolet to his cousin in Chinatown" (35). Bell thus becomes trapped inside the laundry and cannot speak her mind, for Franklin's cigar smoke is always in her throat (57). It is also Franklin who has discouraged Bell from calling her sister in Chicago, afraid that "she'd be getting on a plane and flying out there" (32). Although Ng does not describe Franklin's experience of racial humiliation, it is suggested to the reader by his fear of persecution. For instance, he attributes his sore feet to the fact that he has stopped wanting to go out a long time ago, a physical pain that can be read as a manifestation of psychic pain over racialization. Now Franklin travels through newspapers and shares reports of tragic events with Bell, as though they would justify his fear of the outside world. To be Chinese living in America, in his experience, is to invite trouble. Therefore, one should not broadcast one's ethnicity. Ruby recalls her father taking out the trash. "He was calm when he used a bag from the American supermarket, but when he used a bag from Chinatown, his face would get tight and his hands quick and angry as he turned the bags inside out so that the Chinese lettering didn't show as much" (126). When asked why he turns the Chinese bags inside out, he answers, "So people don't know this is Chinese garbage" (126). Bell in walking the streets of Queens defies her husband's control and braves the world that she is given, despite the risk of racial humiliation. Her newly acquired mobility finally fulfills her destiny—"Bell's mother being the first in her family to have big feet" after the banning of foot binding (27). Bell has inherited her mother's restlessness and "carried it with her all the way to America" (27).

Interestingly, Ruby's wish to take her mother to Florida initiates the change, and her fantasy of rescue bears the fruit of Bell's new mobility. Both women are saved because they are finally able to exercise their freedom independently, and this independence also frees them from each other. Bell's break away from Franklin's control enables Ruby to rid herself of her guilt for her mother's unhappiness and thus enables her to live happily in Manhattan. In turn Ruby's happy independence comforts Bell that her baby has grown into a strong woman. At the end of the novel, their love for each other finds its final expression in food. Ruby calls to ask her mother for a recipe for sea bass, and in such asking she conveys her love for her mother and her connection to her ancestry, for food is their medium of communication. Significantly, the novel ends with Bell's voice on Ruby's voicemail, telling her how to cook a sea bass.

> "First, pick a sea bass with clear eyes, not cloudy. When you get home, wash it in cold water, inside and out. Make sure there's no more scales left. Soak the black beans in some warm water. Put the fish in a bowl, chop garlic, scallion and ginger. Pour a little soy sauce on it, not too much. Then steam it until it's done, maybe twenty minutes. Heat some oil in a pan. Make sure it's hot, but not smoky. Pour it over the top. Watch out for small bones." (252)

Gay versus Queer

Sexual identity has conventionally been conceptualized as a static description of one's sexual essence. This essentialist convention demands that one be either hetero or homo in one's sexual desires. The discourse of "coming out," narrating it as a process in which one becomes increasingly honest about the true nature of one's sexuality, has been shaped more by essentialist sexology than anything else, and ironically, essentialist sexology is the very discourse that gay cultures have been trying to combat. In recent investigations by queer theories, however, there is a concerted effort to distinguish "queer" from "gay" with the intention of infusing queer theories with a fresh critical energy. In her second book, *Tendencies*, Eve Sedgewick defines "queer" this way:

> Queer is a continuing moment, movement, motive—recurrent, eddying, *troublant*. The word "queer" itself means *across*—it comes from the Indo-European root *twerkw*, which also yields the German *quer* (traverse), Latin *torquere* (to twist), English *athwart*. [...] Keenly, it is relational and strange. (xii)

In tracing the etymologies of the word "queer," Sedgewick highlights its translinguistic convergence and invites us to conceptualize queerness as an exercise that troubles, disturbs, twists, resists, and sabotages the regimes of the normal. By this definition, "queer," a noun, a verb, or an adjective, differs from "gay" in that "queer" does not gesture solely toward a sexual identity. First of all, queerness, strictly speaking, is not merely about sexual practices. Sue-Ellen Case puts it succinctly: "Queer theory [...] works not at the site of gender, but at the site of ontology" (3). Second, queerness disturbs identity, for "[t]he queer is the taboo-breaker, the monstrous, the uncanny" (Case 3). Or in Donald Hall's words, queer practices "challenge and undercut any attempt to render 'identity' singular, fixed, or normal" (15).

In the domain of sexuality, being queer, therefore, entails a radically critical position toward sexual normativity, not a specific sexual desire. To truly challenge sexual normativity is to undo a monosexual identity, be it hetero or homo. Fluid sexual identities like bisexuality are fundamentally frustrating to the system of classification because they disrupt the either/or rationality. Bisexual identities are threatening to monosexual identities because they undermine the essentialist bases for monosexual identities. In speaking about the representational bifurcation between hetero and homo, Paula Rust points out, "The reconstruction of relationships to landmarks of both genders implies the destruction of the language that provides people with monosexual identities (79). The discourse of coming-out celebrates the "authentic" self by denouncing the false and dishonest heterosexual self, whereas bisexuals refuse to make up their mind and move on to their "true" selves. Joe Eadie argues that the threat resides within the monosexual identity because the bisexuality threatening to lesbians and gay men is really their own bisexuality. Eadie argues that in denying their own bisexuality, lesbians and gays are not so clearly different from heterosexuals after all (139–170). While the regimes of the normal may reluctantly tolerate gays and lesbians because the coming-out narrative appeals to essence, authenticity, and truth, thus implying lack of choice or agency in one's sexual orientation, bisexuality is an abomination in the general public's eyes, for it stands for willful and insistent challenges to sexual normativity. Bisexuals, fully able yet refusing to choose either hetero or homo, are the truly monstrous and uncanny.

The distinction between gay and queer sexuality is important when reading *Salt* side by side with *Eating*. Although both novels center on the sexual identities of their protagonists, they diverge significantly in their constitution of the desiring subject. Ng's novel, in dramatizing Ruby's queer journey from heterosexual desire troubled by a subconscious homosexual impulse to conscious bisexual desires, may be read as a critique of the monosexual desire and relationships in *Salt*. Such a reading by no means critiques Truong for whatever sexual normalcy she may observe in her historical fiction. Anchored in the mores of the early 1900s when a lesbian relationship was more readily tolerated than male homosexuality, Truong deploys Bình's gay desire as the radical terrain to mobilize a host of critical issues, including sexual normativity, colonialism, patriarchy, class, and race. Reading both texts together, however, invites us to grapple with their different approaches to sexual transgression. What was transgressive in the early 1900s may have become part of the regime of the normal in the 2000s. I wonder why *Eating*, eight years since its publication, has received little critical attention from Asian American scholars. Could it be that its bisexuality is deeply disturbing? It was revealing to watch how my graduate students gravitated to the interpretation that at the end of the novel Ruby is finally awakened to her lesbian self. So seduced and confined by the discourse of coming-out, we often unknowingly reduce a dynamic and large terrain of sexuality to something nameable and containable. The lack of scholarly work on *Eating*, I believe, is one example of our jittery uncertainty about fluid sexualities and our discomfort with Ruby's sexual appetite.

First let me start with *Salt*, in which the Stein and Toklas relationship mirrors that of the historical celebrities who have been extolled as trailblazers of sexual freedom. Their same-sex relationship, even from their era's point of view, however, hardly queers the regimes of the normal, as it largely mirrors the norm of white and propertied heterosexuality in the early twentieth century in the West. Truong, faithful to the historical Stein and Toklas, presents a vivid domestic picture of the pair in *Salt*. The fact that both are female is the only social anomaly in their relationship. Gertrude's endearments for Alice include "Pussy" and "Wifie," while "Lovey" and "Hubbie" are among Alice's for Gertrude. Alice is the wife operating within the domestic sphere, satisfying

Gertrude's culinary and sexual appetites, managing her social life, and serving as her private secretary. Gertrude as the husband pleases Alice by loving her food and her body, by surrendering to her all of the domestic and most of the social decisions, and by maintaining a public presence that makes Alice proud. It is telling that Gertrude almost never enters the kitchen and socializes with women. Simone de Beauvoir remarks, "When Gertrude Stein entertained friends, she conversed only with the men and left to Alice Toklas the duty of talking with the ladies" (423). As pointed out earlier, their arrangement is so agreeable to the institution of marriage that people in their circle refer to them as the Steins.

The two pairs of gay lovers in *Salt,* varying in gender, race, and class, have one thing in common—the irreversible roles of cooks and diners. Alice cooks to please Gertrude on Sundays, and on other days she does so by directing Bình. Spatially, Alice is primarily claimed by garden, market, and kitchen. In this respect Bình is like Alice, fixed in domesticity. With both Alice and Bình cooking for their lovers, Gertrude Stein and Marcus Lattimore are the beneficiaries of the formers' labor. Never vice versa. Such fixed roles mirror the equally fixed sexual roles between the lovers, with Alice performing the role of the traditional wife and Bình the submissive to Lattimore. Revealed in their culinary and sexual relationship is a congealed asymmetrical power relation that is no different from the hegemonic norm of heterosexuality. While one can not freely choose one's sexuality as one pleases, one can conceivably create relationships in which power relations are reversible, permitting fluidity in identities that truly transgress boundaries.

Eating can be read as an interesting critique of the gay relationships in *Salt* in that sexual identities and practices are plural and fluid within one individual. Ng not only faults heterosexuality for people's unhappiness but also removes the stigma from bisexuality by naturalizing it allegorically through metaphors of food and appetite. Ruby's sexuality is not settled once and for all in the novel's resolution. Her conscious desire for Hazel is not arrived at by a denunciation of her desire for men. She may have left Nick for Hazel, but there is no indication that she will not continue having male lovers. In spite of her fear of entrapment by men, Ruby enjoys the sex. "She loved him (Nick) best in bed [...]. [...] And that was the scary part, that in bed it felt good" (122–123). Moreover, the modalities of sexual pleasure for Ruby range between hetero and lesbian, even before she is fully conscious of her desire for women. "What she liked best was to lie at the edge of the bed while he knelt on a pillow on the floor, his mouth between her legs. She liked to come that way" (119). On the other hand, she also finds penetration satisfying. "He pushed into her and she stopped fighting. [...] One minute she was making all kinds of noises and her hips were moving and the next minute she was coming and crying" (124).

Ruby's search is not centered on finding the authentic self between the hetero/homo dichotomy. Rather, her journey arrives at her honesty that she is a queer, desiring subject that cannot choose one sex over the other. She is drawn to women because she desires them and because with them there is no threat of marriage. She is equally attracted to men because she desires them and enjoys them in bed. Nowhere in the novel is the language of hetero/lesbian sexuality evoked. Unlike the narrative movement that firms up Ruby's ethnic identity at the end, the narrative motif on sexuality skirts the notion of identity formation. The novel ends without a clear indication whether Ruby will carry out her fantasy about Hazel. What we know of is her attraction and dinner invitation to Hazel.

Ruby's shyness around women she finds attractive is the consequence of her subject formation in the culture of hegemonic heterosexuality, and her defiance of it is not limited to loving women, for doing so would deny part of herself. And such a denial plays right into the hands of the regime of the normal. To truly trouble the system of classification by which the regime of the normal operates, Ruby must allow herself to love whomever she desires regardless of their sex, resisting the social demand for coherent, singular, and fixed identities. Although Ruby's relationship with a female lover is left to the reader's imagination, we can make an informed conjecture (based on her relationships with Nick and Bell) that it will not be a fixed power relation.

Judith Butler is correct in reminding us that "sexuality cannot be summarily made or unmade, and it would be a mistake to associate 'constructivism' with 'the freedom of a subject to form her/his sexuality as s/he pleases'" (94). Hall is equally correct in qualifying Butler that it has not been proven that "our sexuality is firmly fixed and our potentials for future identifications foreclosed from early childhood" (183). To be queer is to refuse a fixed sexuality and therefore to be shuffled between either and or. To be queer is also to permit chance to take us by surprise.

Epilogue

Can you think of any novel or drama that does not mention food, drinks, and eating? Probably very few of you can at all. Admitted that poetry may be less alimentary than fiction and drama, it invests much significance in food, drinks, and eating when it does employ these imageries. Then why do food studies in literature have a reputation of being "scholarship lite" (Ruark A17)? The first reason probably lies in the conventional notion of intellectual rigor—a rather masculinist concept. While abstract ideas such as race, class, gender, and sexuality have become axiomatic in reading literature, food, in its materiality and dailiness, persists in being associated with the mundane and feminine, and thus is often regarded as undeserving of scholarly attention. Food talk is often thought of as women's conversation. Speaking of the French setting, Priscilla Parkhurst Ferguson remarks, "The attitude has been, Real men don't eat quiche, and real men certainly don't write about quiche" (qtd. in Ruark A17). In American academia, food studies are often perceived as soft, something that only third-rate minds would do. "It's been a disdained and patronized subject, and people who study it have been disdained and patronized" (qtd. in Ruark A17). A couple of years ago, I presented a paper in our college on the subject of appetite and masculinity. A few days later, I found on the door of a male colleague's office the abstract of my paper taped next to a cartoon in which two rats converse about food and deconstruction; standing next to them are three boxes of cereal—Post Modern Toasties, Deconstruction Breakfast, and Foucault Flakes. On my abstract, this colleague had written with a marker, "You thought they were kidding!!!" This colleague did not come to my talk, nor did he ever ask me for a copy of the paper.

Food and Literature

In the *American Studies Association Newsletter* (June 2000), Psyche A. Williams Forson argues that "sophisticated analyses by food scholars unearth hidden terrain—critical contribution to our understanding history, culture (visual and material), literature, philosophy, economics and other disciplines" (19). The fact that food studies need defending is deeply disturbing. As a culture in which overeating and wasting food are pedestrian and in which diet fads pathologize appetite and eating, we have forgotten the cultural and political gravity of food, we have forgotten that wars have been fought because of food, and we choose to forget that starvation is a daily experience of billions. If literary studies are to investigate the human condition and to enlighten us with the human spirit, we cannot ignore food practices as a window into human consciousness and actions. But the fact remains that although more and more respectable journals and presses are publishing articles and books studying food and literature, this union between the two fields continues to experience tension, whereas new frontiers such as queer studies, disability studies, trauma studies, and aging and death studies have become part of the landscape of literary studies.

As a literary food scholar, I don't want to blame this tension simply on others' misunderstandings or prejudices. I want to acknowledge that some publications have treated food in literature superficially as well as coercively. Food scholars are not simply food enthusiasts, waxing their warm, fuzzy feelings about food, kitchen, and women's creativity. Food scholars treat food as a "symbol of power, an aesthetic display, a community ritual, and an expression of ideology or identity" (Ruark A17). What is more important is that responsible critics recognize the constitutive function of food in a literary text—constitutive of its organization, its characters, and its thesis. Any literary text that simply scatters culinary details is not necessarily an ideal object of study. If food does not speak from the core of the text, it is no more than peripheral excess, unessential to the text's organization. In coercing this kind of text to speak through its culinary imageries, one does violence to the text and gives food studies a bad reputation.

To treat food as a signifying system symbiotic with social, cultural, economic, and religious ideologies requires us to study food practices as both produced by and productive of historical and cultural contexts. In other words, food is neither isolated from nor merely symbolic of the operations of the world. For instance, when reading colonial American literature, one may want to place food references in a dialectic relationship with the Christian (Puritan) morality of food and eating. Or in reading nineteenth-century American literature, one may want to contextualize the characters' relationships to food and eating within the discursive context of nutrition and health initiated and constructed by Horace Fletcher.[1] It may strike one as banal to emphasize that food practices are engaged in by human beings who are deeply enmeshed in ideological constraints and struggles, and therefore cannot be interpreted simply as expressions of human creativity. The fact that food practices always function in a dialectical relationship with ideological practices, be they class, race, gender, religion, nationalism, health, or beauty, makes them all the more important to contemporary literary studies that center on human beings as political creatures. To read food in literature as constitutive of characters, plot organizations, and theses requires us to link food references with characters' ontology, psychology, and social environments, with textual patterns and trajectories, and more significantly with a text's central argument or philosophy. In short, food in literature is a stage upon which and through which human dramas act out, and literary human dramas always aim at imparting lessons.

These are the interpretive principles I have put to practice in reading a body of Asian American literary texts in this book. And I think that the same principles are applicable to texts from different literary traditions. When reading Gloria Naylor's *Mama Day* (1988), for example, one recognizes that food references shape the protagonist, Cocoa Day. Having recently moved to New York City, Cocoa manages her fear of the great diversity by cataloguing people with culinary terms: "cherry vanilla," "licorice," "milkshakes," "kumquat" (20–21), "fudge sticks," "bagels," "zucchinis," and "taco" (62). When confronted by her boyfriend George, Cocoa explains, "A whole kaleidoscope of people—nothing's just black and white here like in Willow Springs. Nothing stays put" (63). Cocoa begs us not to settle for the easy accusation that she is racist and homophobic; she invites us to frame her culinary naming of others in the environment in which she was raised. Willow Springs, an island in the Atlantic Ocean that belongs neither to South Carolina nor to Georgia, has been owned by free blacks since 1823. Compared to blacks in the South, people on the island have suffered less racial oppression. It is a place where the darker one is the more accepted one is, where women muster greater power than men, where food occupies a significant communal role. Once we trace Cocoa's formation to the racially homogenous world of women, rituals, and food sharing, we understand that her naming of people as food comes from her heightened sensitivity to differences and the vocabulary available to her in describing these differences. She herself was named Cocoa because of her lighter skin color. With the help of George, Cocoa comes to understand New York City better and acquires a new vocabulary to differentiate people. George remarks to Cocoa, "You'd stopped calling people food. You were learning the difference between a Chinese, a Korean, a Vietnamese, and a Filipino, that Dominicans and Mexicans weren't all Puerto Ricans. You could finally pick out German Jews, Russian Jews, Hasidics, and Israelis" (100). Cocoa's initial habit of naming others as food serves to domesticate the "alien" and the threatening by objectifying people of different races, and her newly acquired ability to recognize and name people by their singularities restores subjectivity to them.

Allow me one more example. Andrea Levy's *Fruit of the Lemon* (1999) is not exactly a culinary novel, but the few references to food are central to the character development of the protagonist, Faith Jackson, and trajectory of the plot. The novel opens with a schoolyard taunting that mortifies Faith as a child: "Your mum and dad came on a banana boat" (3). This reference denotes Faith's Caribbean origin; her parents are from Jamaica, which ships bananas to "the mother country." The taunting shames Faith not only because it castigates her as a "darkie" from a former colony, but also because it associates banana boats with slave ships. Faith imagines "[m]y mum and dad curled up on the floor of a ship, wrapped in a blanket perhaps, trying to find a comfortable spot amongst the spiky prongs of unripe bananas" (4). This image is immediately linked to "the illustrations of slave ships from my history lessons" (4). For the first half of the novel, this conflated image of a banana boat with that of a slave ship casts a dense shadow upon Faith's psychological development. Her difficult relations with her parents as well as white roommates and co-workers display her heightened sensitivity and helplessness toward skin colors and racial hierarchy. Consequently, she quietly suffers from an eroded ego and painful self-consciousness.

In the second half of the novel when Faith visits Jamaica, the story of Cousin Constance (Afria), the last of a series of stories that maps out Faith's genealogy, unfolds to educate her about the absurdity of color hierarchy. In this story the reference to bananas returns to mark Faith's arrival at an ethnic consciousness. Constance, living in England with her white paternal grandparents, pines for bananas—"In every letter she ask for eating bananas" (314). Bananas are the smell and taste of home to Constance born and raised in Jamaica whereas bananas are a source of shame and alienation for Faith born and raised in London. Constance's story thus marks the end of Faith's visit to Jamaica, with the concluding remark, "But she [Constance] is quite happy, Faith—quite happy...until of course she drinks too much rum" (319). Faith's personal journey is therefore sandwiched between the banana boat, by which her parents arrived in England, and bananas as the fruit of Jamaica that carry the meaning of home and nourishment. Upon her return to England, she proclaims, "I was coming home to tell everyone...My mum and dad come to England on a banana boat" (339). With this proclamation, Levy ends the novel, for with the transformation of the meaning of the banana boat free from the association with the slave ship, Faith completes her character development.

The other significant food reference in Levy's novel is lemon. This tropical fruit is a necessity in England at teatime. Lemon in this novel carries dual meanings; on the one hand, lemon signifies whiteness, Englishness, and high class position, and on the other, it suggests a homing journey for Faith enabled by genealogical narratives. Matilda, Constance's mother, a white-looking Jamaican, takes it on herself to teach her darker nieces the ways of the English. "At tea-time she sat them at the table and made them eat lemons. They ate lemons with sugar and a tiny spoon. She assured her small nieces [...] that was how the English eat lemons" (313). In addition, she "made them eat mango, banana, papaya with a knife and fork" (313). Displayed in this misappropriation of the English ways is a racial and class anxiety typical in the colonial scene. Such exaggerated mimicries are doubly alienating, for Matilda can never be English regardless of how pale she looks and how much bitter lemon she eats with sugar, and she cannot and doesn't want to be a Jamaican regardless of her birth.

In the second half of the novel, the image of lemon begins to punctuate stories told Faith by family members, marking the progression of her homeward journey. When she first arrives at Auntie Coral's house in Kingston, Jamaica, Faith notices the lush yard where trees hang with fruit. She rests her gaze particularly on a lemon tree, "with dark leaves and a few yellow drops dangling heavy ready for picking" (201). This image signifies belonging, because this is where lemon grows and ripens. One soon realizes that the lemon tree figures for Faith's family tree, and to become part of that tree is a kind of rebirth for her. As Faith packs to go back to London, she thinks, "They laid a past out in front of me. They wrapped me in a family history and swaddled me tight in its stories. And I was taking that family back to London" (326). Each story, visually begun with a half lemon, grows a new branch in Faith's family tree. By the end of these stories, her family tree comprises eight generations, and she herself becomes one of the "yellow drops dangling heavy ready for picking," echoing the title of the novel, *Fruit of the Lemon*.

Eating Identities

The title of this book suggests the various relationships between food and identities that I have explored in this study—food and ethnicity, food and gender, food and class, food and diaspora, and food and sexuality. "Eating" suggests two sets of meanings different from "food," and the title "Eating Identities" bears multiple connotations. First, eating is a primitive act whereas food is a civilized object. Humans share with all living organisms the most essential act of eating. If we are stripped of all human masks, we are nothing but an eating-defecating organism. The human masks are kept in place partly by the sublimation of eating through styles, manners, utensils, occasions, time and place, and innumerable social significations. In other words, we elevate the act of eating into a social ritual. Second, when paired with the deeply constructionist notion of identity, eating takes on richer connotations than food. Eating entails consuming, internalizing, incorporating, becoming, processing, building, strengthening, corroding, overcoming, and externalizing (excreting).

Therefore, "Eating Identities" yields interesting interpretations, such as acquiring identities through eating, eating up identities, and being eaten by the identities we bear.

In 1825 Jean Anthelme Brillat-Savarin declared, "Tell me what you eat, and I will tell you who you are." Eating is a means of becoming, not simply in the sense of nourishment but more importantly in the sense of what we choose to eat, what we can afford to eat, what we secretly crave but are embarrassed to eat in the presence of others, and how we eat. There is an undeniable relationship between who we are and what and how we eat. Doris Witt in *Black Hunger* clarifies this point: interpretations of food "can help us make sense of how we come to understand ourselves as individual and collective subjects, and therefore also how we come to ally ourselves with and against the prevailing social order" (17). A recent article in *The New York Times* demonstrates the cultural battle ground of culinary desires within the Chinatown of Flushing, New York.

> The clash of cultures is vividly apparent in Flushing, one of the city's new
> Chinatowns. On streets like Roosevelt Avenue, older immigrants still
> throng to traditional Asian markets, with their signs in Chinese, and dine at
> noodle shops where windows fog with steam. Their children, however, are
> increasingly lured by fast food. Along a 100-yard strip of storefronts are a
> McDonald's, a Burger King, a Taco Bell, a Pizza Hut, and a Joe's Best Burger.
> (Santora 4)

The competition between Chinese noodle shops and American fast-food joints is not simply one of business; it is a competition in subject formation that determines one's alliance or opposition to the U.S. hegemonic culture. The older generation, which continues to find satisfaction in Chinese cuisine, is not eager to adopt American ways of life. Their children, however, who "try to fit into their new country by embracing its foods," are eager to stop being identified as Chinese (Santora 4). They believe they can become American, and to a certain extent they do, through the means of desiring and eating hamburgers and french fries. Similarly, Ichiro Yamada in Okada's *No-No Boy* and Stephen Nakane in Kogawa's *Obasan* express self-loathing through disavowing the ethnic eating habits in the face of state-sanctioned racism. In the hope of facing less discrimination and of gaining some acceptance by others, they embrace the dominant foodways. Sterling Lung, Louie's protagonist in *The Barbarians Are Coming*, chooses to cook and eat French in order to be disassociated from his Chinese and class background.

"We are what we eat" also bespeaks the truth that the one who eats is at one with what is eaten. In the Christian eucharist, communicants, by eating Christ's body and drinking his blood, discover themselves assimilated to the one whom they assimilate and recognize inwardly. In head-hunting cultures, with the belief in the existence of a material soul that resides in the head, the headhunter seeks, through decapitation of his enemies, to transfer this soul matter to himself and his community by eating his victims' organs. Li-Young Lee in "The Cleaving" becomes an American transcendentalist by eating/incorporating Emerson and his transparent eyeball. Turning inward into our multiple and sometimes competing selves, we understand that we eat (live on) our identities, for they actualize and sustain our selves. There would not be any self-recognition without the multiple identities we assume. Identities are to our social being what food is to our body. Without them, we do not exist.

As much as we eat identities, identities also eat us. Constructing and maintaining our identities, be they real or fake, consumes us, cuts us up as teeth cut food to be socially processed and metabolized. In psychoanalysis, self-recognition is inaugurated by a child's entry into the symbolic—a particular linguistic system metonymic of social and legal codifications—thus becoming a speaking subject. Coming into the self through language eats us up, because speaking and writing compete with eating. Deleuze and Guattari, in writing about Kafka, explicate,

> The mouth, tongue, and teeth find their primitive territoriality in food. In giving themselves over to the articulation of sounds, the mouth, tongue, and teeth deterritorialize. Thus, there is a certain disjunction between eating and speaking, and even more, despite all appearances, between eating and writing. Undoubtedly, one can write while eating more easily than one can speak while eating, but writing goes further in transforming words into things capable of competing with food. [...] To speak, and above all to write, is to fast. (19–20)

If food is the primitive or natural territory of the mouth, tongue, and teeth, words then can be said to invade and colonize this territory (deterritorialize). Language, symbolic of all norms, initiates us into the social, and by doing so, it regulates our eating and controls our enjoyment. The body parts that are biologically designed for processing food now must be heavily involved in uttering patterns of sounds that are institutionalized as our means of communication and our paths to identities. In light of the remarks by Deleuze and Guattari, we also understand that writing further alienates us from food, because writing transforms words into norms (e.g., beauty and health), rules (e.g., work schedules with fixed intervals between meals and coffee breaks), laws (e.g., food taboos), and codes (e.g., table manners), all of which suffocate appetite, vilify pleasure, suppress desire, and displace gratification. Hence, our identities produced by and productive of the symbolic order indeed devour and consume us.

Social norms are materials from which identities are made. Our racialized, gendered, classed, religious, and sexual-oriented selves are temporal and culturally specific precisely because of the normative power operating in our world. At the same time that we abide by norms, however, we experience the compulsion for and pleasure from nomadic or gypsy behaviors that interrupt and frustrate the daily workings of identities. Ruby Lee in Ng's *Eating Chinese Food Naked* refuses to settle for a fixed sexuality. Ng allegorizes Ruby's bisexual desire by describing her attraction to Chinese cooking as well as American dessert. Her mother's salted fish and sea bass in black bean sauce give her comfort, while apple turnovers and French crullers make her feel free. Her relish for both kinds of food suggests her enjoyment of both male and female lovers.

Recognizing that most of the time we conform to social norms, I believe what makes us truly human is our resistance to normalization. Some of us not only resist norms but also enjoy deviating from norms and exposing norms as arbitrary. Žižek in *On Belief* refers to a surreal scene in Spanish filmmaker Louis Buñuel's *Le fantôme de la liberté* (1974) "in which relations between eating and excreting are inverted: people sit at their toilets around the table, pleasantly talking, and when one of them wants to eat, he silently asks the housekeeper 'Where is that place, you know?' and sneaks away to a small room in the back" (60). Freud's thesis on the anal principle has a heyday in this scene. "[M]an does some really enjoyable things like relieving himself in the toilet, but nevertheless, we should not forget that he has to pay for this by the boring civilized ritual of eating" (Žižek 60). Given this inversion, it can be said that as we eat/consume identities so do we excrete/trash identities. What goes in must come out. It is precisely because of this dialectic between identity formation and identity deconstruction that human life is fraught not only with conflict but also with joy.

Notes

Introduction

1. Robert G. Lee in *Orientals: Asian Americans in Popular Culture* describes in detail the degrading portrayals of the Chinese in nineteenth- and twentieth-century American popular culture, particularly in chapter 1.

2. Amazon.com uses the first sentence to advertise this novel.

3. In *Mother Jones* (January/February 1997), Mukherjee declares, "I choose to describe myself on my own terms, as an American, rather than as an Asian-American. Why is it that hyphenation is imposed only on nonwhite Americans? Rejecting hyphenation is my refusal to categorize the cultural landscape into a center and its peripheries; it is to demand that the American nation deliver the promises of its dream and its Constitution to all its citizens equally." See http://www.motherjones.com/commentary/columns/1997/01/mukherjee.html.

4. "A close reader" might also suggest the connotation of "a closed reader."

Chapter 1: Enjoyment and Ethnic Identity in *No-No Boy* and *Obasan*

1. "Feminine" in Kristeva is not equivalent to "female." Toril Moi defines the "feminine" as a quality acquired through nurture, "female," through nature (108). Moi also points out that Kristeva flatly refuses to define "femininity," for the latter "prefers to see it as a *position*. If femininity can be said to have a definition at all in Kristevan terms, it is simply as 'that which is marginalized by the patriarchal symbolic order'" (Moi 111).

2. The Real is never some amorphous stuff that exists independent of some concrete, incarnate manner of living, even though social rules, roles, desires, and ideologies never can totally control it. It is through fantasy that attempts are made to fill the resistant hole in the social that enjoyment always forces to remain open. Individuals fantasize about living in such a way that both Kant and Sade can be obeyed. The universal imperatives of the law and the personal imperative to enjoy oneself are not met in this fantasized life of success, popularity, and joy. Communities fantasize about a utopian way of life in which social chaos and individual alienation are absent. Persons and communities often are unaware of the fantasies at work in their yearning for unity and peace, but they make them manifest through behavior patterns and the dreams of those sleeping and awake. Although constructed out of social and cultural materials, fantasies,

like the Real, are never simply part of the symbolic world. The desired ontological consistency of personal and communal identities, produced by fantasies bridging the gap between law and enjoyment, is only a fantasy, however. Tension always remains.

3. All male Japanese Americans over the age of seventeen were required to answer two questions: Are you willing to serve in the armed forces of the United States on combat duty wherever ordered? and Will you swear unqualified allegiance to the United States of America and faithfully defend the United States from any form of allegiance to the Japanese emperor, or any other foreign government, power, or organization?

4. Kristeva once defined the semiotic chora this way: "The chora is a womb or a nurse in which elements are without identity and without reason. The *chora* is a *place* of a *chaos* which *is* and which *becomes*, preliminary to the constitution of the first measurable body...the *chora* plays with the body of the mother—of woman—, but in the signifying process" (*Polylogue* 57; this is Kelly Oliver's translation in her *Reading Kristeva* 46).

5. Donna Gabaccia describes the eating habits of early immigrant communities as enclave eating (36–63). She cites the family eating habits of California-born Hiroshi Shikuma: "The family ate Japanese food exclusively—Japanese style rice [...] and fish [...]. Shikuma's mother prepared a wide range of familiar American vegetables Japanese style; the family also raised daikon and napa cabbage, which they viewed as 'Japanese vegetables'" (50). Although Gabaccia dates cross-cultural eating as taking place between the 1900s and 1940s, it is safe to presume that the Japanese immigrant community, facing more isolation than ever during World War II, practiced mainly enclave eating.

Chapter 2: Masculinity, Food, and Appetite in Frank Chin's *Donald Duk* and "The Eat and Run Midnight People"

1. Susan Koshy in "The Fiction of Asian American Literature" sees Chin's early works as a search for independence from white supremacy—an ethnic autonomy that "leads him to formulate such authenticity in purist and separatist terms" (476). Ironically, in the effort to "repudiate the prevailing stereotype of Asians as perpetual foreigners in America," Chin rejects "the Asian part of his identity" and affirms "the experiences of the many Asians in America [...] who are several generations removed from the homeland"—a formulation Koshy describes as an "obsession with the white gaze" (476).

2. Jennifer Ann Ho also centers on this novel's food references, which, she argues "form a system of communication that allows characters to speak to one another and convey messages" (29). In her analysis regarding the protagonist Donald's rite of passage, food stories play a positive role in constituting ethnic and gender pride.

3. See Cheung's "The Woman Warrior versus the Chinaman Pacific: Must a Chinese American Critic Choose between Feminism and Heroism?"

4. Michael Kimmel offers an analysis of the Black Panther Party that made manhood a centerpiece of its appeal (271–272).

5. Shawn Wong, for instance, in his 1996 novel *American Knees* successfully negotiates Chinese American and American masculinities to give his protagonist, Raymond

Ding, a sexy, sensitive, and secure yet vulnerable manhood. Interestingly, Wong, one of Chin's comrades in arms (co-editors of *Aiiieeeee!*) in the war against the humiliating representations of Asian American men in the popular culture, gains control of anger and bitterness. By virtue of that control, Wong's portrayal of the Chinese American character stops being reactionary to that humiliation but is truthful to many Chinese American men, whose gender identity is a daily negotiation among qualities of intelligence, kindness, sexual competence, aggression, and vulnerability.

6. The word "funny" in American culture sometimes signifies homosexuality and queerness. There is that famous scene in the film *Goodfellas* in which Tommy, played by Joe Pesci, confronts Henry Hill in a bar about what he means when he uses the word "funny." (I thank Fred Gardaphe for this connection.) *Funny Boy*, by the Asian Canadian writer Shyam Selvadurai, tells the story of a young Sri Lankan who prefers dressing up as a girl to playing cricket with his older brothers. (I thank David Eng for this connection.)

7. Traditionally speaking, men enjoy cooking when they get to perform for an audience. It is almost always the father, for instance, who carves the Thanksgiving turkey. When men cook, more often than not they make a great mess in the kitchen, and it is women who clean it up afterward. The quintessential national enjoyment of America is men's fanfare of outdoor cooking—flames and smoke with slabs of meat sizzling on the grill. One may think of *Emeril Live* as an American phenomenon of masculine performance. His popularity with men is precisely because of his disdain of (female associated) measurement, moderation, and health consciousness. "Kick it up another notch!" and "Pork fat rules!" are among his sound bites most endearing to the male audience. *The Iron Chef* is also a show about masculine, performative cooking, with its thrill generated by the language of battle.

8. Patricia Chu enters the thickets of *The Three Kingdoms* to highlight its deeply embedded patriarchy and its subordination of women even when they are warriors themselves (177–180). I find it revealing that Chin has such fervor for this classic tale and that he selectively borrows its male characters to be celebrated as mythical heroes in *Donald Duk*.

9. One may perceive my reference to *wen-wu* as an instance of ethnic overdeterminism. But the fact remains that Chin has repeatedly alluded to both *The Three Kingdoms* and *The Water Margin*, both of which are saturated with the *wen-wu* paradigm.

10. The reference Kam Louie makes is from oral and opera traditions in which Diao Chan, an extraordinary beauty, is presented as a gift to Guan Yu. "Instead of accepting her as the spoils of war," he "kills her with his sword" (28).

11. See chapter 42 of a complete translation of *The Water Margin* (e.g., Pearl Buck's *All Men Are Brothers* [754–775]). Chin's own act of disloyalty to Chinese classics makes a joke out of his attack on other Asian American writers for their revision of Chinese myths. He writes, for instance, "Kingston, Hwang, and Tan are the first writers of any race, and certainly the first writers of Asian ancestry, to so boldly fake the best-known

works from the most universally known body of Asian literature and lore in history" (*The Big Aiiieeeee!* 3).

12. I thank Jane Caputi for this insight.

13. Mary Daly presents a feminist reading of some ancient myths in her *Gyn/Ecology: The Metaethics of Radical Feminism* (1–107).

14. For a fascinating, feminist interpretation of ancient myths and religions, see Sjöö and Mor's *The Great Cosmic Mother.*

15. Marx himself has largely ignored domestic work in his analysis of labor and capital. For a feminist critique of Marx, see Juliet Mitchell's *Women's Estate.*

16. Thinly veiled beneath this mocking remark about memoir writing is the intertextuality with Chin's essay "Come All Ye Asian American Writers of the Real and the Fake!" where he castigates Maxine Hong Kingston for having written an autobiography, a genre he associates not only with Christian converts but also with females. Interestingly, Daisy Duk is a Christian (*Donald Duk* 163).

17. One may ask how well Frank Chin is versed in Confucianism and whether the connection with *wen-wu* is forced. To this I would answer that Confucianism so saturates literature, operas, oral traditions, and daily living that few people in China, Taiwan, Hong Kong, Singapore, and Chinatowns, other than Confucian scholars, read *The Analects.*

18. For details see Yiyan Wang's "Mr. Butterfly in *Defunct Capital:* 'Soft' Masculinity and (Mis)engendering China."

19. To achieve "nurture life" or *yang shen,* men are advised to have sex frequently with different partners and without ejaculation and even to "change partners midstream." Men are also advised to choose "childless young women, well-covered with flesh, as partners who offer particularly nourishing *jing* for male collection" (Farquhar 268).

20. This tradition teaches men the methods of producing female orgasm in order to collect and benefit from *jing* emitted by them. Such practice is famed to have ten benefits. "One arousal without orgasm makes the eyes and ears sharp and bright. Two and the voice is clear. Three and the skin is radiant. Four and the back and flanks are strong. Five and the buttocks and thighs become muscular. Six and the water course flows. Seven and the whole body becomes sturdy and strong. Eight and the pores glow. Nine and one achieves spiritual illumination. Ten and the whole body endures" (Wile 78).

21. Chin's particular choice of Lily as former Catholic nun is resonant with his condemnation of the Christian mission, which he describes in his introduction to *The Big Aiiieeeee!* and elsewhere as an instrument of yellow extinction.

22. The Chinese mythology of the Moon Lady, Chang E, has some affinity with the story of the Fall. Chang E stole the peach of immortality from her husband, and her punishment was her eternal loneliness on the Moon. I thank Cheng Lok Chua for this connection.

23. Mary Daly points out that Catholicism stole this cauldron symbol and made it the holy chalice (81–83).

Chapter 3: Class and Cuisine in David Wong Louie's *The Barbarians Are Coming*

1. Examples: John R. Hall, ed., *Reworking Class* (Ithaca: Cornell University Press, 1997); Beverley Skeggs, *Class, Self, Culture* (New York: Routledge, 2004); Rick Olin Wright, *Class Counts: Comparative Studies in Class Analysis* (New York: Cambridge University Press, 1997); Stanley Aronowitz, *How Class Works: Power and Social Movement;* Janet Zandy, *Hands: Physical Labor, Class, and Cultural Work,* and the collection she edited, *What We Hold in Common: An Introduction to Working-Class Studies.*

2. Almost from its beginning, Asian American literary study focused on the racial castration of Asian American males. In the 1970s, emulating African Americans, the Asian American movement adopted manhood as a master trope of protest against racial inequality. The editors of the first anthology of Asian American literature, *Aiiieeeee!* (1974), used race and masculinity to forge an Asian American solidarity in combat with mainstream culture. Two years later Maxine Hong Kingston published her memoir, *The Woman Warrior,* which engendered an Asian American feminist discourse. Kingston began the book with her mother's injunction for silence and her breaking of that silence. The silencing of Asian American women, therefore, became a new trope for the cultural condition of Asian Americans. In response to the success of a number of Asian American writers, particularly Kingston and Amy Tan, the editors of *Aiiieeeee!* produced a second edition that further heightened its potency by prefixing it with "big." *The Big Aiiieeeee!* (1991) decisively pitted the discourse of masculinity against that of feminism, a paper war still being waged. From this point on gender and race began to dominate the discussion in this field.

3. Such a textual organization by no means suggests that these two sets of issues are independent of each other.

4. Robert Perucci and Earl Wysong define "skill capital" as "the specialized knowledge that people accumulate through their work experience, training, or education. [...] Skilled capital is exchanged in a labor market, just as investment capital is used in connection with a financial market" (14).

5. See "Success Story of One Minority Group in U.S.," *U.S. News and World Report,* December 26, 1966: 73–76.

6. Professional jobs didn't exist for Asian Americans until the mid 1970s, when Asian immigration patterns changed.

7. Sau-ling Cynthia Wong postulates "two contrasting modes of existence and operation" in her discussion of Asian American literature: Necessity and Extravagance (*Reading Asian American Literature* 13). She elaborates that Necessity is "contained, survival-driven and conservation-minded," whereas Extravagance is "attracted to freedom, excess, emotional expressiveness, and autotelism" (13). Wong associates Necessity chiefly with the first generation of Asian immigrants and Extravagance with their American-born children. The latter's desire to belong leads to their attraction to the mainstream lifestyle as well as their shame over the parents'.

8. There are several stories of the wolf boy in the world. Benedictine monks told the story of the wolf boy of Hesse—a boy aged about seven or eight had been living with wolves since he was taken by them at the age of three. The dates are unclear, ranging from 1304 to 1744. In *Arcana Microcosmi* (1652), Alexander Ross gave an account of the wolf boy as well. Louie's allusion is most likely to Rudyard Kipling's novel *The Jungle Book* (1894–1895), which created the unforgettable character of the wolf boy Mowgli.

9. Zandy mentions several examples including Richard Wright's "I Have Seen Black Hands," Agnes Smedley's *Daughter of Earth,* Maxine Hong Kingston's *China Men,* and Tillie Olsen's *Yonnondio (Hands* 1).

10. In chapter 2 I made the case that food and women are interchangeable in the masculinist discourse of consumption and consummation.

11. The Page Law of 1875 prohibited the immigration of Asian women on the grounds of morality.

12. Sterling is an example of Chinese American men who find Chinese women undesirable. He thinks, "[I]n my heart every Chinese woman registers as an aunt, my mother, my sisters, or the Hong Kong girl whose picture my mother keeps taped to the kitchen mirror. They hold no romantic interest for me" (7).

13. See James H. Mittelman and Norani Othman, eds., *Capturing Globalization.*

Chapter 4: Diaspora, Transcendentalism, and Ethnic Gastronomy in the Works of Li-Young Lee

1. Apparent in Hall's theorization of the position of enunciation, "place" here has little relationship to physical locations. Rather, it is a semantic nexus from which one articulates unifying motifs or imageries, which in turn offer the ground for a self-representation. In Lee's case, the position of enunciation is more than a semantic one as food straddles the semantic and the semiotic in that it is both a system of representation (the symbolic) and *jouissance* (the semiotic). Therefore, it is more appropriate to describe this place in Lee's poetry as a semantic/semiotic nexus.

2. I'm referring to the Lacanian notion of the divided subject. Žižek aptly explains it in differentiation of the poststructuralist notion of the subject-position. He writes, "If we subtract all the richness of the different modes of subjectivation, all the fullness of experience present in the way the individuals are 'living' their subject-positions, what remains is an empty place which was filled out with this richness; this original void, this lack of symbolic structure, *is* the subject, the subject of the signifier. The *subject* is therefore to be strictly opposed to the effect of *subjectivation*: what the subjectivation masks is not a pre- or trans-subjective process of writing but a lack in the structure, a lack which is the subject" (*The Sublime Object of Ideology* 175).

3. See John Durham Peters, "Exile, Nomadism, and Diaspora" (23).

4. The ancient trade routes "stretched from China to the Atlantic, whose terminals were the Chinese and Roman Empires" (Miller 119). Before the European merchants began to travel to the East Indies, spices, silk, and other commodities reached Europe

via Byzantium and Venice. For the history of the ancient spice trade, see Miller, *The Spice Trade of the Roman Empire*.

5. For an account of the relationship between the East India Company and the opium trade, and its consequent wars between China and Europe, see Xu, "The Opium Trade and *Little Dorrit*."

6. What the townspeople might have seen on the Lees' back porch were probably eels. Two pages later, he recalls a scene in which his nanny in Jakarta chases and kills eels in the grass for that evening's soup.

7. See Timothy Yu in his "Form and Identity in Language Poetry and Asian American Poetry." He critiques David Mura's attempt at ethnic identification via commodified ethnic food signs.

8. One may argue that such aestheticizing of eating fish heads satisfies the mainstream reader's desire for the exotic. I think, however, it succeeds in crossing the threshold of the exotic to the other side of the gross, the shocking, and the abject. In American culture fish heads are often associated with poverty and punishment. Remember Americans' astonishment and outrage at the story that American POWs were fed fish-head soup in the Japanese camps.

9. Vendler's notion that "everything said in a poem was a metaphor for something in my inner life" advocates a humanistic universal identification (*Soul Says* 3). Vendler herself, however, would probably find it gross and hard to swallow that Lee writes about eating fish heads, their brains and eyeballs, with loving detail.

10. See Rob Wilson, *American Sublime: The Genealogy of a Poetic Genre*, for a Foucaultian interpretation of the American poetic tradition that offers an excellent examination of the ideological underpinnings of the American sublime.

11. In speaking of "the Jewish prohibition to fill out God's Name with a positive content," Žižek writes, "[P]re-Jewish, pagan gods belong to the Real: we gain access to them only through sacred *jouissance* (ritualistic orgies)." See his *Tarrying with the Negative* (190).

12. For a good reading of Lee's use of Song of Songs, see Hesford's "*The City in Which I Love You*: Li-Young Lee's Excellent Song."

13. On the strength of the horticultural history of persimmons in China, he deems "grafting" to be a more fitting term in describing Lee's cross-cultural poetics (Yao 20). Yao's convincing argument is anchored in a careful analysis as to how English language and poetics override Chinese in Lee's "Persimmons."

14. This strategy may further prove Yao's argument that Lee's knowledge of Chinese is so meager that English dominates the poetics of "Persimmons." He writes, "The poem offers the voyeuristic appeal of a seemingly intimate glimpse into Chinese culture, while at the same time compensating for any ignorance on the part of readers about Chinese language or cultural practices" (6).

15. Centered on this legend, there is an interesting intertextuality between two other Chinese American writers. In Maxine Hong Kingston, the words of revenge that

Yue Fei's mother tattooed on his back become transferred to the back of the female protagonist in "The White Tiger" of *The Woman Warrior.* Chin, embattled about ethnic authenticity, faults Kingston for feminizing the legendary figure and retells the legend to cement the Chinese heroic tradition (*Big Aiiieeeee!* 3). In *Donald Duk* Chin makes use of this legend in the context of food to cement the adolescent protagonist's ethnic and gender pride (140).

16. I use "impression" to indicate that Lee is fundamentally opposed to such a notion as ethnic authenticity. This will be made apparent near the end of my discussion.

17. Such as T. K. Seung, *Semiotics and Thematics in Hermeneutics* (189), and Terry Eagleton, *Literary Theory* (72), who interpret Gadamer's notion of fusion of horizons as expounding the impossible homogenization of incommensurate worlds of differences. David Hoy, however, points out that the background of a text or a reader is not a substance that can be fully fused together. See Hoy and McCarthy (188–200).

18. About Emerson's racism, see Cornell West, *The American Evasion of Philosophy* (29–35).

19. Jeffrey Partridge traces the original source of Emerson's racial remarks. "Emerson entered these comments on the Chinese in his private journal at the age of twenty during a period in which, as Robert D. Richardson Jr. describes, he was in a 'gloomy and petulant' mood (55). His information about the Chinese came from one secondary source, a book he had just read called *Journal of the Late Embassy to China*" (115). Partridge contextualizes Emerson's remark in the writing of his formative years that he revised or contradicted in his mature writing.

20. Lee uses "face" here repeatedly to make us hear an echo of the words "effaced and effacer" a few lines earlier (*City* 86).

Chapter 5: Sexuality, Colonialism, and Ethnicity in Monique Truong's *The Book of Salt* and Mei Ng's *Eating Chinese Food Naked*

1. I define "queer" in the last section of this chapter.

2. Gertrude Stein returned to America on a lecture tour in the summer of 1934.

3. I further elaborate on this in the last section of this chapter.

4. I use "displace" because the old object-choice can never be erased by replacement, for a new attachment is able only to make the loss tolerable.

5. Ho was a kitchen assistant at the Ritz in 1919 when he submitted the petition to the Paris Peace Conference for an independent Vietnam. See http://www.moreorless. au.com/heroes/ho.html for further biographical details.

6. See chapter 1 of *Ho Chi Minh: The Missing Years 1919–1941* by Sophie Quinn-Judge.

7. Ho lived in England between 1913 and 1917, and trained as a pastry chef under the legendary French master Escoffier at the Carlton Hotel in the Haymarket, Westminster. See http://en.wikipedia.org/wiki/Ho_Chi_Minh. Quinn-Judge refutes this particular detail while confirming that Ho worked in a kitchen in London. She writes, "[T]here is no

contemporary evidence that he worked as an assistant to Escoffier at the Carlton Hotel, as is claimed in the Tran Dan Tien book" (25).

8. Quinn-Judge documents that Ho shared living quarters with other compatriots "at 6 Villa des Gobelins" (20).

9. See http://www.vietquoc.com/0006vq.htm.

10. Ho's significance to Bình is made clear at the end of the novel. When Bình goes to the photographer to purchase the photograph of himself with Sweet Sunday Man, he discovers a picture of Ho hanging on the wall of the shop. He decides to buy Ho's photograph instead, for he admires him as "a traveler whose heart has wisely never left home" (247).

Epilogue

1. Horace Fletcher (1849–1919) was an American health-food faddist who initiated the discourse of health and mastication. He earned his nicknames The Great Masticator and The Chew-Chew Man by arguing that food should be chewed thirty two times—or about a hundred times per minute—before being swallowed. Fletcher and his followers even claimed that liquids, too, had to be chewed in order to be properly mixed with saliva. Fletcher advised against eating before being "good and hungry" or while angry or sad. He also advocated a low-protein diet as a means to health and well-being. He promoted his theories for decades on lecture circuits. Upton Sinclair, Henry James, and John D. Rockefeller were among those who gave the fad a try. Henry James and Mark Twain were house guests at his home in Venice.

Bibliography

Adams, Carol. *The Sexual Politics of Meat*. New York: Continuum, 1990.

Addams, Jane. *Democracy and Social Ethics*. New York: Macmillan, 1902.

Anderson, Benedict. *Imagined Communities*. London: Verso, 1991.

Aronowitz, Stanley. *How Class Works: Power and Social Movement*. New Haven: Yale University Press, 2003.

Ashley, Bob; Joanne Hollows; Steve Jones; and Ben Taylor. *Food and Cultural Studies*. London: Routledge, 2004.

Baxter, Janeen, and Mark Western. *Reconfigurations of Class and Gender*. Stanford: Stanford University Press, 2001.

Beauvoir, Simone de. *The Second Sex*. New York: Vintage, 1989.

Beck, Marianna. "Only Food." In *Eating Culture*, ed. Ron Scapp and Brian Seitz, 89–91. New York: State University of New York Press, 1998.

Bhabha, Homi K. *The Location of Culture*. New York: Routledge, 1994.

Bloom, Harold. *Agon*. New York: Oxford University Press, 1982.

Bourdieu, Pierre. *Distinction: A Social Critique of Judgment of Taste*. Trans. Richard Nice. Cambridge: Harvard University Press, 1984.

———. *The Logic of Practice*. Cambridge: Polity Press, 1990.

Buck, Pearl S. *All Men Are Brothers*. New York: Grove, 1937.

Butler, Judith. *Bodies That Matter: On the Discursive Limits of "Sex."* New York: Routledge, 1993.

Cacho, Lisa Marie. "Book Review: *Hunger, The Barbarians Are Coming*." *Journal of Asian American Studies* 3.3 (2000): 378–382.

Cao, Lan, and Himilce Novas. *Everything You Need to Know about Asian American History*. New York: Penguin, 1996.

Case, Sue-Ellen. "Tracking the Vampire." *Differences* 3.2 (1991): 1–20.

Cauti, Camille. "'Pass the Identity, Please': Culinary Passing in America." In *A Tavola: Food, Tradition, and Community among Italian Americans*, ed. Edvige Giunta and Samuel J. Patti, 10–19. Staten Island, N.Y.: Italian American Association, 1998.

Chan, Jachinson. *Chinese American Masculinities: From Fu Manchu to Bruce Lee.* New York: Routledge, 2001.

Chang, Iris. *The Chinese in America: A Narrative History.* New York: Viking, 2003.

Chen, Jack. *The Chinese of America.* New York: Harper and Row, 1980.

Chen, Jianguo. "'Cultural Difference' and Trans/national Identification—the Problematic of Contemporary Chinese Diaspora." In *Aspects of Diaspora,* ed. Lucie Bernier, 79–100. New York: Peter Lang, 2000.

Cheng, Anne Anlin. *The Melancholy of Race.* New York: Oxford University Press, 2000.

Cheung, King-kok. "The Woman Warrior versus the Chinaman Pacific: Must a Chinese American Critic Choose between Feminism and Heroism?" In *Asian American Studies: A Reader,* ed. Jean Yu-wen Shen Wu and Min Song, 307–323. New Brunswick: Rutgers University Press. 2000.

Chin, Frank. *The Chickencoop Chinaman.* In *The Chickencoop Chinaman/The Year of the Dragon,* 4–66. Seattle: University of Washington Press, 1981.

———. "Come All Ye Asian American Writers of the Real and the Fake!" In *The Big Aiiieeeee! An Anthology of Chinese American and Japanese American Literature,* ed. Jeffrey Paul Chan, Frank Chin, Lawson Fusao Inada, and Shawn Hsu Wong, 1–92. New York: Meridian, 1991.

———. *Donald Duk.* Minneapolis: Coffee House Press, 1991.

———. "The Eat and Run Midnight People." In *The Chinaman Pacific & Frisco R.R. Co.: Eight Short Stories by Frank Chin,* 8–23. Minneapolis: Coffee House Press, 1988.

———. "Railroad Standard Time." *The Chinaman Pacific & Frisco R.R. Co,* 1–7.

———. "Riding the Rails with Chickencoop Slim." *Greenfield Review* 6.1–2 (1977): 80–89.

———, and Jeffrey Paul Chan. "Racist Love." In *Seeing Through Shuck,* ed. Richard Kostelanetz, 65–79. New York: Ballantine, 1972.

Chiu, Monica. *Filthy Fiction: Asian American Literature by Women.* New York: Altamira Press, 2004.

Chu, Patricia P. *Assimilating Asians: Gendered Strategies of Authorship in Asian America.* Durham: Duke University Press, 2000.

Connell, R. W. *Masculinities.* Berkeley: University of California Press, 1995.

Counihan, Carol M. "An Anthropological View of Western Women's Prodigious Fasting: A Review Essay." In *Food and Gender: Identity and Power,* ed. Carol M. Counihan and Steven L. Kaplan, 99–123. Amsterdam: Hardwood Academic Publishers, 1998.

Curtin, Deane W., and Lisa M. Heldke, eds. *Cooking, Eating, Thinking: Transformative Philosophies of Food.* Bloomington: Indiana University Press, 1992.

Daly, Mary. *Gyn/Ecology: The Metaethics of Radical Feminism.* Boston: Beacon, 1990.

Dason, Shymala B. "All the Necessary Things." *Massachusetts Review* 45.3 (Autumn 2004): 229–240.

Davis, Carole Boyce. *Black Women, Writing, and Identity: Migrations of the Subject.* New York: Routledge, 1994.

Deleuze, Gilles, and Félix Guattari. *Kafka: Toward a Minor Literature.* Trans. Dana Polan. Minneapolis: University of Minnesota Press, 1986.

Douglas, Mary. *Purity and Danger: An Analysis of Concepts of Pollution and Taboo.* London: Routledge and Kegan Paul, 1966.

Eadie, Joe. "Activating Bisexuality: Towards a Bi/Sexual Politics." In *Activating Theory: Lesbian, Gay, Bisexual Politics,* ed. Joseph Bristow and Angela R. Wilson, 139–170. London: Lawrence and Wishart, 1993.

Eagleton, Terry. "Edible écriture." In *Consuming Passions,* ed. Sian Griffiths and Jennifer Wallace, 203–208. Manchester: Mandolin, 1998.

———. *Literary Theory.* Minneapolis: University of Minnesota Press, 1983.

Ellison, Ralph. *Invisible Man.* New York: Vintage-Random, 1995.

Eng, David L. *Racial Castration: Managing Masculinity in Asian America.* Durham: Duke University Press, 2001.

Engles, Tim. "Lee's 'Persimmons.'" *Explicator* 54.3 (1996 Spring): 191–192.

Fanon, Frantz. *Black Skin, White Masks.* New York: Grove Press, 1967.

———. *The Wretched of the Earth.* Trans. Constance Farrington. New York: Grove Weidenfeld, 1963.

Farquhar, Judith. *Appetites: Food and Sex in Postsocialist China.* Durham: Duke University Press, 2002.

Fischler, Claude. "Food, Self and Identity." *Social Science Information* 27.2 (1988): 275–292.

Forson, Psyche A. William. "Perspectives in Material Culture: Make Room for Food Studies." *American Studies Association Newsletter,* June 2000: 19–20.

Foucault, Michel. "Sexual Choice, Sexual Act." In *Michel Foucault: Ethics, Subjectivity, and Truth. Essential Works of Foucault,* ed. Paul Rabinow, 1:141–156. New York: New Press, 1997.

Freud, Sigmund. "Mourning and Melancholia." In *The Standard Edition of the Complete Psychological Works of Sigmund Freud,* trans. James Strachey, 239–260. London: Hogarth, 1955.

Fung, Eileen Chia-Ching. "'To Eat the Flesh of His Dead Mother': Hunger, Masculinity, and Nationalism in Frank Chin's Donald Duk." *LIT: Literature, Interpretation, Theory* 10 (1999): 255–274.

Fung, Richard. "Looking for My Penis." In *Queer in Asian America,* ed. David L. Eng and Alice Y. Hom, 115–134. Philadelphia: Temple University Press, 1998.

Gabaccia, Donna R. *We Are What We Eat: Ethnic Food and the Making of Americans.* Cambridge: Harvard University Press, 1998.

Gadamer, Hans-Georg. *Truth and Method.* New York: Continuum, 1975.

Georges, Robert A. "You Often Eat What Others Think You Are: Food as an Index of Other's Conceptions of Who One Is." *Western Folklore* 43.4 (October 1984): 249–255.

Goldstein-Shirley, David. "'The Dragon Is a Lantern': Frank Chin's Counter-Hegemonic *Donald Duk.*" *49th Parallel* 6:1–11.

Gribben, Bryn. "The Mother That Won't Reflect Back: Situating Psychoanalysis and the Japanese Mother in *No-No Boy.*" *MELUS* 28.2 (Summer 2003): 31–46.

Hall, Donald E. *Queer Theories.* New York: Palgrave, 2003.

Hall, Stuart. "Cultural Identity and Diaspora." In *Colonial Discourse and Post-Colonial Theory: A Reader,* ed. Patrick Williams and Laura Chrisman, 392–403. New York: Columbia University Press, 1994.

———. "The Spectacle of the 'Other.'" In *Representation: Cultural Representations and Signifying Practices,* ed. Stuart Hall, 223–290. London: Sage, 1997.

Hawley, John C. "Gus Lee, Chang-Rae Lee, and Li-Young Lee: The Search for the Father in Asian American Literature." In *Ideas of Home: Literature of Asian Migration,* ed. Geoffrey Kain, 183–195. East Lansing: Michigan State University Press, 1997.

Heidegger, Martin. "The Origin of a Work of Art." In *Poetry, Language, Thought,* trans. Albert Hofstadter, 17–87. New York: Harper and Row, 1971.

Heldke, Lisa. *Exotic Appetites: Ruminations of a Food Adventurer.* New York: Routledge, 2003.

Hesford, Walter A. "*The City in Which I Love You:* Li-Young Lee's Excellent Song." *Christianity and Literature* 46.1 (Autumn 1996): 37–60.

Hirose, Stacey Yukari. "David Wong Louie." In *Words Matter: Conversations with Asian American Writers,* ed. King-kok Cheung, 189–213. Honolulu: University of Hawai'i Press, 2000.

Ho, Jennifer Ann. *Consumption and Identity in Asian American Coming-of-Age Novels.* New York: Routledge, 2005.

Hooks, Bell. *Black Looks: Race and Representation.* Boston: South End Press, 1992.

Hoy, David Cousens, and Thomas McCarthy. *Critical Theory.* Cambridge: Blackwell, 1994.

Huang, Yibing. "Li-Young Lee's *The Winged Seed: A Remembrance.*" *Amerasia Journal* 24.2 (1998): 189–191.

Jameson, Fredric. *The Political Unconscious.* Ithaca: Cornell University Press, 1981.

Jen, Gish. *Typical American.* New York: Penguin, 1991.

Kim, Daniel Y. "The Strange Love of Frank Chin." In *Q & A: Queer in Asian America,* ed. David L. Eng and Alice Y. Hom, 270–303. Philadelphia: Temple University Press, 1998.

Kimmel, Michael. *Manhood in America.* New York: Free Press, 1996.

Kingston, Maxine Hong. *The Woman Warrior: Memoirs of a Girlhood among Ghosts.* New York: Vintage, 1989.

Kitchen, Judith. "Li-Young Lee's *The City in Which I Love You.*" *Georgia Review* 45 (Spring 1991): 154–169.

Kogawa, Joy. *Obasan*. New York: Anchor, 1982.

Koshy, Susan. "The Fiction of Asian American Literature." In *Asian American Studies: A Reader,* ed. Jean Yu-wen Shen Wu and Min Song, 467–495. New Brunswick: Rutgers University Press, 2000.

Kristeva, Julia. *Polylogue*. Paris: Seuil, 1977.

———. *Powers of Horror, an Essay on Abjection*. Trans. Leon S. Roudiez. New York: Columbia University Press, 1982.

Kwong, Peter. "Asian Americans Need Class Analysis." In *Privileging Positions: The Sites of Asian American Studies*, ed. Gary Y. Okihiro et al., 75–81. Pullman: Washington State University Press, 1995.

Lacan, Jacques. *Ecrits: A Selection*. Trans. Alan Sheridan. New York: Norton, 1977.

Lahiri, Jhumpa. *The Namesake*. New York: Houghton Mifflin, 2003.

Lau, D. C., trans. *Confucius: The Analects*. London: Penguin Books, 1979.

Lee, Chang-Rae. *Native Speaker*. New York: Riverhead Books, 1995.

Lee, James Kyung-Jin. "Li-Young Lee." In *Words Matter: Conversations with Asian American Writers,* ed. King-Kok Cheung, 270–280. Honolulu: University of Hawai'i Press, 2000.

Lee, Li-Young. *Book of My Nights*. Rochester: Boa Edition, 2001.

———. *The City in Which I Love You*. Rochester: Boa Edition, 1990.

———. *Rose*. Rochester: Boa Edition, 1986.

———. *The Winged Seed: A Remembrance*. Saint Paul: Hungry Mind Press, 1995.

Lee, Robert, G. *Orientals: Asian Americans in Popular Culture*. Philadelphia: Temple University Press, 1999.

Leich, Vincent. "Theory Ends." In *Profession 2005,* ed. Rosemary G. Feal, 122–128. New York: Modern Language Association of America, 2005.

Levenkron, Steven. *Cutting: Understanding and Overcoming Self-Mutilation*. New York: Norton, 1998.

Levinas, Emmanuel. *Outside the Subject*. Trans. Michael B. Smith. Stanford: Stanford University Press, 1994.

Levy, Andrea. *Fruit of the Lemon*. London: Review, 1999.

Lim, Shirley Geok-lin. "Identifying Foods, Identifying Selves." *Massachusetts Review* 45.3 (Autumn 2004): 297–306.

Lin, Yutang. *My Country and My People*. New York: Reynal and Hitchcock, 1935.

Ling, Jinqi. *Narrating Nationalisms: Ideology and Form in Asian American Literature*. New York: Oxford University Press, 1998.

———. "Race, Power, and Cultural Politics in John Okada's *No-No Boy*." *American Literature* 67.2 (June 1995): 359–381.

Louie, David Wong. *The Barbarians Are Coming*. New York: Berkley Books, 2000.

———. *Pangs of Love*. New York: Knopf, 1991.

Louie, Kam. *Theorising Chinese Masculinity: Society and Gender in China*. Cambridge: University of Cambridge Press, 2002.

Lowe, Lisa. *Immigrant Acts: On Asian American Cultural Politics.* Durham: Duke University Press, 1996.

Lukanuski, Mary. "A Place at the Counter: The Onus of Oneness." In *Eating Culture,* ed. Ron Scapp and Brian Seitz, 112–120. New York: State University of New York Press, 1993.

Lupton, Deborah. *Food, the Body, and the Self.* London: Sage, 1996.

Mannur, Anita. "Culinary Fictions: Immigrant Foodways and Race in Indian American Literature." In *Asian American Studies after Critical Mass,* ed. Ken A. Ono, 56–70. New York: Blackwell, 2004.

———. "Food Matters: An Introduction." *Massachusetts Review* 45.3 (Autumn 2004): 209–215.

———. "Model Minority Can Cook: Fusion Cuisine in Asian America." In *East Main Street: Asian American Popular Culture,* ed. Shilpa Dave, 72–94. New York: New York University Press, 2005.

Marable, Manning. *How Capitalism Underdeveloped Black America.* Cambridge: South End Press, 2000.

Marshall, Tod. "To Witness the Invisible: A Talk with Li-Young Lee." *Kenyon Review* 22.1 (Winter 2000): 129–147.

McDonald, Dorothy Ritsuko. "Introduction." In Frank Chin, *The Chickencoop Chinamen/ The Year of the Dragon,* ix–xxix. Seattle: University of Washington Press, 1981.

Miller, J. Innes. *The Spice Trade of the Roman Empire.* New York: Oxford at the Clarendon Press, 1969.

Milton, Giles. *Nathaniel's Nutmeg.* New York: Penguin, 1999.

Mitchell, Juliet. *Women's Estate.* New York: Pantheon Books, 1971.

Mittelman, James H., and Norani Othman, eds. *Capturing Globalization.* London: Routledge, 2001.

Moberg, Mark, and J. Stephen Thomas. "Class Segmentation and Divided Labor: Asian Workers in the Gulf of Mexico Seafood Industry." In *Asians in America: The Peoples of East, Southeast, and South Asia in American Life and Culture,* ed. Franklin Ng, 43–55. New York: Garland, 1998.

Moeser, Daniel. "Lee's 'Eating Alone.'" *Explicator* 60.2 (Winter 2002): 117–119.

Moi, Toril. "Feminist, Female, Feminine." In *The Feminist Reader: Essays in Gender and the Politics of Literary Criticism,* ed. Catherine Belsey and Jane Moore, 104–116. Malden: Blackwell, 1997.

Moyers, Bill. *The Language of Life: A Festival of Poets.* New York: Doubleday, 1995.

Naylor, Gloria. *Mama Day.* New York: Vintage, 1993.

Neumann, Erich. *The Great Mother: An Analysis of the Archetype.* Trans. Ralph Manheim. Princeton: Princeton University Press, 1972.

Ng, Fae Myenne. *Bone.* New York: Hyperion, 1993.

Ng, Mei. *Eating Chinese Food Naked.* New York: Scribner, 1998.

Nguyen, Lan N. "The Ming Attraction." *A. Magazine: Inside Asian America*, February–March 2001: 30–33.

Nguyen, Viet Thah. "The Remasculinization of Chinese America: Race, Violence, and the Novel." *American Literary History* 12.1–2 (2000): 130–157.

Okada, John. *No-No Boy.* Seattle: University of Washington Press, 1976.

Oliver, Kelly. *Reading Kristeva.* Bloomington: Indiana University Press, 1993.

Ozeki, Ruth L. *My Year of Meats.* New York: Penguin, 1999.

Partridge, Jeffrey F. L. "The Politics of Ethnic Authorship: Li-Young Lee, Emerson, and Whitman at the Banquet Table." *Studies in the Literary Imagination* 37.1 (Spring 2004): 101–125.

Perrucci, Robert, and Earl Wysong. *The New Class Society: Goodbye American Dream?* New York: Rowman and Littlefield, 2003.

Peters, John Durham. "Exile, Nomadism, and Diaspora: The Stakes of Mobility in the Western Canon." In *Home, Exile, Homeland: Film, Media, and the Politics of Place,* ed. Hamid Naficy, 17–41. New York: Routledge, 1999.

Potter, Robin. "Moral—in Whose Sense? Joy Kogawa's *Obasan* and Julia Kristeva's *Powers of Horror.*" *Studies in Canadian Literature* 15.1 (1990): 117–139.

Quinn-Judge, Sophie. *Ho Chi Minh: The Missing Years 1919–1941.* Berkeley: University of California Press, 2002.

Raussert, Wilfried. "Minority Discourse, Foodways, and Aspects of Gender: Contemporary Writings by Asian-American Women." *Journal x: A Journal in Culture and Criticism* 7.2 (2003 Spring): 183–204.

Reiter, Ester. *Making Fast Food: From the Frying Pan into the Fryer.* Montreal: McGill-Queen's University Press, 1991.

Ruark, Jennifer K. "A Place at the Table." *Chronicle of Higher Education,* July 9, 1999: A17.

Ruf, Henry L. *Postmodern Rationality, Social Criticism, and Religion.* St. Paul: Paragon House, 2005.

Rushdie, Salman. *Imaginary Homelands: Essays and Criticism 1981–1991.* London: Granta Books, 1991.

Rust, Paula C. "Sexual Identity and Bisexual Identities: The Struggle for Self-Description in a Changing Sexual Landscape." In *Queer Studies: A Lesbian, Gay, Bisexual, and Transgender Anthology,* ed. Brett Beemyn and Mickey Eliason, 64–86. New York: New York University Press, 1996.

Said, Edward. *The Edward Said Reader.* Ed. Moustafa Bayoumi and Andrew Rubin. New York: Vintage, 2000.

———. "The Mind in Winter: Reflections on Life in Exile." *Harper's* 269 (September 1984): 49–55.

———. *Orientalism.* New York: Vintage, 1979.

Santora, Marc. "East Meets West, Adding Pounds and Peril." *New York Times.* January 12,

2006. http://www.nytimes.com/2006/01/12/nyregion/nyregionspecial5/12diabetes.html?

Savage, Mike. *Class Analysis and Social Transformation*. Buckingham: Open University Press, 2000.

Sedgewick, Eve Kosofsky. *Tendencies*. Durham: Duke University Press, 1993.

Selvadurai, Shyam. *Funny Boy*. New York: Penguin Books, 1994.

Sen, Sharmila. "Looking for Doubles in the Caribbean." *Massachusetts Review* 45.3 (Autumn 2004): 241–257.

Seung, T.E. *Semiotics and Thematics in Hermeneutics*. New York: Columbia University Press, 1982.

Sjöö, Monica, and Barbara Mor. *The Great Cosmic Mother: Rediscovering the Religion of the Earth*. New York: Harper Collins, 1991.

Stein, Gertrude. *Everybody's Autobiography*. New York: Cooper Square Publishers, 1971.

Symons, Michael. *One Continuous Picnic: A History of Eating in Australia*. Ringwood, Victoria: Penguin, 1984.

Toklas, Alice B. *The Alice B. Toklas Cook Book*. New York: Harper and Brothers, 1954.

Tourino, Christina. "Ethnic Reproduction and the Amniotic Deep: Joy Kogawa's *Obasan*." *Frontiers: A Journal of Women Studies* 24.1 (2003): 134–153.

Truong, Monique. *The Book of Salt*. New York: Houghton Mifflin, 2003.

Van Gulik, R.H. *Sexual Life in Ancient China*. Leiden: E.J. Brill, 1961.

Vendler, Helen. *Part of Nature, Part of Us: Modern American Poets*. Cambridge: Harvard University Press, 1980.

———. "Poetry for the People." *New York Times Book Review*, June 18, 1995: 14–15.

———. *Soul Says: On Recent Poetry*. Cambridge: Harvard University Press, 1995.

Waller, Nicole. "Past and Repast: Food as Historiography in Fae Myenne Ng's *Bone* and Frank Chin's *Donald Duk*." *Amerikastudien/American Studies* 40.3 (1996): 485–502.

Wang, Yiyan. "Mr. Butterfly in *Defunct Capital*: 'Soft' Masculinity and (Mis)engendering China." In *Asian Masculinities: The Meaning and Practice of Manhood in China and Japan*, ed. Kam Louie and Morris Low, 41–58. New York: Routledge, 2003.

Waters, Lindsay. "Literary Aesthetics: The Very Idea." *Chronicle Review*, December 15, 2005: B6–B9.

West, Cornell. *The American Evasion of Philosophy*. Madison: The University of Wisconsin Press, 1989.

Wile, Douglas. *Art of the Bedchamber: The Chinese Sexual Yoga Classics, including Women's Solo Meditation Texts*. Albany: State University of New York Press, 1992.

Wilson, Rob. *American Sublime: The Genealogy of a Poetic Genre*. Madison: The University of Wisconsin Press, 1991.

Witt, Doris. *Black Hunger: Food and the Politics of U.S. Identity*. New York: Oxford University Press, 1999.

———. "Soul Food: Where the Chitterling Hits the (Primal) Pan." In *Eating Culture,* ed. Ron Scapp and Brian Seitz, 258–287. New York: State University of New York Pess, 1998.

Wong, Sau-ling Cynthia. "Chinese/Asian American Men in the 1990s: Displacement, Impersonation, Paternity, and Extinction in David Wong Louie's *Pangs of Love.*" In *Privileging Positions: The Sites of Asian American Studies,* ed. Gary Y. Okihiro et al., 181–191. Pullman: Washington State University Press, 1995.

———. Reading Asian American Literature: From Necessity to *Extravagance.* Princeton: Princeton University Press, 1993.

Wong, Shawn. *American Knees.* New York: Simon and Schuster, 1995.

Wu, Jean Yu-wen Sheng, and Min Song, eds. *Asian American Studies: A Reader.* New Brunswick: Rutgers University Press, 2000.

Xu, Wenying. "Making Use of European Theory in the Teaching of Multicultural Literature." *Modern Language Studies* 24.4 (Fall 1996): 47–58.

———. "The Opium Trade and *Little Dorrit:* A Case of Reading Silences." *Victorian Literature and Culture* 25 (1996): 53–66.

Yao, Steven G. "The Precision of Persimmons: Hybridity, Grafting and the Case of Li-Young Lee." *LIT: Literature, Interpretation, Theory* 12 (2001): 1–23.

Yogi, Stan. "The Collapse of Difference: Dysfunctional and Inverted Celebrations in John Okada's *No-No Boy.*" *Revue Française d' Etudes Americaines* 52 (August 1992): 233–244.

Yu, Timothy. "Form and Identity in Language Poetry and Asian American Poetry." *Contemporary Literature* 41.1 (Spring 2000): 422–461.

Zandy, Janet. *Hands: Physical Labor, Class, and Cultural Work.* New Brunswick: Rutgers University Press, 2004.

———, ed. *What We Hold in Common: An Introduction to Working-Class Studies.* New York: Feminist Press, 2001.

Zhou, Xiaojing. "Inheritance and Invention in Li-Young Lee's Poetry." *MELUS* 21.1 (Spring 1996): 113–133.

———. " 'Your otherness is perfect as my death': The Ethics and Aesthetics of Li-Young Lee's Poetry." In *Textual Ethos Studies or Locating Ethics,* ed. Anna Fahraeus and AnnKatrin Jonsson, 297–314. Amsterdam: Rodopi, 2005.

Ziff, Larzer, ed. *Ralph Waldo Emerson: Selected Essays.* New York: Penguin, 1982.

Žižek, Slavoj. *Looking Awry.* Cambridge: MIT Press, 1992.

———. *On Belief.* London: Routledge, 2001.

———. *The Sublime Object of Ideology.* New York: Verso, 1989.

———.*Tarrying with the Negative: Kant, Hegel, and the Critique of Ideology.* Durham: Duke University Press 1993.

Index

abjection, 20, 23, 102; self-, 19, 139, 143
Adams, Carol, 49
Addams, Jane, 77
agency, 52, 140–141, 143
alienation, 39, 67, 73–74, 90, 93, 103, 110;
    self-, 67, 71, 75–76
ambivalence: toward ethnicity in *No-No*
    Boy, 24–25; toward the female body in
    Donald Duk, 60
American Dream, the, 14, 63, 71, 86–87, 93
American sublime, the, 112–113
Analects, The, 53
Anderson, Benedict, 3
appetite, 4, 43, 47–48, 53–56, 122;
    disciplined, 53; indiscriminate, 53, 61;
    and sexuality, 15, 55; undisciplined,
    47, 48, 53
Asian American fatherhood, 88–90
assimilation, 9, 21, 26–27, 40, 89, 93, 121;
    American, 24–25; discourse of, 75;
    gustatory, 70; ideology of, 43, 65, 66,
    74, 106
Astaire, Fred, 41, 43, 45

Beauvoir, Simone de, 160
Bhabha, Homi, 129, 139
bisexuality, 127, 151, 158–160. *See also*
    sexuality
Bloom, Harold, 112
body, 31, 114, 119, 126, 168; consumption
    of female, 54, 56; female, 59–60; male,

54–55, 59; mind and, 4, 120; of the
    mother, 172n. 4; politic, 42; racialized,
    141; sexual, 141
Bourdieu, Pierre, 5, 67
Brillat-Savarin, Jean Anthelme, 167
Buck, Pearl, 48, 173n. 11
Buddhism, in *No-No Boy* and *Obasan,* 36
Buñuel, Louis, *Le fantôme de la liberté,* 169
Butler, Judith, 161

capital, 7, 51, 63, 66, 175n. 4
capitalism, 6–7, 66, 74, 85; global, 7, 75,
    93; transnational, 150–151
Case, Sue-Ellen, 158
Cauti, Camille, 40
Chan, Jachinson, 38
Chang E (the Moon Lady), 174n. 22
Chen, Jack, 10–11
Cheng, Anne Anlin, 43, 44, 65, 69, 137
Cheung, King-kok, 38
Chin, Frank, 15, 37–39; *The Big Aiiieeeee!*
    53, 173n. 11, 175n. 2, 177n. 15; *The*
    Chickencoop Chinaman, 37, 54, 57,
    89; "Come All Ye Asian American
    Writers of the Real and the Fake!" 37,
    53; *Donald Duk,* 15, 37–61; "The Eat
    and Run Midnight People," 15, 38, 49,
    53–61; "Racist Love," 37; "Railroad
    Standard Time," 55; "Riding the Rails
    with Chickencoop Slim," 47
Chinese *ars erotica,* 55, 60

Chiu, Monica, 14, 65
chop suey, 11
Christianity, 49, 110–111
Chu, Patricia, 173n. 8
class, 15–16, 52–53, 61–66, 73, 134;
    analysis, 62–63, 175n. 1; anxiety, 70,
    166; aspiration, 15, 69, 72; conflict,
    63, 66; consciousness, 64, 68, 71; envy,
    69, 86; exploitation, 85; food and,
    6–7; identification, 64; ideology, 65;
    oppression, 62, 86; position, 61, 64,
    71, 77, 86, 148–150, 165; preference,
    65; privileges, 84; solidarity, 85;
    struggle, 64, 71; system, 68;
    unconsciousness, 68, 81, 86; working,
    5, 64, 82–83, 87, 93
colonialism, 39, 96–98, 139, 141, 147, 159;
    cultural food, 9
communal bathing, in Obasan, 30–31
community, 18–21, 36, 101, 104–105; Asian
    American, 42, 63, 93; Chinese, 79, 94;
    ethnic, 24–27; food and, 3–4; Japanese
    American, 21, 31
Confucianism, 53, 114, 174n. 17. See also
    Analects, The; Spring and Autumn
    Annals
Connell, Robert, 38
Counihan, Carol, 55
culinary: desires, 26, 167; multiculturalism,
    9; nationalism, 5; passing, 40
culturally estranged, the, 40
Curb Your Enthusiasm, 8
Curtin, Deane, 4
cutter, 141–143

Daly, Mary, 174nn. 13, 23
Davis, Carol Boyce, 101
Deleuze, Gilles, 168
desiring subject, 129, 135, 159, 161
desiring subjectivity, 126–127
diaspora, 93, 95–98, 110; Chinese, 101
diasporic Asia, 92–93
dietary accusation against Asians, 8

displacement, 90, 97, 100–101, 103,
    104–106, 119; linguistic, 118
Douglas, Mary, 102
dream motif, in Obasan, 28, 30, 32–34
dream scenarios, in Donald Duk, 41–42, 48

Eadie, Joe, 158
Eagleton, Terry, 3, 178n. 17
Ellison, Ralph, Invisible Man, 6
emasculation, 15, 54, 62, 81, 84, 91; racial,
    62, 86
Emeril Live, 82, 173n. 7
Emerson, Ralph Waldo, 94, 111–113, 168,
    178n. 19
enclave eating, 26, 172n. 5
Eng, David, 41, 141, 173n. 19
Engles, Tim, 118
enjoyment, 3, 19–21, 25, 27, 29–31; ethnic,
    36. See also jouissance
eroticism, 106, 117, 135; homo-, 143
ethnic exoticism, 75
ethnic identity, 19, 21, 50, 81, 101, 118,
    124; disavowal of, 72, 93, 114, 126
eucharist, 167–168
exile, 94–96, 98–101, 104–111, 140–147;
    aesthetics of the, 105, 147; internal,
    96; self-, 70
exilic intellectual, 96–97

Fanon, Frantz, 39–40, 133
Farquhar, Judith, 55, 174n. 19
fear of female power, 59–60
femininity, 5, 20, 24, 83, 171n. 1
feminization, 43, 84
Ferguson, Pricilla Parkhurst, 162
filth, 6–7, 20, 33–34, 65, 102
Fischler, Claude, 2, 59, 102, 122
Fletcher, Horace, 163, 179n. 1
food: and Asian Americans, 10–12; and
    eroticism, 129–131, 135–136; and
    identity, 2–7, 14; studies, 2, 162–163;
    taboo in Eating Chinese Food Naked, 153
Forson, Psyche A. William, 162

Levinas, Emmanuel, 125
Levy, Andrea, *Fruit of the Lemon*, 165–166
liao zhai zhi yi, 60–61
Lim, Shirley Geok-lin, 5
Lin, Yutang, 19
Ling, Jinqi, 24, 38, 62
literary reading (close reading), 16–17
Lot's wife, 104
Louie, David Wong: *The Barbarians Are Coming*, 15, 62–93, 149, 167; *Pangs of Love*, 89–90
Louie, Kam, 46, 53, 173n. 10
Lowe, Lisa, 7, 66
Lukanuski, Mary, 3, 4
Lupton, Deborah, 4, 5, 34, 37

male cannibalism, 49
male hysteria, 141–142
manhood, 35, 39, 83; Asian American, 15, 38–40 passim, 47, 57; black, 20; Chinese American, 37, 38; white, 41. *See also* masculinity
Mannur, Anita, 9, 14, 16, 26
Marable, Manning, 6–7
masculinity, 36–39, 45, 48, 53, 57, 82–83; Asian American, 15, 39, 54, 175n. 2; Confucian, 54; contained, 47; hegemonic masculinity, 38, 39, 85; normative, 54; property-based, 85; soft, 53. *See also* manhood
masochism, 71, 86, 140
maternal, the, 14, 19, 20–36, 49, 81
melancholia, 43, 62, 71, 133, 137–139, 143
metaphysics, 110, 114, 124
Milton, Giles, 98
mirror stage, the, 23
Moberg, Mark, 12
model minority, 7, 9, 63, 64, 89
Moeser, Daniel, 107
monkey-brain feast, in *The Woman Warrior*, 13
monosexual identity, 158–159
Mor, Barbara, 49

Mother Goddess, 49
Mukherjee, Bharati, 15, 171n. 3

national ideal, the, 65–66
Naylor, Gloria, *Mama Day*, 164–165
Neumann, Erich, 59
Ng, Mei, *Eating Chinese Food Naked*, 16, 127, 147–157, 160–161, 169
Nguyen, Viet Thah, 42, 57
nostalgia, 96, 104, 147

Okada, John, *No-No Boy*, 14, 21–30, 35–36
Oliver, Kelly, 19, 172n. 4
Opium War, the, 2
orality, 121, 123
Ozeki, Ruth L., *My Year of Meats*, 141

patriarchal religion, 49
patriarchy, 39, 60, 61, 139, 159
Partridge, Jeffrey, 14, 103, 108, 123, 178n. 19
Peters, John Durham, 95–96
pigeons, in *Book of Salt*, 143–145
ponytail, the, in *The Barbarians Are Coming*, 83–84
Potter, Robin, 30
Puck, Wolfgang, 8–9

queer, 127, 157–161
queerness, 132, 135, 154, 155, 173n. 6

Real, the, 19, 22, 30–31, 34, 114, 123, 171n. 2
repression, 28, 29, 32, 35
Ruf, Henry, 114
Rushdie, Salman, 104
Rust, Paula, 158

Said, Edward, 96, 99–100, 101
salt, 79, 104–105
Savage, Mike, 64
scholar-and-beauty romance, 54,
Sedgewick, Eve Kosofsky, 158

self-loathing, 26, 39, 40, 41, 76, 78
self-mutilation, 143. *See also* cutter
Selvadurai, Shyam, *Funny Boy*, 173n. 6
semiotic, the, 19–21, 25, 30, 33–35, 114, 172n. 4, 176n. 1
sex and food, 56
sexuality, 24, 127, 129, 148, 158, 159, 161; and consumption, 49; appetite and, 55; food and, 135, 152; male, 59. *See also* bisexuality; heterosexuality
sexual metabolism, 56–57
Sjöö, Monica, 49
Social Darwinism, 77
Song of Songs, 97, 117
soul food, 6, 7, 20
spice trade, 98
Spring and Autumn Annals, 53
Stein, Gertrude, 128–129
stone bread, in *Obasan*, 28–29
sublime, the, 112–113
Symbolic, the, 20–36, 114, 123, 168

Tan, Amy, *The Joy Luck Club*, 101
Thanksgiving, 70–71
Thomas, J. Stephen, 12
Three Kingdoms, The, 42, 46, 173n. 8
Toklas, Alice, 128–129
Tourino, Christina, 31, 32
trains as male violence and virility, in "Eat and Run", 57–59

transcendentalism, 94, 95, 110, 123, 124
Truong, Monique, *The Book of Salt*, 16, 127–147, 159–150
Tsai, Ming, 9–10

Van Gulik, R. H., 55
Vendler, Helen, 108, 109, 112, 126, 177n. 9
violence and sex, 38, 49, 57–59, 61, 86, 131

Water Margin, The, 46, 47, 173n. 11
Waters, Lindsay, 16, 17
wen-wu, 46, 54, 173n. 9, 174n. 17
Wile, Douglas, 174n. 20
Wilson, Rob, 112, 113, 126
Witt, Doris, 6, 20, 167
Wong, Sau-ling Cynthia, 26, 90, 124, 175n. 7
Wong, Shawn, *American Knees*, 172n. 5

Yao, Steven, 111, 114, 116–119, 177n. 13
Yogi, Stan, 27
Yue Fei, 121, 177n. 15

Zandy, Janet, 83, 175n. 1, 176n. 9. See also *Hands: Physical Labor, Class, and Cultural Work*
Zhou, Xiaojing, 111, 125
Žižek, Slavoj, 3, 19–25, 30, 36, 114, 142, 169, 176n. 2, 177n. 11

About the Author

Wenying Xu is associate professor of English at Florida Atlantic University. She received her Ph.D. from the University of Pittsburgh in 1994. She is the author of *Ethics and Aesthetics of Freedom in American and Chinese Realism* and of numerous articles that have appeared in such journals as *boundary 2, Cultural Critique, Modern Language Studies, LIT, MELUS, Victorian Literature and Culture, Philosophy and Social Action,* and *Paintbrush.* She has also contributed essays to *Blackwell Companion of the American Short Story* and *Canon Debates and Multiethnic Literature.* Her creative writings have appeared in *Prairie Schooner, Room of One's Own, Sistersong,* and *AIM.* Her fiction "Nai Nai's Memory," which was published in *Prairie Schooner,* won the 1991 Reader's Choice Award. In 2001 she received a Fulbright Lectureship to China. She served as Vice President/Program Chair of MELUS in 2002–2006. She is a third-degree black belt in Taekwon-Do.

Production Notes for Xu EATING IDENTITIES

Cover designed by April Leidig-Higgins

Interior designed by Paul Herr in Berkeley,
with display type in Gill Sans

Composition by Lucille C. Aono

Printing and binding by Versa Press, Inc.

Printed on 55# Glatfelter Offset Book B18, 360 ppi

CPSIA information can be obtained
at www.ICGtesting.com
Printed in the USA
BVHW080238281118
534168BV00001B/96/P